Advancing Public Management: New Developments in Theory, Methods, and Practice

ADVANCING PUBLIC MANAGEMENT: New Developments in Theory, Methods, and Practice

Jeffrey L. Brudney
Laurence J. O'Toole, Jr.
Hal G. Rainey

Georgetown University Press, Washington, D.C.

Printed in the United States of America

10 9 8 7 6 5 4 3 2 1 2000

This volume is printed on acid-free offset book paper.

Library of Congress Cataloging-in-Publication Data

Brudney, Jeffrey L.

Advancing public management : new developments in theory, methods, and practice / Jeffrey L. Brudney, Laurence J. O'Toole, Jr., Hal G. Rainey.

p. cm.

Includes bibliographical references and index.

ISBN 0-87840-760-X (cloth : alk. paper)

1. Public administration. 2. Administrative agencies—Management. 3. Technological innovations—Management. I. O'Toole, Laurence J., 1948– . II. Rainey, Hal G. (Hal Griffin), 1946– . III. Title.

JF1351.B76 2000 351—dc21 99-38857

CIP

Contents

Preface

This book presents valuable contributions by scholars working to advance the theory and practice of public management. The parts and chapters of the book are based on papers presented at the Fourth National Public Management Research Conference that met at the University of Georgia in Athens, Georgia, in late October through early November of 1997. As described in the introductory chapter that follows, that conference was the latest in a series of conferences that have brought together leading scholars from diverse settings who share the conviction that we need to advance our knowledge of a recently developing field that we call "public management." The scholars working in this area agree that these advancements are important because the field addresses the need to devote more attention to management than one finds in the literature on public administration, and more attention to the public sector context of management than one finds in the literature on business management.

In working to blend attention to management with attention to the public sector context, the National Public Management Research Conferences have pursued an array of interesting and important questions. What is distinctive about the context of public management, and how can we analyze this context to understand the ways in which public managers can influence important events? What methods should we use to study public management? What conceptual frameworks and models should we use? Governments have continually undertaken reforms and changes in their administrative branches throughout this century, and this recurrent pattern leads public management scholars to analyze such change processes. How can we better understand these processes in order to provide managers with advice about successful change and reform?

Authors at the conference in Athens focused on these questions and many others and presented many more excellent papers than we could include in a single book. We selected a set of papers that worked well together in addressing major themes developing in the literature on public management and that the questions above suggest. These included the nature, impact, and context of the public manager's role; the methodology for studying public management and conceptual frameworks and models for such analysis; and the analysis of reform, change, and innovation in public management.

In addressing these topics, the parts and chapters of the book also cover many concepts and ideas of current importance in public management research and practice. Among others, these include "formal modeling" techniques, organizational culture, managing in networks, "partnering," "reinvention," the "reinvention laboratories" in the National Performance Review, "quasi markets" (use of market-like arrangements in government), a new "Substantively Weighted Least Squares" technique for statistical analysis of governmental performance data, the behavior of "street-level" public servants, "privatization" in Medicaid reform, and the framework employed in the internationally significant Government Performance Project. We hope that readers unfamiliar with any of these topics and terms, or familiar with them but eager for more current information on the rapid developments surrounding them, will experience the same excitement we feel in getting to learn more about them from our colleagues, these accomplished scholars and experts who have written the chapters presented in this book.

Acknowledgments

We are grateful to Dean Wyatt Anderson of the Franklin College of Arts and Sciences and Professor Thomas P. Lauth, chairperson of the Department of Political Science, University of Georgia, for financial support for the Fourth National Public Management Research Conference. We also thank the members of the Organizing Committee of the series of Public Management Research Conferences. The authors extend special thanks to Michele L. Ross for the excellent, highly professional administrative and personal skills she devoted to managing the organizational arrangements for the conference and to helping conceive its intellectual organization and content. We owe thanks to Kelly See for a fine job in handling the word processing of the manuscript, including innumerable details in keeping it organized and properly presented. Thanks also to Sarah Visser for assembling the combined references. We also owe gratitude to John Samples of Georgetown University Press for his support of this book project and his expert editorial guidance. Finally, we thank everyone who joined us in Athens, Georgia, in the fall of 1997 to make the Fourth National Public Management Research Conference a credit to its predecessors and a very tough act to follow for its successors.

Jeffrey L. Brudney
Laurence J. O'Toole, Jr.
Hal G. Rainey
Athens, Georgia
March 1999

Chapter 1

Introduction: Public Management in an Era of Complexity and Challenge

Jeffrey L. Brudney, Laurence J. O'Toole, Jr., and Hal G. Rainey
The University of Georgia

How much of the performance delivered by important public programs can be attributed to the efforts of public managers, those who organize people and resources to get the job done? Which kinds of managerial actions, aimed at which other actors or variables and from which levels in the governing apparatus, can be expected to have consequence? How can we decide which managers or agencies or programs have outperformed the rest and deserve closer study and emulation by others? What has all the fuss about "reinvention" and "reform" in public management and governance amounted to? What do these terms really mean? In a world in which devolution, contracting, privatization, and other such instruments increasingly occupy center stage, what is the role of public management in "making a mesh of things," to borrow Paul Appleby's (1949) classic aphorism? What models and frameworks best capture the key features of the public-managerial task under such conditions?

These questions and a host of others press upon thoughtful managers in the United States and other countries at century's end. In an era of expanding policy agendas, of increasingly intergovernmental, international, and third-sector interdependence, and of constrained financial resources, the challenge of advancing public management in practice is linked to researchers' ability to frame the right questions and begin to deliver some sensible answers. This volume offers a sampling of contributions united by a shared objective: to assist in the development of such advancements and to stimulate still further efforts toward the same goal.

The Fourth National Public Management Research Conference

In late fall of 1997 many of the most respected scholars in the field of public management gathered at the University of Georgia in Athens to share their latest thinking and research on such issues. As with several previous conferences of this type, these scholars came together because they shared the conviction that public management is a central topic that urgently needs further development. While the term "public management" has been in use for a long time, these scholars saw it as a relatively new or distinctive topic. As described below, the scholars meeting in Athens saw public management as a topic that brings together public administration and general or business management to develop, in new and original ways, the theory and practice of managing governments and their agencies and programs. Many of those at the conference felt that the research literature in general management does not cover managing in the public sector as well as it needs to and that public administration does not cover important topics in management as well as it should. Whether or not they all agreed about these limits of the related fields, they shared the conviction that public management plays an essential role in all nations and needs continuing development of theory and practical guidance to support it.

In pursuit of this objective, the collection of articles in this book presents some of the fruits of their discussion, interaction, and study at the Fourth National Public Management Research Conference. Like the three biennial meetings that preceded it, a series that began in 1991 at the Maxwell School of Syracuse University, approximately 100 leading scholars attended the Athens meeting and contributed to the success of the event. Each of the previous meetings resulted in an edited volume that attempted to summarize and characterize the state of public management and to lay out challenges for the future (Bozeman 1993; Kettl and Milward 1996; Frederickson and Johnston 1999).

The present collection of papers, from the Fourth National Public Management Research Conference, follows in this tradition and extends it. From the fifty-five papers delivered at the meeting, representing a total of sixty-five authors, the editors selected twelve to be included in this volume. Our task was not an easy one, for the by-invitation conference attracts top scholars, and the biennial time frame encourages authors to develop innovative, ambitious work for the public management community. The chapters in this volume bear testimony to that assessment. The quality is underscored further by the many other papers presented in Athens that have already found their way into some of the best journals and edited books available, or that will soon do so.

Because of space limitations, we selected from among the best papers a set that works together well in representing several major themes that have been developing in the literature on public management. One central theme concerns the nature and impact of the public manager's role, and part I of the book includes chapters about the nature, impact, and context of that role. Another major issue concerns methodology and how we study public management. Part II presents chapters covering new and interesting methods for public management research, and other sections include papers with important methodological themes as well. Reform, change, and innovation have been major topics in the administrative branch of government for a long time and, if anything, have grown in significance in recent decades as waves of reform have swept governments around the world (Light 1997). Such reforms have been so recurrent in the U.S. that, as one observer comments, contemporary public administration has become virtually synonymous with reform (Frederickson and Johnston 1999). Part III includes chapters covering important current topics in reform, change, and innovation. Another major theme concerns the quest for models and frameworks to guide analysis of public management, and part IV contains chapters reporting on two new approaches to developing such models. Moreover, a careful reader will see many interrelations and cross-cutting themes among these parts and the chapters in them, to which we return in the concluding chapter.

In covering these major themes, the chapters also present a rich sampling of many important topics in public management research and practice. One chapter illustrates the use of "formal modeling" techniques, now widely employed in the social sciences, to analyze public managers' influence on policy decisions. Other chapters apply to public management some of the most current concepts in the social and administrative sciences, such as organizational culture, networks, "partnering," and many of the recent concepts pertaining to change and reform, such as "reinvention" and "quasi markets" (use of market-like arrangements in government). Another chapter describes the highly innovative "Substantively Weighted Least Squares" technique for statistical analysis of government performance data. In addition the book includes an extension of a research tradition of studying "street-level" or frontline public servants, applying to public management research qualitative techniques widely used in the social sciences. Still other authors cover the reinvention laboratories set up by some federal agencies as part of the National Performance Review, a recent federal reform initiative that experts consider historically significant. Another chapter analyzes the use of "privatization" to reform Medicaid, thus not only covering this important government program but also introducing the topic of privatization, a major reform movement in the United States and around the world in recent decades. A chapter also covers the framework employed in the Government Performance Project, an innovative initiative to provide performance assessments and ratings of governments around the nation. This project is currently receiving a great deal of national and international attention. In sum, in covering a set of major themes represented by the parts of the book and the chapters, the book also addresses many current and significant concepts and developments in the research and practice of public management.

In so doing the volume is designed to document and add to the advancement of public management. We take up this theme again at the conclusion of the collection, where we revisit the chapters to distill the advances documented, or at least presaged, in these pages. In the remainder of this introduction we offer a context for the readings to follow. We clarify the subject of common investigation and the important role played by the National Public Management Research Conferences over the past decade in helping the field to mature. We then discuss the organization of the volume and the contributions contained in the upcoming chapters.

The Rise of Public Management as a Field of Study

During the 1980s numerous prominent scholars with a variety of academic orientations began to converge on a new topic called "public management." Several distinct groups pursued this subject from their own perspectives without a great deal of communication and cross-fertilization, much to the detriment of theoretical and practical advancement of the field. The National Public Management Research Conference originated to bridge these academic chasms. This series of conferences brings together scholars from different disciplines, but with a common interest in public management, to promote the sharing and integration of streams of research that will enrich and stimulate the field.

One group consists of researchers in public administration, usually associated with the American Society for Public Administration (ASPA) and the American Political Science Association (APSA). They pointed out that the literature in their field very often had concentrated on normative discourse about such matters as administrative responsibility, ethics, and social equity. While they regarded this work as valuable, they also saw in the field of general management/business management additional concepts and analysis that had practical relevance for operational management of organizations. The general management field, they noted, provided much more elaborate development of such topics as leadership, strategic management, organizational design, employee motivation and work attitudes, and individual and organizational productivity, performance, and effectiveness. At the same time, however, these scholars found the business management literature deficient in its coverage of the distinctive aspects of management in the public sector, with too little attention to political influences and dynamics and to the political and governmental institutions that give public management its unique context and challenge. These scholars began to develop the topic of public management to unite the strengths of business and general management with those of political science and public administration, with the goal of developing a body of knowledge that would provide theoretical insights as well as useful guidelines for practicing public managers.

A second group of scholars pursued this same synthesis from the opposite direction. Housed in schools of business or management and not closely linked to public administration, yet interested in the public and nonprofit sectors, they too sought to build a new field of public management that would blend their own disciplinary roots in business administration with the knowledge of governmental processes and institutions provided by scholars of public administration and political science. They often encountered public administration scholars and worked with them in such venues as the Public and Nonprofit Sector Division of the Academy of Management. This institution is the leading association of scholars of general organizational management—organizational theory and behavior, strategic management, and human resource management—most of whom are located in business schools.

Meanwhile, a third group of faculty in schools of public affairs and public policy also devoted attention to the topic of public management, albeit with a different audience in mind. For the most part, these schools were established with a mission to provide education for high-level governmental officials and their top advisors, with related research and scholarly activity to generate a supporting knowledge base. Given their focus on executive policy making and strategic leadership, these schools and their faculty usually disassociated themselves from a field of "public administration" that they saw as concentrated on employees located at less lofty levels and on the more routine bureaucratic functions. They joined in the formation of a new Association for Public Policy Analysis and Management (APPAM) to pursue this interest. This group found that the literature on government policy making and its analysis and evaluation, while very valuable in support of the policy-making responsibilities of public officials, did little to address their leadership and managerial roles. These academics, some of whom had significant backgrounds as practicing public officials, added to the diverse groups interested in the study of public management. Thus the field of "public management" has come to be recognized as a unifying theme for researchers and students who examine related issues and challenges from these different but overlapping perspectives.

The National Public Management Research Conferences

As these diverse and far-flung groups produced more research, their professional separations became more evident and less logical for the study and development of public management (Lynn 1996). While valuable work appeared at the professional meetings and in the journals of the various academic associations, individual scholars interested in public management were seldom active in all of these venues. They struggled to learn about and keep up with public management research in the outlets with which they did not maintain close contacts. Both the research enterprise and the advancement of public management in practice were shortchanged by this lack of cross-fertilization.

To surmount these difficulties, in the early 1990s a network of scholars coalesced around the idea of bringing together these disparate groups and building a collective discourse and research agenda for the study of public management. They organized a major national conference intended to draw outstanding representatives from all groups and perspectives with an interest in the topic, regardless of their associational or institutional affiliation. Under the leadership of Barry Bozeman, the First National Public Management Research Conference convened at the Maxwell School of Syracuse University in 1991. This gathering was highly successful in attracting leading researchers from the relevant fields, and the proceedings led to a published collection of selected papers from the conference (Bozeman 1993). Many other contributions from the meeting were published elsewhere, and a renewed set of less formal, cross-specialty interchanges had begun. Because the attendees were highly enthusiastic regarding both the need for and the success of these meetings, a conference advisory committee agreed to hold the conference on a regular basis, every two years at a leading public management institution. The Second National Public Management Research Conference followed at the University of Wisconsin–Madison in 1993 and led to another published volume (Kettl and Milward 1996). A third conference was held two years later at the University of Kansas and has also produced a published volume (Frederickson and Johnston 1999).

The fourth conference in this series convened on 30 October–1 November 1997. As a leading research and graduate educational center in the field, the University of Georgia provided a congenial, facilitative, and fitting setting for the Fourth National Public Management Research Conference. The meeting has now become a regular and much anticipated event, with the Fifth National Public Management Research Conference scheduled for Texas A&M University, at the recently founded George Bush School of Government, in December 1999.

Organization of the Book

An earlier version of each of the chapters in this volume was presented at the Georgia meeting. All of the papers have been revised in light of the discussion, commentary, and interaction at the conference and later reviews by the editors. As noted earlier, the chapters are organized around four major themes.

The first part, concerning the role and context of public management, is aptly titled, "In Government, Does Management Matter?" Laurence E. Lynn, Jr., organized and chaired a panel on this crucial issue at the conference. His introduction, written for this volume, accompanies the papers from the panel.

In this section, Laurence J. O'Toole, Jr., and Anne M. Khademian address the effect of two central variables on the management of public organizations, structural context and organizational culture, respectively. They reach parallel results. O'Toole argues that the rise of service-delivery and other organizational networks for conducting the public's business opens up new avenues and approaches for managerial influence as well as the need for it. The management of such "networks" and "partnering" processes has emerged as a major issue in public management since governmental activities so often involve complex interrelationships with other actors and organizations in the public, private, and nonprofit sectors. Despite the opportunity and need for public management in such settings, however, O'Toole is dubious regarding our ability to measure, test, and predict its effects. Similarly, based on an excellent review of the voluminous literature on the topic, Khademian finds that organizational culture matters a lot for public management, but that the ability of the manager or executive to manipulate or shape culture, to use Khademian's metaphor, as if it were "Silly Putty," has been oversold. Organizational culture is one of the most widely used concepts in contemporary management in all sectors, and the chapter extends it to the arena of public management. Despite popular exhortations for executives and managers to alter existing organizational cultures, the chapter demonstrates that many factors, such as organizational context and environment, severely curtail the permeability of culture to public management. Khademian sketches some salient research questions that follow from this analysis, issues that should be of central interest to those who seek to know the extent of the opportunities available to managers to have substantial impact on performance.

The final paper in part I, by Thomas H. Hammond and Jack H. Knott, presents a challenging formal model of policy choice at the highest reaches of public organizations. Formal modeling techniques are widely used in the theory-driven social sciences, and a major issue for public management concerns how they might be employed in analysis for improving practice. Consistent with the heterogeneity of research in public management discussed above, the Hammond and Knott analysis is geared to political executives rather than agency managers and focuses almost entirely on strategic interactions with the environment rather than "management" of the internal organization. While Hammond and Knott identify important constraints in the agency policy space, they are relatively optimistic concerning the opportunities for political executives to exert leadership and policy choice.

A second organizing theme is represented in part II, titled "Methodological Frontiers in Understanding Public Management." Although this part of the book is somewhat mislabeled—chapters throughout the book make important substantive as well as methodological contributions—we wanted to emphasize the degree to which the field of public management has stimulated the development of new methods. This topic is a particularly significant one. In a review of the published collection from the 1995 National Public Management Research Conference, Fred Thompson (1997) argued that innovations and applications in advanced methodology and measurement techniques related to performance are sorely needed in this field but thus far not much in evidence. The chapters in part II demonstrate some of the progress that has been made in this domain.

The most noteworthy is the extension of substantively weighted least squares (SWLS) analysis provided in the chapter by Kenneth J. Meier, Jeff Gill, and George Waller. Introduced by Meier and Lael R. Keiser (1996), this family of techniques is designed to isolate cases of exceptional agency performance for descriptive and prescriptive purposes. Thus the approach has considerable promise for connecting careful statistical analyses more directly and practically with efforts to improve the performance of government. The chapter shows how to identify agencies that perform better than average, given the constraints encountered, or that avoid failure in the face of complex tasks and unforgiving environments—conditions of central interest to scholars and practitioners of public management.

The next chapter, by Gordon Kingsley and Julia Melkers, takes yet a different methodological turn. Based on science and technology agencies, they employ an embedded case study design to see how two states, Alaska and New York, attempted to influence the adoption of innovations among networks of organizations when the state agency was in a weak position to do so. Their concern is how public agencies can move networks of organizations in which government lacks formal membership status, the means or authority to coerce behavior, and munificent resources—not an uncommon situation.

The final chapter in part II, by Steven Maynard-Moody and Suzanne Leland, also presents a novel though quite different method. The authors show how stories told by frontline service agents, in this case vocational rehabilitation counselors, concerning their interactions with clients can elucidate the norms, mores, and procedures followed by these officials. A central issue in public management is the responsible use of discretion and judgment by field-level and other employees. In contrast to certain stereotypes that characterize service agents as either shirking their duties or acting arbitrarily, this chapter suggests that at least in this service domain many are highly principled decision makers. As noted earlier, this chapter also represents a stream of research on "street-level" or frontline public servants, and it raises the issue of what levels of organization are most appropriate for investigating public management. Some researchers focus on the structural peak—the executives and top managers. Scholars of management and organizations from business administration, sociology, and psychology, however, regularly study frontline workers and first-level supervisors. They readily accept the importance of understanding people at those levels as part of a comprehensive analysis of management, and Maynard-Moody and Leland raise the issue of how much public-management researchers should focus on this level.

A third major theme is represented in part III, titled "Reform, Reinvention, Innovation, and Change." Many of the papers presented at the Fourth National Public Management Research Conference dealt with this topic, and the four chapters in the section provide excellent examples. Eugene B. McGregor, Jr., offers the most global analysis of change in the public sector: His chapter, "Making Sense of Change", shows the interrelationships among the many "R" words (and others) used to characterize and understand this phenomenon, such as reinvention, restructuring, right-sizing, reform, redesign, reengineering, and so forth.

In their chapter, "Local Heroes? Reinvention Labs in the Department of Defense," Mark T. Green, Lawrence R. Jones, and Fred Thompson focus on perhaps the most prominent of the "R words." Experts regard the National Performance Review (NPR) as one of the several most important efforts at administrative reform in the history of the U.S. government, and the creation of reinvention labs has been one of the most interesting and successful initiatives within the NPR. Over one-third of the reinvention laboratories that were inaugurated by the NPR to experiment with novel means of achieving improved customer service and enhanced mission performance at lower cost are concentrated in the Department of Defense (DoD). While their analysis of reinvention laboratories identifies some successes, these authors also find serious obstacles in the DoD that limit the prospects for planned change and innovation. More sobering, Green, Jones, and Thompson believe that "most of the problems faced by DoD's reinvention labs are ubiquitous. They must be overcome in all organizations for innovation to take place."

The remaining two chapters in part III look at other examples of change in government. The first, by Barbara S. Romzek and Jocelyn M. Johnston, examines change in a service delivery network toward "Reforming State Social Services through Contracting: Linking Implementation and Organizational Culture." In this change effort, three popular proposals coalesce: privatization and contracting out, government downsizing, and social welfare reform. Privatization of public services has been a growing trend and one of the most widely discussed and enacted reforms in government around the world during the last two decades. Medicaid is a large U.S. government program in financial terms and one of the most sensitive and controversial because of severe challenges in controlling its size and cost due to the growing elderly population and abuses of the program. Romzek and Johnston show that the result of the Medicaid reforms has been a highly stressful period for some participating nonprofit organizations as they attempt to cope with the significant increases in administration and workload occasioned by new, market-oriented relationships at the expense of their traditional advocacy function.

The last chapter in part III is concerned with "Quasi Markets and Strategic Change in Public Organizations," that is, the use of market-like arrangements such as internal contracts or pricing mechanisms to effect change in government bureaucracies. James R. Thompson shows the frequency and importance of such initiatives by drawing from international experience, especially in Great Britain under Prime

Minister Margaret Thatcher's "Next Steps" program and to a lesser extent in New Zealand. Thompson concludes that introducing market-like features into public bureaucracies has achieved some performance improvements in those countries. He is skeptical, however, that more limited change efforts under way in the United States, such as the Government Performance and Results Act, can successfully dislodge organizational cultures and power structures to achieve lasting impact.

The final part of the book turns to the fourth major theme, broad models and approaches to the study of public management, and presents two new ones. Nancy C. Roberts proposes "Organizational Configurations" as a novel way to conceive governmental agencies. Rather than focusing on the individual parts or elements of organizations, this approach suggests that we consider organizations as "constellations of interconnected parts." These coherent patterns or configurations can and should be understood in their entirety, as coherent wholes, rather than as sets of discrete properties or elements amenable to individual adjustment. As Roberts points out, from the perspective of governmental change or reform—an issue crucial to contemporary public management—the key question is whether proposed changes "fit" or are compatible with the various configurations. When neither is the case, performance can be expected to suffer rather than improve.

Patricia W. Ingraham and Amy E. Kneedler present another new approach to the study of public management. They attempt to dissect the "black box" of public management by proposing a model of government performance and discussing approaches to measuring management effectiveness. The model is the centerpiece of the Government Peformance Project (GPP), a major research effort underway at the Alan K. Campbell Public Affairs Institute at Syracuse University, funded by the Pew Charitable Trusts. This ambitious project seeks to address three important questions of interest to scholars, practitioners, and citizens alike: How well do governments perform? What is the relationship of public management to performance? Can public management and government performance be improved? The model offers a basis for assessments of the performance of state governments and of state and federal agencies around the nation. Results of the assessments are being prominently published (for instance, see the February 1999 issue of *Governing* magazine for a summary of the project's state "report cards" for management capacity; and the February 1999 edition of *Government Executive* for similar reports on a number of federal agencies). This project and its assessments will continue to receive serious attention and discussion by a host of practitioners, and everyone interested in public management needs to be aware of it. The chapter presents a fitting conclusion to the contributions toward advancement represented in this volume. It builds a case for a clear, coherent, and measurable conception of public management as a central element explaining any government's ability to deliver on what it promises.

Part I

A Symposium: In Government, Does Management Matter?

Introduction to Part I

Laurence E. Lynn, Jr. The University of Chicago

Do public managers contribute in systematic ways to the effectiveness of government? As Larry O'Toole notes in his paper for this symposium, no serious scholar of public management doubts the importance of the question or even the answer—yes. Yet, he says, there has been surprisingly little energy devoted to a disinterested exploration of the issue.

The purpose of this symposium is to promote such disinterested exploration. Authors were invited to address some or all of the following questions:

1. How can we define "management" for purposes of empirical research?
2. Conceptually and empirically, how can we compare the contributions to governmental performance (e.g., of a given agency or program) of "management" as compared with factors such as structures, policy designs, resource dependencies, tasks, technologies, political environments, and the like?
3. Within a multivariate framework, how can we distinguish effective from ineffective management?
4. To what extent is it possible or useful to generalize across institutions, cultures, and contexts?
5. With respect to the question, "Does management matter," what do we know and how do we know it?

Management may be defined as the exercise of judgment or discretion by actors in managerial roles. Following Moore (1995), we might further distinguish between managing "outward" toward the political environment, managing "upward" toward superior authority, and managing "downward" toward the organization's work and outputs. In these terms, much of the recent literature on public management has been prescriptive, oriented toward identifying and advocating "best practices" or toward employing various conceptual heuristics, e.g., principal-agent models, to delineate generic problems of public management. There has been little effort to situate management in a conceptual framework that incorporates other determinants of government performance or to conduct empirical research that investigates competing explanations for governmental outcomes.

The more basic questions are often finessed in prescriptive public management studies by appeals to the "short run" inhabited by outward-oriented political appointees or downward-oriented program managers, for whom contextual and structural factors are a "given." Short shrift is given a more malleable longer run inhabited by officials who see themselves as confronting a wider array of variables, circumstances, and opportunities. This tendency to assume away structural considerations has the odd effect of banishing the design of policies, structures, and institutions from the realm of public management research. Thus the environment of public management is relegated by default to the drafters of statutes and rules, to the stakeholders who influence them, and to the scholars of public choice and political economy who study them. Public managers are assumed to operate—ideally according to best practices—within spheres of autonomy intentionally or unintentionally granted to them by these drafters and stakeholders.

Writ large, this shrunken view of public management has in recent years reached a *reductio ad nullus* at the hands of proponents of the New Public Management (NPM), in which, in effect, there is no management at all. Instead, in this view there is highly instrumented role playing by the assembly line workers of performance-oriented government who, at best, are engaged in continuous quality improvement.

The authors of the three symposium papers that follow make important progress toward rejoining the study of public management and theories of political institutions and policy choice that provide intellectual foundations for a more ambitious, longer-run view of public management. Each paper employs a different style of analysis. Hammond and Knott use a formal spatial model to explore the domain of managerial influence. O'Toole explores various social science literatures, including his own political economy of networks, to develop notions of managerial opportunities and constraints. Khademian draws on organizational culture literature and on literatures from other domains to establish relationships among institutional environments, organizational cultures, and management behavior. Despite these differences in approach, all three papers contribute the same fundamental insight: management matters to the extent that managers comprehend the institutional contexts in which they operate and the opportunities for influence these contexts afford.

For Hammond and Knott, public management is managing outward, i.e., policy management. Managers must correctly identify their domains of autonomy. The size of such a domain—in effect, the size of the policy space within which the manager operates—depends on the extent of divergence among the preferences of an agency's powerful external actors. "To realize the potential for influence when the external actors' preferences diverge, the agency head needs to take into account the location of the status quo policy, the location of his own ideal policy, and the location of the ideal policies of the other critical actors." Four skills are associated with moving policy in the direction of the manager's preferences: identifying what is politically possible; acquiring political allies, i.e., persuading powerful actors to share the manager's preferences; acquiring and exercising a good sense of political timing; and framing issues in a way that enables other actors to see advantages in the manager's preferred positions. When the domain of possibilities is narrow, Hammond and Knott argue, managers are precluded from an independent influence on public policy; when the domain is wide, managers cannot help but be policy makers.

Khademian also emphasizes the importance of the institutional environment to managerial autonomy, but her argument is a different one and focuses on managing downward. The primary influence of the institutional environment, she argues, is on an organization's culture. Culture, in turn, affects the possibilities for organizational governance: " . . . the role of the leader in an organization," she says, "varies according to the significance of culture for its governance." She adds content to this proposition by noting its resonance with arguments advanced both in the political economy literature concerning the impossibility of optimal incentives, focal points, and clan governance and in the literatures of institutional sociology and political science. Thus understanding organizational cultures and their significance is fundamental to understanding how management might matter.

O'Toole makes the interesting argument that public management's significance may be greater in agencies for which a network of relationships with other organizations is important to achieving agency goals: " . . . network contexts increase the range of potentially manipulable variables subject to managerial influence" to the extent that public management may be "more consequential in its impacts on government performance in network contexts. . . . " At the same time, however, even more actors are capable of having influence on agency performance in network settings. Thus empirical research based on causal models is difficult to do well because possibilities for isolating the management contribution in linear, additive models are reduced.

Does management matter? These authors say yes, perhaps greatly, but the extent of managerial contributions depends on the possibilities inherent in the policy environment, on the strength of institutional influences on agency cultures, and on the extent and complexity of an agency's network relationships. Among the skills public managers must possess, then, is the ability to identify and evaluate contextual factors having a bearing on their preferred strategies.

What are the implications of this line of argument for public management research? Many public management scholars recoil from the notion that the reductive tools of positive social science can be used to address public management issues, thus accounting for the popularity of case-based research. The more "post positive" among them favor interpretive analyses of managerial effectiveness and argue for the importance of tacit knowledge to managerial effectiveness. Positive researchers, in their turn, acknowledge the value of "practice wisdom" but recoil from the self-serving quality of much that passes for knowledge in public management, urging, instead, that researchers submit their ideas to tests that could potentially refute their theories.

This symposium, then, helps us toward a better understanding not only of public management but of the necessity for further development of models and methods for public management research.

Chapter 2

*Different Public Managements? Implications of Structural Context in Hierarchies and Networks**

Laurence J. O'Toole, Jr. The University of Georgia

This chapter outlines a claim that public management in emerging networked contexts is consequential—more so, indeed, than in more traditionally bureaucratic settings. Unfortunately, the argument also includes a sobering and challenging corollary: efforts to verify this proposition empirically can be expected to be highly problematic.

Précis

What is known about public management's significance in different places and varied policy settings? The answer, unfortunately, is: not much. One implication is that the addressing of context at present is a task that must necessarily be approached in a broad and largely deductive way rather than on the basis of a mass of extant and easily integrated evidence.

What approach is likely to be helpful in elucidating how context influences public management's importance? Consideration of context and causality requires addressing how to distinguish management from context, including structural context, and how then to understand the impact of public management on the intended or unintended results of managerial effort. Importantly, the former question tends to confound the latter in ways that will be explained below.

But to consider public management broadly—including managerial efforts to affect not just operational behavior and the flow of standard processes but also the kinds of assumptions adopted as fixtures (or variables treated as moveable) in shifting government

*Support for the preparation of this paper was provided by the Pew Charitable Trusts. This support is gratefully acknowledged. The analysis is the responsibility of the author alone.

from idea into action—this requires consideration of the structural context as a central factor. And while the field has been largely built on the basic structural assumption of hierarchy, the real world of public management contains considerably more variability. The different structural contexts, in turn, carry implications for whether and how public management matters.

In particular, the increasing importance of networks as a context for public management introduces structural elements that, in turn, alter the possibilities available to public managers. In brief, network contexts increase the range of potentially manipulable variables subject to managerial influence. At the same time, however, networks also increase uncertainty and decrease institutional fixedness for *all* actors in the setting. Managers have more levers available, but so do others.

Among the implications of this more complex and dynamic structural context, two in particular stand out. One is that the very notion of public management may need to be broadened in networks, where many actors share potential for management functions and influences. And second, devising clear answers to the core question—Does public management matter?—becomes substantially more difficult. The closer to network the context becomes, the more likely it is that management matters but the less possible it is to demonstrate this conclusion with convincing empirical evidence.

Prelude: Does Public Management Matter? The State of the Discussion

No serious scholar of public management doubts the importance of the core question. And it is easy to identify plenty of work consistent with the proposition that public management matters, in highly consequential ways. Yet a good deal of the scholarship on the subject avoids, or assumes away the need for, direct investigation. Still, as Golembiewski (1995) has pungently commented, "hollowers" and "hallowers"—those seeking drastic diminishment of the administrative institutions of governance and those defending and praising the actors and institutions under attack, respectively—are not enough. Performance, considered broadly, needs to be viewed as central; and public management performance should be assessed fairly, critically, and with an eye toward improvement.

But to assess public management performance, at least two difficult questions must be faced. The first is conceptual: What is to be considered part of public management? Even relatively straightforward managerial options raise this background question. Is the designing of incentive systems by managers to be included? Or as an institutional adjustment that reaches beyond the coordination efforts typically treated as managerial? This kind of question refers to the longitudinal dimension and, therefore, to public managers of different projected likely tenures (and thus positions) as well as the related issue of the extent to which managers themselves can leverage influence (and thence performance) indirectly, by manipulating such factors as structures rather than merely operations.

The second is the empirical question. How much impact does public management actually have? Research offers considerably less enlightenment than might be imagined. There *are* studies of the impacts of public management; and, depending on how broadly one decides to cast the net, a great deal of the field's scholarship speaks in some fashion to the subject. But there are significant gaps and much less serious investigation than many might suppose.

One obvious vein of scholarship is the rich lode of findings on public-private differences. But for all its strengths, this line of inquiry focuses almost exclusively on organizational comparisons rather than on systematic exploration of management impact per se.

In another chapter of this book, Ingraham and Kneedler conclude similarly on the paucity of extant research on public management capacity and its link to performance. Indeed, the Government Performance Project, undertaken under Ingraham's direction, represents a large-scale initiative to alter this state of affairs in significant ways.

Clearly, the field could benefit from more intensive exploration of the core question as well as a set of logically entailed subsidiary issues. One element of the picture is examined in this chapter: the contingent impact of structural context on the importance of—and preferred approaches for—those engaged in public management. It is helpful to begin by circumscribing the territory encompassed by the notion of public management.

Purview: What Is Public Management?

Management refers to the set of conscious efforts to concert actors and resources to carry out established collective purposes. The management function consists of, among other things (for example, acquiring resources, crafting information systems, and so forth), motivating and coordinating actors toward performance consistent with established intent. While this notion includes much from the venerable POSDCORB tradition, it is substantially broader. Furthermore, it treats management—à la Simon (1976)—as significantly "a problem of social psychology" while also allowing room for a recognition of the importance of institutional context for the managerial challenge.

More specifically, management in this sense does not necessarily assume coordination exclusively in or through the institutional setting of a formal hierarchy. This point may seem obvious, although almost all discussions of management assume such a context. But efforts to coordinate do not necessarily carry these entanglements, as students of self-governing institutional arrangements have emphasized (Ostrom 1990). Indeed, network settings are prime locales for managerial needs and challenges.

The term "networks" is used here to refer to structures of interdependence involving multiple organizations, or parts thereof, where one unit is not merely the formal subordinate of others in a larger superior-subordinate arrangement (O'Toole 1997b). The networks of interest are those that involve public managers as significant actors, public agencies or parts of agencies as constituent units, and/or the execution of public policy by others.

The idea of "management" in networks can carry diverse connotations. To some observers, the very notion is a contradiction in terms since it may seem to imply a degree of controllability over interunit actions that is unlikely and may be undesirable. Nevertheless, the question of how the behavior of interdependent units might be influenced is important (Bardach 1998; Gage and Mandell 1990; O'Toole 1983). There is general recognition of the importance of the linking, mediating, and coordinating function in networks, even if there is little agreement regarding the precise activities being embraced or the requisites for their successful fulfillment. In this chapter, the term "management" is employed to include the function specified above, without assuming a priori managerial control, formal managerial authority over all necessary participants, or managerial hierarchy as the institutional backdrop.

What are the boundaries of *public* management? Lynn (1996, 2–3) correctly cautions not to draw too "parochial" a set of limitations—in particular with respect to hierarchical level or identification of governmental branch. The point can be broadened. Particularly for managers operating within network settings, challenges on the part of government's programs reach considerably beyond the boundaries of their own formal jurisdiction. Reference to the increasing attention given to intergovernmental and public-private arrangements indicates that the reach of public management now extends far beyond internal bureau-managerial issues.

Nor is the subject likely to be only incrementally different—extended, for instance, by the consideration of a few bilateral ties, or multiple principals, or managers who must mediate between an internal agency and an "environment." The managerial world is often structurally much more complex, and the literatures on intergovernmental relations and contracting are often simplified to produce misleading inferences. Nor can the theories on these subjects be expected to be accurate. It can be shown, in fact, that these greatly expanded structures of interdependence signify not merely differences of scale but fundamental modifications in the institutions through which public goods and services are provided. One cannot understand and explain behavior in these complex arrays through simple extrapolation (see Scharpf 1997). Those tasked with public management must often seek to operate on structurally more uncertain terrain, firmament that can include regular ties with patterns of not-for-profits and profit-seeking entities as well as multiple formally governmental institutions. For the analysis in this chapter, this broadened concept of public management is the one employed.

Such a concept is more justified than one treating managers and managers' formal organizations as the relevant units of analysis—one that assumes managers' responsibilities, jurisdictions, and authority are coterminous with the compass of the agency. A portion of the field's literature, of course, is devoted to complications for managers that derive from "limitations" on their control, for instance, public managers' severely restricted authority to hire, fire, and determine material rewards for subordinates. But theoretically explicit and central treatment of the more intricately patterned structures of interdependence has been rare. Understanding management in these arrays is an important challenge for the field.

This point is suggested, for instance, in what is probably the most highly regarded public management text—by Rainey (1997). The author introduces the topic of the multiactor, interlinked character of the public management setting (especially pp. 113–21) and then comments on research related to the "'too many cooks' problem": such scholarship has "not yet addressed many of the managerial issues that the remaining chapters take up. Analyzing the relationship to the problems of [policy] implementation remains a challenge for the field" (Rainey 1997, 121; see also 193).

This assessment provides a perspective that informs the present analysis. This chapter sketches some of the public-managerial implications of structural context, particularly insofar as these affect answers to the question of how much public management matters.

Presentation: Hierarchy, Network, and the Structural Context of Public Management

What difference does structural context make in public management? To a significant extent, the answer to this question depends on differentiating public management as a causal force from other influences.

For present purposes, it is useful to focus especially on one of the implied complications: the relationship between public management and structural context.

Structures are relatively stable patterns of social relations that provide channels within which action in and on the world of practice takes place. Bureaucratic agencies provide some, but only some, of the structural context for public management; and even bureaucratic structure is dynamic, shaped by numerous factors including management itself.

Structure matters, as new institutionalists have been arguing and demonstrating for some time. And yet the public managers who operate within the bounds of structure also have a hand in shaping the constraints within which they and others must operate. The point, and the bidirectional causality, have long been recognized by some students of the subject.

Consider, for example, the prescient words of Simon alluding to the issue. In his remarkable study, *Administrative Behavior,* Simon refers to the constraints of structure while also emphasizing the possibility—indeed, necessity—of working to redesign and improve the structural controls enabling management in the first place:

> The highest level of integration [means-end rationality] that man achieves consists in taking an existing set of institutions as one alternative and comparing it with other sets. That is, when man turns his attention to the institutional setting which, in turn, provides the framework within which his own mental processes operate, he is truly considering the consequences of behavior alternatives at the very highest level of integration. [1976, 101]

The conceptual and empirical aspects of this issue are important complications. It can be helpful to address two issues in this regard. One is the common confusion in assuming that the set of what "public managers" do is public management, and therefore no one else participates in this activity (and all of this activity constitutes management). The second is the empirical point: how to establish or explore the independent or additional contributions by managers and management to governmental performance.

On the former issue, the perspective offered by some public choice theorists can be helpful. Actors and kinds of action are related but distinct topics. A given set of actors can partake of actions at one or several levels or "worlds" of action (Kiser and Ostrom 1982)—what Ostrom and colleagues call the operational (acting directly on and in the world), collective choice (acting on the rules that in turn channel operational actions), and constitutional (acting to craft the rules to be used in shaping collective choice itself) levels.

While it might seem sensible to equate the task of coordinating operational action with management, doing so would constitute a public choice-phrased restating of the old politics-administration dichotomy. For public managers can be expected to make moves at the collective-choice level as well. (For simplicity, constitutional action is ignored in this discussion.) And what of collective choice? In the realm of governance, such rule sets would seem to consist primarily of two kinds: structural attributes and policy choices (note also the discussion of trust and collective choice below). Policy choices are typically recognized as actions in which public managers participate; structural design, however, is often ignored. But, as Simon suggests, shaping the context of operations can be a management task of a high order. And some recent analysts have devoted attention to the different levels of significant managerial actions (see, for instance, Klijn 1996).

Structure, therefore, offers another channel of simultaneous managerial constraint-cum-influence. And beyond structure and policy—in the realm even of culture—managers can carry weight. Here additional public management tasks can be consequential, particularly over the long term, even if they do not directly drive operations. Consider, for example, the significance of trust for the performance of government. Even in a formal treatment of bureaucratic structures, and without considering complications created by larger variations in structural context, Miller has shown that management in the narrow cannot be expected to maximize efficiency of production; tasks such as the building of trust can be critical (Miller 1992). And, as LaPorte and colleagues have recently shown (LaPorte and Keller 1996; LaPorte and Metlay 1996), trust is not only crucial but also extremely fragile, even in relatively standard structural contexts. High levels of trust, often important to governmental performance for a number of reasons, are difficult to generate. And if weakened, trust in such a setting is exceedingly difficult to regenerate.

Public managers, therefore, are necessarily involved in an array of tasks extending far beyond the narrow notions of management often discussed. Public managers, even if simply interested in accomplishing management tasks, typically become active in collective choice.

The entanglement of management-as-coordinating-operations with management-as-crafting-of-structure in the same individuals and roles makes assessing the relative importance of different causal factors exceedingly difficult. (This point holds even more in some contextual settings and concludes the present analysis.) And those usually considered as the public managers may not be the only actors performing public management tasks. This complication further confuses the empirical task.

If the same actors can make moves nearly simultaneously in different realms or levels of action—indeed, if particular moves may themselves carry impacts at multiple levels—the task of tracing causality becomes obscure. One can examine the results of narrowly managerial efforts and ignore such more subtle but potentially consequential attempts to shape managerial structure or catalyze trust, but doing so would force a systematic underestimation of the importance of the managerial function in governance. One could explore only short-run impacts of managerial action and ignore longer-term effects, including those traceable to institution building by managers, but such an approach is guaranteed to miss several types and channels of managerial influence.

Second, those formally designated as managers are not necessarily the only actors involved in undertaking coordination. They may be aided or hindered by the "managerial" actions of others. This point reinforces the preceding one. Tracing the impact of formal managers can be important, but others may also be involved, particularly outside the more traditional structural contexts. All in all, then, solving the empirical challenge is likely to be extremely difficult.

Indeed, the present argument extends analysis of such difficulties in an additional direction by a more intensive examination of the structural context of public management, one of the complicating elements already introduced.

Paradox: Public Management in Emerging Network Settings

As argued elsewhere (for instance, O'Toole 1996, 1997a, 1997b), a strong case can be made that the typical structural context assumed in much of the literature of public management approximates a hierarchy in which managers are provided with some, albeit limited, formal authority over those whom they must seek to coordinate. But increasing evidence suggests a shift in the structural context within which many public managers operate. It is not so much that networks have *replaced* hierarchies but more that standard hierarchical arrays, or parts of them, have often been enmeshed in lattices of complex network arrangements. And many public managers inhabit hierarchies as organizational homes while managing programs and agendas that span several other units. So the structural context has shifted to a more complicated pattern while the vertical links have usually been retained.

Such developments may be particularly significant because the structural setting carries implications for the relative importance of public management in influencing performance. To make such a claim plausible, it is crucial to build on a solid theoretical foundation. Unfortunately, the field's understanding of network settings is relatively limited thus far.

Still, the topic has not been completely neglected. One possibility is provided by interorganizational theory. Thus far, however, there has been little integration with the needs and perspectives of public management. And most contributions focus on explaining interunit arrays rather than their outputs (see Provan and Milward 1995, for more detail). Explaining and improving production within or through networks have been mostly neglected.

Likewise, transaction-cost economics and the new institutionalism have sought to understand the proliferation of organizational units within business. Explanation of the conditions under which firms undertake a function internally or contract out for its provision has generated a provocative line of theoretical development with the potential for public sector insights (Williamson 1985; Powell 1990). It shares, however, the limitations of other perspectives based squarely in economics. It hardly offers accurate coverage of the public administrative setting, wherein a broader set of forces encourages continued proliferation of networking (Simon 1995; O'Toole 1997b). The markets-and-hierarchies conceptualization is too narrow for understanding networks in public management.

What theoretical tools can be helpful? Among the promising approaches are: game theory, especially as appropriately simplified to take into account features of governance and management settings; institutional rational choice, the perspective crafted by Elinor Ostrom and colleagues (see Ostrom 1996); actor-centered institutionalism, an approach drawing in part on each of the other two just mentioned (Mayntz and Scharpf 1995; Scharpf 1997); an advocacy coalition framework (Sabatier and Jenkins-Smith 1996); and more inductively generated, resource dependence-based network theory (Provan and Milward 1995).

This chapter is not the place for a careful review of these approaches. What can be noted, nonetheless, is a set of shared characteristics. They all deemphasize causal forces emanating from the "top" via authority, including from or through "managers." Models of causation are, rather, multipath and reciprocal, in ways not often seen in earlier perspectives on determinants of governmental performance. And yet all suggest, explicitly or otherwise, the likelihood of expansion in the kinds of moves available to public managers, as shifts are made from predominantly hierarchical to heavily networked settings. All indicate that even modest shifts in interunit structure can have drastic changes in the outcomes affecting performance. (This point is driven home especially clearly in the work of Scharpf, Ostrom, and proponents of game theory.)

What do these observations mean? The theoretical lines of development converge on a portrait of public management as potentially more consequential in its impacts on governmental performance in network contexts than in the standard portrait of hierarchical structure. In the latter, public managers may acquire some formal authority through position and via the limited set of incentives and sanctions that hierarchy and relatively set structure can support. But even in the medium to long run, the transparent nature of the array; the support of law, regulation, and precedent for setting standards of accountability; the reinforcement of structure through managerial patterns built over time—all these and the controls exercised by political overseers mean the managerial role has real but clearly limited impact on decisions at the collective-choice level. Structure operates primarily as a constraint on managerial options, rather than as a variable in the public-managerial toolkit.

As demonstrated elsewhere, at least two important characteristics accompany structural shifts from hierarchy to network: increases in uncertainty and decreases in institutionalization that follow from the less clearly demarcated, monitored, and decomposable interorganizational structure when taken as a whole (O'Toole 1996, 1997a, 1997b). Network settings provide more opportunities for freeriding as well as freewheeling, fewer reliable reporting mechanisms for political overseers, and less overall clarity regarding expectations. Patterns and channels are more fluid, interunit links are less decipherable. These characteristics carry implications for public management in that managers are thereby presented with more opportunities, and at different levels of action, to have impact on governmental performance.

Earlier work has used the heuristic of games and game theory to sketch the array of possible moves in outline form. Here it is useful to note that several of the most important moves available to public managers in network structures involve action beyond the operational level. "Playing the game," including assisting in the challenging tasks of coordinating actors toward authorized lines of impact, can be significant in network settings, and public managers have several levers close at hand to have such influence. But these are supplemented by options of at least three other sorts.

One has to do with the possibilities created by structural fluidity to link ostensibly unrelated streams of action to build support for performance. The converse, untying linked but unproductive interdependencies, is also an option. (These abstract phrasings encompass a host of more concrete management possibilities.) Moves to connect or disconnect are not completely absent from standard hierarchies, but the opportunities are especially plentiful in networks. And such moves can be quite potent. They can convert unplayable games into positive-sum circumstances for all parties involved.

A second set of possibilities is not so easily tied to one level of action, although research on institutional analysis has demonstrated its importance to successful performance (Ostrom 1990): the enhancement of trust. Influencing trust is not a directly structural move, but it can have structural ramifications. Trust is likely to be threatened more seriously in networks; uncertainty and complexity can be expected to drive instability and related difficulties in determining causality for opportunistic action. But managers can have impact on performance as well as on relations. Trust in a network can be potent in trimming uncertainty and thereby making performance games more playable, and it also has direct impact on discount rates (that is, how steeply to discount expected payoffs available later when one makes decisions now), lengthening the shadow of the future on present actions, as seen in the eyes of the network actors. In highly significant ways, then, managerial moves on the trust-preserving or -enhancing properties of networks can make relatively more difference in networks.

Perhaps most interestingly, public managers in networks have ample opportunity to work on the collective choice level by crafting structure more directly. Network arrays are less stable and certain, more subject to a variety of forces as they are shaped and reworked, by accident or design. Public managers in networks have a great deal of opportunity to alter structural properties of the arrays in which they operate. Although some network participants, and some of their authority and links, may be stipulated by statute or contract or other explicit agreement or policy, typical situations present possibilities for managers to add, or remove, actors from the array. Less drastically, public managers can often shift greatly the regular connections among participating units, moving some into more central roles and others to the periphery. While managers have options moderately resembling these within hierarchies as well as between them, the restrictions are typically much more significant in hierarchical context. Similarly, flows of information and other resources are greatly subject to influence by managers in networks, so that resource management can quickly result in structural dynamics.

Furthermore, such shifts in network membership, relations, and resource flows can be combined with the other, less drastically structural moves to magnify impacts on both short-term and (especially) long-term performance. All in all, then, a strong deductive argument can be made that public management is likely to be particularly consequential when the structural context shifts from hierarchical to network-like characteristics.

Does this line of analysis mean, then, that different structural contexts are likely to experience, or enable, different public managements? The answer is no, at least insofar as the core meaning of the public management function is concerned. The coordination challenge remains, whether the setting is Weberian bureaucracy or fluid and intricate network. The needed forms of management, however, are likely to be somewhat different in network settings—generally speaking, moves at the collective-choice level are likely to be more abundant, feasible, even necessary—and management actions useful in networks may be counterintuitive, from more traditional perspectives implicitly based on hierarchy as backdrop (O'Toole 1997b). For instance, in network settings, more than in simpler hierarchical arrays, giving orders can actually weaken authority; bargaining knowledge and skills are more prized; and, especially, a range of additional moves, of the sort outlined above, must be part of the standard repertoire. Structural context itself becomes more pliant and thus public management becomes a potentially more significant force, particularly over the longer run.

Nevertheless, it is important to turn as well to a complication engendered by the same set of factors. The loosened structural context enables influence from many points, in many directions. That is the meaning of the relative lack of institutionalization in networks, a feature rendering action through them difficult to anticipate (Tsebelis 1990) but also accessible to influence at multiple points.

What are the implications? The fact that public management (and the actions of "public managers") can be more consequential in networks than in hierarchies must be seen in the light of the enhanced possibilities for influence on the part of *many* actors, with many interests, in network settings. The uncertainty and lack of institutionalization, features that create opportunities for public management to function to craft the games leading to governmental performance, are also characteristics enabling influence—including toward evasion, disruption, or coordination in contrary directions—by and from others. The significant commonality of the theoretical approaches mentioned above lies in their emphasis on *multi*directional action and on interaction as primary in understanding performance.

Therefore, as chances for public management mattering grow, so too do chances for other factors—and other actors—to be consequential. The emergence of performance, however measured, is less clearly traceable to what managers per se do and how management per se functions. The result is a paradox. As structural context moves toward network features and public management acquires the potential for more influence, the means of documenting that influence become stretched and other actors also acquire the potential for more influence. The empirical task of tracing governmental performance, or underperformance, to management becomes inherently less feasible.

Prospects: Conclusion and Challenge

This chapter has sketched an argument leading to an ambiguous conclusion regarding the central question. A persuasive case can be made that public management matters even more for governmental performance in network settings. The influence of certain contextual factors, like relatively stable structure, is less; the opportunities for altering performance are more numerous and more consequential; and designated public managers are often situated in key positions to have substantial leverage on results. Even small shifts in network contexts can have large impacts on coordination patterns and thus governmental performance.

Not merely time and place matter in deciphering the answer to the public management riddle; structural context matters as well. And this context is shifting on the public management landscape. It may be important to learn, or relearn, the craft of management for these newer, less familiar settings. Public management is likely to be more influential in networks and should therefore be at the center of sustained attention for those interested in improving governmental performance in the future.

And yet the weight of this argument has fallen on theory and deduction, a point that connects this conclusion less optimistically to the question of how one can determine empirically the impact of public management. Unfortunately, the same theoretical line that suggests the importance of the management function suggests as well that even more points of potential leverage present themselves in networks, and even more actors are capable of having competing influence.

The solution to this issue lies partially in a careful stipulation of the concept of public management and careful crafting of research designs so as to avoid examining phenomena that may not map closely onto the function of interest. But the empirical challenge of specifying causality in settings inherently multidirectional and interactive, where simultaneous moves by multiple parties or institutions determine the outcome, and thus governmental performance, can be difficult or perhaps impossible. After all, an implication of the theories referred to earlier is that it is the *pooled* character of the action that must be at the center of analytic attention. This point in turn means that it is wise to focus on public-management-in-relation (to borrow a phrase from Mary Parker Follett), rather than as a separate factor, in assessing and explaining results. And it means as well that at its most effective public management must engage multiple other parties in concerted efforts at coordination. But the kinds of research designs to be used in answering effectively, with convincing evidence, the skeptic's question are difficult to envision.

As Ingraham and Kneedler suggest, some new techniques, such as the substantively weighted least-squares refinement to standard multiple regression introduced recently by Meier and Keiser (1996), can provide some assistance in isolating the management function, in more typical contexts at least. But to the extent that the present analysis has implicitly challenged linear, additive specifications of models for network settings, it is clear that this adjustment alone cannot do the job; nor can the issue be finessed simply by adding an interaction term or two. In these conceptual, theoretical, and empirical directions, substantial research energy and talent must therefore be placed. The issues are likely to become ever more consequential.

Chapter 3

Is Silly Putty Manageable? Looking for the Links between Culture, Management, and Context

Anne M. Khademian

Crack open a small, plastic, egg-shaped container painted in contrasting colors of yellow and blue, or red and green. A light tan putty rests in one half of the egg. Flatten the putty in your hand and press it to the Sunday comics page of the paper, a magazine, or book; the image is transferred to the putty. Stretch it lightly, pull it from the middle, let it dangle, twist, and turn and the image becomes distorted, hard to decipher. Fold it over, work it with your hands, and the putty is clean.

As a toy, Silly Putty's utility is limited. The pressing, stretching, molding, twisting, and throwing wears thin rapidly. As a metaphor for organizational culture, it might have potential. Indeed it is precisely the perceived malleability of culture that makes it an attractive tool for organizational leaders. Culture, it is argued, can be molded and stretched, and if the cultural image becomes distorted, unworkable, or at odds with the intentions of leaders, it can, like Silly Putty, be folded over, flattened, impressed again, and, if necessary, "thrown at the wall," thereby giving the leader a clean slate with which to work.

Public management seems to have accepted and adopted this "corporate culture" approach to organizational culture. But a critical look at the study of organizational culture suggests caution when using it as a management tool. In this paper I first examine conceptual and methodological problems with the study of culture that public management must weigh heavily before applying the findings to the management and reform of public organizations.

Second, I argue that the value of organizational culture for management practitioners and scholars might rest not with its potential as a management tool per se, but as a means to understand the context (constraints and opportunities) within which managers manage and how management matters. Much of the corporate culture literature places great weight on the actions organizational leaders take to shape, manage, and change culture without giving much attention to the thick institutional contexts within which cultures develop and in which top executives and other managers operate. A similar critique is aimed at "best practice" research in the public management literature more generally (Lynn 1994). Discovering the interdependencies between leadership and context is a critical challenge for public management scholarship (Fountain 1994b), and I argue that the study of culture in the new institutional literature provides a conceptual means to begin the investigation. Specifically, the critical relationship between culture and context must be understood before developing the capacity to *manage* organizational culture.

Culture as a Management Tool

In 1938 Chester Barnard argued that the "informal organization" and its "personality" can harmonize work within an organization. Culture can be a strong source of motivation and behavioral control toward collective ends, "subordinating individual interest and the minor dictates of personal codes to the good of the cooperative whole" (1938, 279). Barnard also argued that maintenance of the organizational personality by "inculcating points of view, fundamental attitudes, [and] loyalties" was the "distinguishing mark of the executive responsibility" (1938, 279). Viewed as a tool to motivate and control, Barnard argued its effectiveness can exceed the exercise of sanctions, the implementation of structured processes, or the use of material rewards.

Today's "corporate culture" literature (see Smircich 1983) builds upon Barnard's argument (Scott 1990, 41–44). As with Barnard, this literature views organizations as adaptive systems where culture is an integrating feature that provides a source of employee identification, motivation, and coordination, giving strength (and, when necessary, flexibility) to organizational procedures. Culture is manifest as commonly held "focal points" (Kreps 1990), "basic assumptions and beliefs" (Schein 1990), or as symbols such as "rituals" (Deal and Kennedy 1982). Members of an organization draw upon these beliefs or symbols to identify the organization's view of itself and its environment and to identify an appropriate pattern of behavior for a variety of situations (Schein 1990). Ideally, the culture will also contribute to an overall reputation (Kreps 1990) that other organizations, shareholders, or customers can use to assess the organization as a potential partner, agent, or producer.

Barnard's emphasis upon culture as a *tool* of leadership to enhance organizational performance is also central to this literature.

Edgar Schein argues that the creation, maintenance, and change of an organization's culture is the leader's primary responsibility. Utilizing "primary embedding mechanisms," leaders define culture by what they "pay attention to, measure, and control," how they handle crises, how they allocate rewards and sanctions, and how they recruit, promote, and deal with retirement and even excommunication (1990, 115). Similarly, Jeffrey Pfeffer links the strategic use of "symbolic actions" with the exercise of power and influence in organizations. "We exercise power and influence," he argues, "when we do it successfully, through the subtle use of language, symbols, ceremonies, and settings that make people feel good about what they are doing" (1992, 279). Others link the performance of an organization to the presence of a particular type of strong culture or deeply held organizational commitments to quality (Deming 1986) or excellence (Peters and Waterman 1982; Deal and Kennedy 1982), and identify ways in which leaders can create, preserve, or change cultures (Trice and Beyer 1993, chapter 7). Cultural change in particular rests with the "words and deeds" of leaders, including "redesigns or reconfigurations of the organization's processes, structures, and resource allocations" (Huber and Glick 1993).

Culture and Public Management

In practice and research, public management also increasingly incorporates culture as a manageable variable for bringing about organizational reform (Rainey 1997) Michael Barzelay and Babak Armajani, for example, conclude that "creating an uplifting mission and organizational culture" is one of the many "role concepts" the informed public manager must practice to break through the traditional bureaucratic paradigm (1992, 132). Others link the building of "trustworthy government" (Carnevale 1995, 73), "institutional constancy," a "repeatedly high performance" (La Porte and Metlay 1996, 344–45), and the capacity to change in public organizations (Denhardt 1993, 21) to supportive cultures cultivated primarily by organizational leaders.

Leadership that can transform dysfunctional cultures is also targeted as key to improved performance. Donald Kettl examines the dysfunctional clash of political, managerial, and technical cultures in agencies responsible for managing the procurement of complex goods and services. He argues that political leadership at the top of an organization can "begin to change the culture inside out" by creating conditions for organizational learning (1993b, 211–12). Similarly, Mark Moore's assessment of the Houston Police Department (HPD) in 1982 focuses on the dysfunctional role of the HPD's "subterranean culture" that isolated police from the community (1995, 225–26).

Police chief Lee Brown reformed the department through fundamental changes in the organization's culture brought about by what Moore calls the "techniques of operational management."

Culture is also a central component in much of the current effort to reform the national government. Development of the concept is extremely limited, but throughout National Performance Review (NPR) publications culture pops up as a facilitator of a variety of reforms from strategic planning to the devolution of authority and the creation of an entrepreneurial spirit in government (Gore 1994; NPR 1997).

Is the Leap from Corporate Culture Appropriate?

The argument that culture can be managed and put to a variety of productive uses—coordinating work, motivating employees, guiding behavior, providing a sense of organizational identity, and ensuring accountability within and without, to name a few—is appealing. Organizational change is tough, particularly in the public sector, and there are limits to reform that can flow from changes in structure and process alone. Early interest in organizational culture as a focus for analysis and as a tool for management grew in part from a frustration with the knowledge base built by organizational and management studies emphasizing structure and process (Ott 1989). But the ease with which public management has accepted culture as a management tool should be tempered by three conceptual and methodological questions.

What Is Culture and What Is Its Primary Organizational Role?

At a broad disciplinary level, there is no consensus as to what culture is. Like Silly Putty, it is twisted, stretched, and impressed with meaning by research orientations across disciplines. In an analysis of organizational culture studies, Linda Smircich identifies as many as five concepts of culture (1983, 342). When culture and organizational analysis are combined, culture can be viewed as a variable within an organizational system, as in the corporate culture literature, or as a variable external to organizations but with significance for performance within (Hickson 1993). It can also be viewed as a "root metaphor," shifting the researcher's focus "from concerns about what do organizations accomplish and how may they accomplish it more efficiently to how organization is accomplished and what does it mean to be organized?" (Smircich 1983).

The role that culture may play within an organization is also hotly disputed. The argument that culture serves an integrating role in organizations is challenged by alternative approaches that emphasize the strength and significance of subcultures within organizations (Rouse and Fleising 1995) or the fragmented and ambiguous nature of organizational culture (Feldman 1989). Where the corporate culture literature focuses on culture as a means of reducing ambiguity, replacing it with consensus and harmony, Joanne Martin argues that a "differentiation" perspective looks past possible integrating efforts at a broad organizational level, focusing instead upon strong subcultures that provide islands of consensus. The primary emphasis in this approach is the dissonance created by power differentials and the subsequent development of management versus employee subcultures (1992, 85). In their analysis of the miner and manager subcultures in a British Columbia coal mine, for example, Michael Rouse and Usher Fleising argue that despite the "common destiny tied to world demand for coal" shared by both groups, "[T]he difference in epistemologies, values, assumptions, time horizons, histories, intuitions, and goals provide ample opportunity for disagreement, misunderstanding, and conflict." (1995, 248)

Beyond the dichotomies of differentiation is a view of culture in constant flux. New understandings or simple ambiguity are created for members of an organization subject to inconsistencies between symbols, organizational ideology or "content themes," and organizational practice—all of which are argued to be the source of harmonizing behavior within the integration perspective (Martin 1992, 141–52). An organization whose leader emphasizes interpersonal communication to facilitate cooperation, for example, might nevertheless communicate strictly by memorandums that pass through the hierarchy.

These deep differences in the conceptualization and understanding of culture suggest caution before embracing the phenomenon as commonly held organizational commitments, defined by leaders, that can guide behavior in an integrating manner.

How Should We Study Culture?

"Quality" is used to identify the interest in organizational culture both in terms of how we study organizations (the methods) and as an argument for how they ought to be managed (see below). Some have made the case for a more qualitative approach to the study of organizations (Trice and Beyer 1993; Ott 1989). As Ott argues, "quantitative quasi-experimental research methods . . . have produced very little useful knowledge about organizations over the last twenty years" (1989, 4). Others have argued that through the study of organizational culture, qualitative methods such as clinical research and the use of open-ended and structured interviews have become more acceptable means to understand organizational behavior (Schein 1993; Martin 1992, 65).

Nevertheless, the qualitative approach raises important methodological challenges that are familiar for public management. Corporate culture researchers tend to focus on "best practice" organizations or those that are successful in accomplishing goals or bringing about significant change. Hence, the same criticisms of research focused on the best practices of public executives more generally (Lynn 1994) can be applied to the study of culture as a manageable variable.

First, the problem of identifying good and particularly the "best" practicing organizations is the subjectivity of the choice. Janet Weiss (1994, 283) argues, "'Best' is a political judgment that is often in dispute by stakeholders viewing any given episode of public management." Similarly, the identification of "ideal" cultures that facilitate "quality" organizational performance is a highly subjective process. While we cannot ultimately escape the subjectivity of choice, we can sample broadly across the public organization landscape for cultural comparisons rather than exclusively target the particularly innovative, customer-driven agencies with "entrepreneurial" leaders, as the current thrust of reform encourages.

The methodological concern is similar once an organization(s) is selected and data collection begins. If it is assumed that a single culture drives the work of successful organizations, researchers will look for that single culture. If it is assumed that this culture is defined and directed from above, then researchers will interview and spend time with upper division management and leaders. And if it is assumed that culture plays an integrating role in organizations, then non-integrating elements of culture might not be examined (see Martin 1992, 65–67). In short, what one finds depends in part upon where one looks (Hummel 1994, 495).

A second criticism of best practice research, and case analysis more generally, is that we must select cases with an eye toward the development of theory (Yin 1984), not just the identification of good management efforts (Weiss 1994). If an ultimate goal is a theory of organizational culture that can guide public management practice, organizations that demonstrate various levels of performance, whose cultures are possibly diverse (integrated, differentiated, and fragmented) and whose cultures appear differentially connected to organizational performance, must all be examined.

Can (and Should) "Quality" Cultures Replace Hierarchy?

Yet another quality problem is the more normative concern for how to build "quality" organizations and the role for culture. Within the total quality management (TQM) literature, culture is viewed as an integrating component of the organization manifest as the strong commitments to (or beliefs in) quality principles championed by organizational leaders and held by members. TQM's central premise is that the quality of a service or product is most important (Deming 1986). Quality is produced by empowered employees working and communicating in an open and flexible setting and focused on continuous improvements in results for their customers. An organizational commitment to (or belief in) "quality" practices establishes a culture that is the glue as well as the motivation necessary to coordinate an organization that rejects hierarchical systems of control (Peters and Waterman 1982; Denhardt 1993, 17–18).

The quality approach has been eagerly embraced by government reformers and academics, some applying Deming's TQM explicitly (Rago 1996), and others focusing on the key principles of customer service, empowered and innovative employees, and results-driven improvement efforts (Barzelay 1992; Kamensky 1996). Just as enthusiastic have been the criticisms of this new approach to governance. While some focus on the appropriateness or fit of the quality reform movement with the public sector (Moe 1994), another challenge rests with the coherence of reform ideas and the lack of concern among reformers for the institutional context that might influence quality reform efforts. Both criticisms highlight the significance of culture in the debate as well as its indiscriminate application to reform efforts.

Coherence and Culture

In his review of reform efforts across the globe, Donald Kettl (1997) argues that reform in the United States embraces two contradictory ideas. On the one hand, the quality notions of empowerment flow throughout NPR literature. If we "let the managers manage," they can focus on problems free of the procedures and red tape that can inhibit performance (1997, 447). Another strand of reform focuses on "making the managers manage" (1997, 448). Drawing upon principal-agent theory, the argument is that exposure to market incentives will force managers to be better managers. Reform is framed from above by politicians who design individual and organizational performance agreements that offer rewards and punishments for results, but facilitated by competition with the private sector. This tension between reform through management freedom versus reform through market-based incentive systems is further exacerbated by the inclination to centrally coordinate and control programs, budgets, and policies within the executive branch (Peters and Savoie 1996). Here the thrust is neither to make managers manage through market exposure nor to let them manage, but to control outcomes within the broader goals of fiscal conservatism, regulatory restraint, and economic growth.

The implications of these reform tensions for culture are two. First, if a coherent integrating culture is to facilitate the reform effort, ideas that pull in opposite directions could inhibit the development of such a culture and perhaps create ambiguity identified in the cultural fragmentation literature. What we need to know are the connections between reform philosophies (as articulated across a government more generally, and within an organization by a leader) and the evolution of organizational cultures and just how essential a coherent integrating culture actually is to reform efforts.

Second, if the culture of quality is distinctively different from a culture based upon centralized control, rationalization, and efficiency above all else, how does a leader replace one with the other? This is of particular concern if executive management agencies (such as an Office of Management and Budget) adhere to the concerns of control and efficiency (Peters and Savoie 1996). Indeed critics of the quality reform movement argue that a "managerial metamyth" continues to linger in organizations bent on quality reform. Eventually the emphasis upon control, the rationalization of work, the means rather than the ends, and the importance of efficiency above all else will suppress the empowered employee and the organizational commitments to quality (Ingersoll and Adams 1992; Hummel 1994).

There might indeed be one culture in organizations (the "metamyth"), perhaps dominant across public organizations, but changing that culture can be difficult if it is to be done in anything but a superficial manner. The driving pace of the economic market, traditional conceptions of management control, or even a broader social context imbued with distrust for large organizations might weigh more heavily in determining "the way work is done" within an organization than a leader trying to define a quality approach with a supportive culture. The questions for public management would seem to be: is there in fact a managerial culture of control (the managerial metamyth), does it exist throughout government agencies, and, if so, can it be replaced and under what circumstances? If not, is there room for a co-culture or is the result ambiguity and confusion?

Context and Culture

A second criticism put to the quality reform (and public management more generally) is its emphasis upon the behavior of top executives as the key source of reform. The institutional context within which leaders operate—the formal and informal "rules and requirements to which individual organizations must conform if they are to receive support and legitimacy from the environment" (Scott and Meyer 1983, 40)—is typically neglected. Early public administration roped off the political world with the politics-administration dichotomy, focusing instead upon the internal and formal structures and processes of government organizations as the key to effective performance. The field of public management rejects the politics-administration dichotomy and much of the empirical (structural) focus of the past. Top executives in particular are considered "constantly and inescapably involved in political work" (Roberts 1995, 292). Hence an effective management strategy includes management of the political context within which the agency rests as well as management of the organization (Moore 1995). But the problem is that we know very little about what is manageable outside of the organization. Nor do we know how the outside world interacts with management efforts to influence internal factors such as the development of a culture.

A body of research in political science suggests that organizational cultures are connected to institutional environments, reflecting the nature of a task, professional priorities, past management efforts, and the constraints imposed by the political world (Wilson 1989; Kaufman 1981). Rather than portray culture as putty that is shaped into an integrating force, this literature views culture as putty that can clog management innovation. Herbert Kaufman argues, "Each new leader after the first one enters an organization with a history of managed learning permeating its personnel. . . . A new chief is therefore likely to feel sharply constrained by what was deliberately infused into his work force by his organization before his accession to office" (1981, 118). Beyond constraint, culture is also viewed as an influence on management efforts, rather than the other way around (Derthick 1990; Ban 1995).

This literature is a premise (often unrecognized) from which public management can identify the management constraints and the opportunities presented by the political environment (Ellwood 1996). But it is a frustrating start for public management practitioners and researchers interested in the "possible" and the "manageable" and the significance of management efforts in the world of public policy. A sharp critique of James Q. Wilson's *Bureaucracy* (1989) by eight practicing executives is illustrative, arguing that his emphasis on constraints and negative incentives offers nothing "positive . . . about the roles and rewards of managers in the public service" (Buck et al. 1992, 406)

So where do we go from here? One weakness of the political science "management constraint" literature might simply be the particular managers studied, perhaps constrained by traditional management philosophies (Kamensky 1996), overwhelmed by time constraints and demands of the job (Kaufman 1981), or simply refusing to make creative efforts (Ban 1995)—including the transformation of culture. Part of the problem might also be the type of institutional contexts upon which practitioners and researchers have focused.

A variety of methods for operationalizing the institutional environment are offered by the new institutionalism (see below). Institutional environments can present constraints as well as opportunities for managers, and perhaps one place to look for the significance of the institutional environment for management efforts is organizational culture. In the new institutionalism a link between the environment and the development of organizational culture is present, suggesting, as Wilson, Derthick, and Kaufman do, a depth to culture beyond efforts of the top executive. If culture is to be managed, this literature indicates we must understand connections between culture and context.

Culture, Management, and the New Institutionalism

Across the social sciences there is a renewed interest in institutions as phenomena that are important for understanding behavior in political, economic, and social settings (March and Olsen 1989; Williamson 1990; Powell and DiMaggio 1991). Explanations for where institutions come from, how and why they change, and ultimately why they are important for political, economic, and social behavior are as diverse as the disciplines themselves (Powell and DiMaggio 1991, 7–11; March and Olsen 1989, 2–16). But the literature's treatment of the environment and its relationship to organizational culture is surprisingly similar. The treatment of leadership, on the other hand, and its connections to culture is ambiguous. Together, the two points suggest an agenda for public management research.

Environment and Organizational Culture

First, the new institutionalism views organizations as institutions (or as potential institutions) whose environments are important for how they develop. An important component of institutionalization is the development of something akin to a culture for coping with that environment. Consider the work of sociologist Philip Selznick (1957)—whose work some label "old institutionalism"—in conjunction with that of Wilkins and Ouchi (1983), who incorporate economic theory. Both focus on the relevance of environmental uncertainty for the way organizations operate and the role of an organizational culture in that process.

For Selznick not all organizations become "institutions." The transition to institutionalization and the accompanying evolution of a culture (or "character") depends upon the uniqueness of a task, the clarity of the goal, and the availability of standardized information. Some organizations can be maintained as machine-like tools "[w]hen the goals of the organization are clear-cut and when most choices can be made on the basis of known and objective technical criteria" (1957, 137). When these conditions do not apply, "[o]rganizations become infused with value . . . prized . . . as sources of direct personal gratification and vehicles of group integrity" (40). The infusion of values is manifest through the "elaboration of commitments—ways of acting that can be changed, if at all, only at the risk of severe internal crisis." These commitments provide a "social integration [for the organization] that goes well beyond formal co-ordination and command" (40).

Wilkins and Ouchi (1983) also argue that environmental certainty (or uncertainty) matters for the operation of an organization and the development of a culture, but they incorporate transaction cost theory to make their case. Organization depends upon the mediation of an "interdependent exchange" in which individuals give something of value (such as their labor) with the expectation they will receive value in return (such as money). Mediating this transaction in a manner equitable to all parties is the primary source of transaction costs for organizations, and environmental certainty and complexity are key to the mediation process. Organizational governance will range from "market" to "bureaucratic" to "clan" models as the determination of value and identification of an equitable interdependent exchange become more complex and uncertain. At the height of complexity and uncertainty the "clan" substitutes performance measurement and control with a "social understanding" of the organization's objectives, methods, and values, and, hence, a means to identify equity or justice in the exchange of value in the long run.

Others within the new institutionalism identify relevant institutional environments for organizations, giving greater substance to the "uncertainty" and "complexity" of the environments presented by Selznick (1957) and Wilkins and Ouchi (1983). Within sociology, an "institutional" perspective examines interorganizational connections (DiMaggio 1986), the ways in which organizations in a similar "field" influence each other (Scott and Meyer 1983), and the more general impact of institutional (symbolic) environments upon organizations. Different types of organizations are also associated with different thicknesses of environmental institutionalization.

Elaborations of the institutional environment focus on formal rules and structures, such as the formal processes by which government agencies are held accountable, or the "mores, customs, and established practices" which have significance for organizational behavior (Scott 1990). Symbolism and systems of meaning take on significance not only within the organization as sources of meaning and motivation (as the corporate culture literature argues), but as forces outside the organization with relevance for its behavior. Organizations might incorporate elements from the institutional environment to confer legitimacy, such as the incorporation of a professional group, or the establishment of a particular office, such as an equal employment opportunity office in a firm (Scott 1990).

Within government, for example, the adoption of policy-analytic offices across virtually all government agencies can be viewed not only as a response to congressional mandates for analyses such as benefit-cost assessments (part of the organization's formal institutional environment), but as conferring legitimacy upon agency decision making in a policymaking process increasingly embedded in the language of "rationality" and "efficiency" (Stone 1997). While the transfer has taken place, however, the relevance of the policy-analytic information for organizational performance and the quality of public policy is questionable (Feldman 1989). What organizations do for external legitimization, in other words, does not necessarily mesh with efficiency or performance enhancement as defined within economics.

The bottom line of this diverse research is that the institutional environment can matter a great deal for the evolution of a culture. Public organizations are embedded in rich institutional contexts within which managers must manage particular tasks with various employees. The new institutionalism suggests that a culture represents (in part) the meshing of task, personnel, and environment (Khademian 1996)—perhaps in an efficient integrating manner, perhaps simply as a coping mechanism, or perhaps in something of an ad hoc manner with high levels of ambiguity. Whatever its form, it may be that culture takes on greater significance for the performance of an organization as the institutional context becomes more thick, i.e., as intricate decision-making procedures and processes of accountability substitute for goal clarity, as interorganizational connections increase, and as broader social values relevant for a policy area become more competitive and complex. Yet, the increased significance of culture for organizational governance does not necessarily mean an inability to manage. Reliance upon culture may be the only viable way to manage some organizations. Discovering how deeply embedded cultures might be managed, or how to manage around such cultures, is a key challenge for public management research. This literature suggests that managers might have to look to, understand and work with the institutional environment before beginning to make fundamental adjustments in culture.

Leadership and Culture

A second characteristic common to the diverse field of new institutionalism is the uncertainty associated with the role of leaders in the development of organizations (as institutions) and, more specifically, in the development of a culture. In fact, it ranges from the definitive impact of a leader to the remote. Selznick (1957) and Wilkins and Ouchi (1983) again exhibit common ground, suggesting that the role of the leader in an organization varies according to the significance of culture for its governance. Both suggest that leadership has greater significance for those organizations operating in complex environments in which the work of the organization is distinctive and difficult to assess as to its value. Organizations governed by a clan, for example, rather than the market or a bureaucracy (Wilkins and Ouchi 1983), or organizations that no longer simply *do* something but *become* something distinctive (Selznick 1957) are more difficult to lead. In these organizations, leaders must direct the socialization process, identify sources of motivation, and build and reinforce loyalty and trust.

Perhaps the strongest statement of the role leaders can play in shaping organizations and cultures is based in economic theory, but it is much less concerned with the external environment as a constraint. Gary Miller (1992), for example, combines an economic literature focused on formal incentive/control systems as a form of governance in organizations with literatures in sociology, psychology, and political science that emphasize the importance of leadership to inspire employees to reach beyond self-interest for the good of the organization. In a review of high-involvement management, Miller argues that corporate cultures defined by "strong norms of cooperation and effort within work groups" were encouraged to grow in companies where leaders drew upon formal structure and incentives to empower workers with real "property rights" (1992, 211). David Kreps (1990) presents a similar notion of leadership as the key to organizational development and its culture. "Focal points," he argues, are the basis of corporate culture. They serve as a "principle or rule individuals use naturally to select a mode of behavior in a situation with many possible equilibrium behaviors" (121). While Kreps argues that focal points arise in part due to "evolutionary fitness," it is less clear how the environment interacts with the decisions of leaders for producing focal points.

What is also unclear is the relevance for the public sector of these leadership actions, aimed at building norms of cooperation that facilitate organizational efficiency. How "property rights" are shared within a public organization can be a very political decision. Efforts by Reagan appointees in several regulatory agencies to move economists into key decision-making positions, replacing attorneys, and the consequent uproar in Congress and across powerful interest groups are illustrative (Eisner 1991). The relationship between leadership and the institutional context again seems critical for understanding the influence a leader might have on the development of culture. To the extent that a leader can create some autonomy for organizational operations, perhaps by heightening the value of the organization's expertise for policy making (March and Olsen 1989, 30–34) or by creating a public expectation for and support of the organization's work (Meyer and Rowan 1991), the likelihood of influencing organizational culture and using it as a management tool might increase.

Finally, the work of "institutionalists" within sociology suggests a remote role for leaders in shaping organizational cultures (Powell and DiMaggio 1991). Leadership is not absent in these analyses, but a broader "organizational" effort to conform with, fit, or derive legitimacy from the institutional environment drives explanations for how organizations grow and change and where cultures come from. There is, in fact, a close parallel between the work of political scientists focused on the political context of bureaucracies and the impact upon bureaucratic performance (Derthick 1990; Wilson 1989) and the institutionalists within sociology. Both view external institutional forces as exerting greater influence than organizational leadership over organizational behavior and the development of culture.

Culture and Public Management: A Few Cautions and Suggestions

Is culture the Silly Putty of an organization? Can it be shaped, impressed, stretched, and twisted by a committed and focused leader to integrate work in an organization? Interdisciplinary disagreements as to what exactly a culture is, the role it might play in an organization, the appropriate methods for analysis, and the relevance of an organizational culture in the context of broader more dominant cultures suggest a cautious approach to culture as a tool for public management. Reform efforts aimed at creating "quality" cultures in government organizations highlight some of the challenges posed by the premise that culture is a management tool—specifically, the little known links between culture, management efforts, and the environment or context within which managers manage.

A growing institutional literature, however, is identifying some of the connections between context and culture in particular. For public management, the new institutionalism suggests that the ability to *manage* organizational culture will depend in part on an understanding of the interaction between culture and context. Public management might therefore approach the study of culture in a manner that is (a) more mindful of the institutional context of agencies, (b) interdependent in its conceptualization, and (c) attentive to the potentially varied strengths and weaknesses of cultures in organizations.

This initiative might begin with a creative effort to conceptualize the relevant institutional context for any given agency. Beyond the formal rules, structures and processes are norms, values, customs, informal relations with organizations and constituencies, and public perceptions. Judgments about an agency's contribution, its value as a source of expertise, and its responsiveness to its clientele, for example, turn on less formal parameters, but these parameters are nevertheless important for the ability of an agency to carry out its mission. Consider the work of Ingram and Schneider (1993) on the social construction of groups targeted by public policy. Judgments by society about the value of the target population are embedded in public programs. These judgments have consequences not only for the targeted populations, but for the ways in which political overseers communicate with an agency responsible for the program, check its actions, and intervene on behalf of constituencies.

A broader understanding of the institutional context suggests that we think about the influences upon culture as varied and interdependent, including the role of an executive. The world of the public manager, as Ellen Schall (1995) has described it, is something of a "swamp." Internally a culture can mire leadership efforts, bogging down even the most incremental efforts at reform. Externally, the demands of political overseers, constituents, professional groups, and the assessments of the press and public can flood an agency, leaving a murky film over a special project or reform. But when a leader clears a spot in the swamp, pulling away weeds and scum, the water stirs elsewhere. Just as the institutional environment of an agency can influence the evolution of a culture, so too can a leader's efforts to alter or improve the context within which an agency operates have consequences for the culture.

Finally, we might also think about culture in terms of varied strengths, perhaps having varied levels of significance for organizational performance and being more or less manageable. For example, if an organization has increased control over its internal operations, do the internal priorities of an organization, such as professional goals, become more manifest in the culture? The cultures of agencies that have experienced periods of high political conflict as well as several years of relative anonymity might be examined for possible changes in cultural emphasis and priorities. Does the "technical" clarity of an organization's environment reduce the significance of a culture for organizational operations? Organizations with missions narrowly defined, performing tasks that are familiar, might draw less upon a culture and more upon technical routines as a source of guidance. Finally, do the cultures of agencies with private sector competitors (or other public sector competitors) reflect efforts to demonstrate a distinctiveness about their work, or does the presence of competitors and hence a more standardized way to do the task reduce the significance of a culture?

The inclination to view culture as putty in the hands of an executive is strong. As a potential source of organizational motivation, coordination, reputation, and control, culture is an enticing tool for managers trying to achieve difficult goals with minimal resources within a web of constraints. Yet, as John Ellwood has argued, if the research agenda is "driven by the needs of practitioners" in the short term, we forgo an effort to "improve our understanding of public management (writ large) . . . " (1996, 57). To this might be added that if the agenda is driven by an assumption that every dimension of an organization is manageable (or malleable) in the hands of a "successful" manager, we forgo an opportunity to better understand the complexities of public management in rich institutional and organizational settings.

Chapter 4

*Public Management, Administrative Leadership, and Policy Change**

Thomas H. Hammond Michigan State University
Jack H. Knott The University of Illinois

Introduction

To what extent can top-level appointed political executives make significant policy choices? Participants in the debate over this question within the field of public management have taken a variety of positions. At one extreme are arguments that public managers are so constrained by large-scale political and institutional forces that they have little room for significant choice. The Organizational Process model of Allison (1969) is a well-known representative of this school of thought: in this view, the choices of top-level executives are limited to the menu of routines supplied by their subordinate organizations. Wilson (1989) similarly argues that it is not the top-level executives but the mid- and lower-level managers, as well as the professional and organizational constraints under which these managers work, which play the critical role in determining organizational effectiveness.

External constituencies impose equally important constraints on the ability of political executives to choose their own course of action. Public agencies operate in an "embedded hierarchy" of other agencies, interest groups, and branches of government that limit the autonomy of agency executives (Moe 1990). Legislatures also impose administrative constraints on public agencies; while intended to maintain accountability, they also contribute to the growth of bureaucratic rules and "red tape" (Warwick 1975). The consequence, Kaufman asserts (1981, 174), is that political executives generally have relatively little impact on policies and programs: "They certainly do

*The authors thank Laurence Lynn for sponsoring the original version of this paper. Thanks also go to Don Hammond for drawing the figures and to Jay Verkuilen for his very helpful comments and corrections on an earlier draft of the paper.

calculate and negotiate to accomplish all they can. But they make their mark in inches, not miles, and only as others allow."

At the other extreme, however, are accounts of political executives who were able to forge great changes in public policies and so appear to have been less constrained by political and institutional forces; see, e.g., Caro (1974), Lewis (1980), Doig and Hargrove (1987), and Behn (1991). These political executives successfully altered the relationships between their organizations and their political environments and shaped the activities of their mid- and lower-level managers. Indeed, Doig and Hargrove (1987) were able to compile a substantial series of case studies of political executives who were unusually effective.

In this chapter we explore the implications of a formal theory of political institutions and policy choice for gaining a better understanding of the constraints and opportunities faced by senior political executives. While realizing the importance of internal institutional constraints, we focus here on the emphasis in the public management literature on the importance of the external political environments of the executive agencies. As Bozeman and Straussman (1990, 214) point out: "Public management is, to a large extent, management of the external environment of the organization." We are interested in particular in a better understanding of the conditions under which political executives can achieve their policy goals. Are some environments so rigid that political executives can make little difference? Are other environments more malleable such that political executives can employ leadership strategies to achieve their goals? Which leadership strategies work best under these differing conditions?

In the first part of this chapter we use our model of multi-institutional policy making—see Hammond and Knott (1996)—to characterize the different kinds of external environments which political executives might face. We show that some environments are more constraining than others and that the strategies of political executives, and the executives' influence on the choice of policies, should be expected to vary accordingly. The second and third parts of the chapter take the questions raised by the public management literature on leadership as their starting point. We modify our model so as to clarify the conditions under which political executives might be able to change their political environments, thereby overcoming the constraints which prevent them from choosing the policies they most desire.

Policy Equilibria in Political Institutions

Bolman and Deal (1991, 411) summarize the literature on the contingency theory of leadership as indicating that "good leadership is situational, that is, what works in one setting will not necessarily work in a different one." We will use our multi-institutional model to demonstrate that the impact of political executives on policy choice can be expected to vary quite considerably, just as Bolman and Deal suggest. That is, under some conditions political executives can be expected to have a large impact on policy choice, while under other conditions the same executives could be expected to have little impact at all.

Because our purposes here involve illustration and interpretation, we will use a simplified version of our model. We will assume that there are just three institutions which are important to agency policymaking: the House floor, the Senate floor, and the president. We assume that this policymaking by the House, Senate, and president takes place in a two-dimensional issue space. This means that, as far as the individual actors are concerned, all politically significant features or aspects of public policies can be meaningfully represented on two orthogonal issue dimensions—that is, on the X- and Y-dimensions.

Each individual actor is assumed to have a most-preferred policy in this two-dimensional issue space; this individual's most-preferred policy is referred to as his or her "ideal point." Each individual's goal is to get a policy adopted which is as close as possible to his or her own ideal point. Assume for simplicity that each individual actor cares equally about the two issue dimensions. This means that the set of policies which yield a utility equal to the status quo policy, or SQ, can be represented by a circle through SQ and centered on the individual's ideal point; this circle is called the individual's "indifference curve" through SQ.

For any SQ considered by a chamber, the set of options which defeat it with the support of a majority of the chamber is called the *win set* of SQ, or W...(SQ). We subscript W with the initials of the body that is considering SQ. Thus, W_{HF}(SQ) is the set of options that a majority of the House floor prefers to SQ, and W_{SF}(SQ) is the set of options that a majority of the Senate floor prefers to SQ. The set of options which the president prefers to SQ is the president's *preferred-to set* of SQ; for consistency in notation, we abbreviate it as W_P(SQ).

A *core* is the set of options which cannot be upset in a body, given the rules governing policymaking in that body. Thus, we can speak of a *floor core,* which is the set of points that cannot be upset by any floor majority. The House and Senate floor cores are $CORE_{HF}$ and $CORE_{SF}$, respectively. If SQ lies in a core, this means (by definition) that there is no other option which can defeat SQ via the prescribed rules. Thus, if SQ is in a core, W...(SQ) must be empty. If SQ is not in a core, then W...(SQ) is not empty.

To further simplify the diagrams used to illustrate our arguments, we will assume that there is just one House member and one Senate member plus the president. The ideal points of the House member, Senate member, and president are indicated by H, S, and P, respectively. If the ideal points of the House, Senate, and president form a triangle, then the area within the triangle, including its border, is $CORE_{HSP}$ (see Fig. 1a). An SQ lying anywhere in this $CORE_{HSP}$ is in equilibrium, which means that there exists no coalition of the House, Senate, and president which can upset any such SQ. That is, there exists no region in which the indifference curves through SQ of the House, Senate, and president all overlap; at most, the indifference curves of only two actors at a time would overlap. Since for constitutional reasons it takes all three actors to replace SQ with some other policy, this SQ is thus in equilibrium. Similarly, if the ideal points of the House, president, and Senate form a straight line, then the line from H to S (including P) is $CORE_{HSP}$ (see Fig. 1b). For an SQ on this straight-line $CORE_{HSP}$ there exists no line segment for which the indifference curves of the House, Senate, and president through SQ all overlap; at most, the indifference curves of only two actors at a time overlap. Hence, this SQ is also in equilibrium.

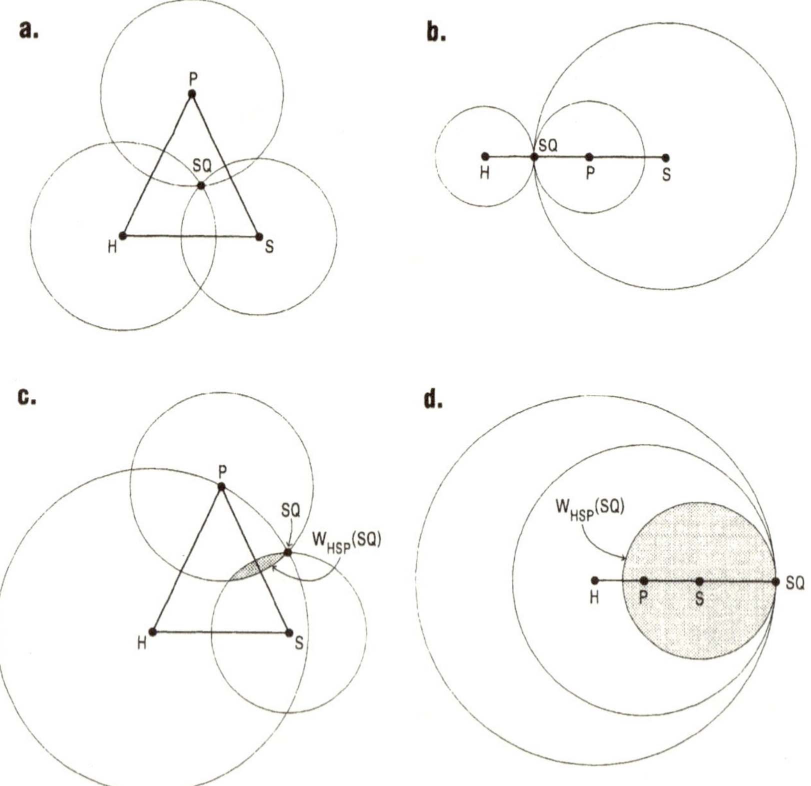

Figure 1. Win Sets for Triangular and Straight-Line Cores

In contrast, if SQ lies outside $CORE_{HSP}$, then the president, House, and Senate can all join together in a coalition to replace SQ with some other policy in $W_{HSP}(SQ)$. In Figure 1, c and d, for example, the shaded areas show where the indifference curves of all three actors overlap for these triangular and straight-line cores. The actors can replace SQ with some policy in the shaded areas, and they would all find a policy *within* $CORE_{HSP}$ to be most beneficial. In effect, then, the House, Senate, and president can always upset any SQ outside $CORE_{HSP}$ and agree to replace it with a new policy inside $CORE_{HSP}$.

Political Constraints on the Autonomy of Political Executives

Our model of policy making focuses just on relations among the House, Senate, president and an appointed political executive. We will now assume that the agency of interest is an independent regulatory body with broad legal jurisdiction and that there is one person who serves as the agency head for a fixed term and who cannot be fired by the president.[1]

The literature on public management emphasizes the importance of political executives' knowledge of how their actions are constrained by the political environment as well as their skill in selecting beneficial courses of action within these constraints. For example, Yates (1991, 40) maintains that an understanding of the agency's environment is "the starting point of any successful diagnosis of the problems that exist and the strategies that are likely to work in any management context." Similarly, Cohen and Eimicke (1995, 29) suggest that, "The best managers are those who understand their organization's environment. They are able to project the effect that their actions will have on that environment. They also have a keen understanding of how these outside forces constrain and influence their organization's activities." Let us use our formal model to clarify what some of these constraints and influences might be.

Given the agency head's policy preferences at any particular time, policymaking for the agency head is a problem of *constrained optimization*; that is, given the constraints imposed by the preferences of the president and legislators, the agency head has only one best choice, which we will label SQ* (and sometimes even SQ**) and which is his most preferred option in $CORE_{HSP}$. We will consider various possible locations for the agency head's ideal point in relation to $CORE_{HSP}$; for each case we will determine the best action the agency head could take.

The location of SQ will affect whether the agency head will be able to unilaterally make an improvement in policy. Imagine a situation in which the agency head's ideal point, A, lies outside $CORE_{HSP}$, and the initial SQ lies on the boundary of $CORE_{HSP}$ nearest to A. Since the agency head's optimal policy, SQ*, is located at the same point as SQ, the agency head can make no improvement in the location of SQ. In contrast, imagine a situation in which SQ lies in a part of $CORE_{HSP}$ which is relatively far away from A (and thus far from SQ*). The agency head can now unilaterally make a substantial improvement in policy, moving it from its initial location at SQ to a new location at SQ*. Since SQ* is in equilibrium (recall that it lies in $CORE_{HSP}$), it cannot be upset by any joint action of the House, Senate, and president. A similar situation arises when the agency head's ideal point lies inside $CORE_{HSP}$ and SQ lies inside $CORE_{HSP}$ but far away from A. The agency head can again unilaterally make a substantial improvement in policy, moving it from SQ to SQ*.

If the agency head's preferences change over time, the agency's political autonomy is determined by the extent to which the agency head can abandon some current policy and unilaterally adopt something else. An agency's political autonomy thus refers to the existence of a set of policies, any one of which the agency head could select without his choice being reversed by the president and Congress. In our model, as long as the agency head selects a policy in $CORE_{HSP}$, the chosen policy will be invulnerable to upset by the president and Congress. That is, the agency's political autonomy is defined by the set of equilibrium choices that are available to any possible agency head.

This means that the appropriate measure of the amount of political autonomy for an agency is simply the size of $CORE_{HSP}$. A configuration of actor preferences which creates a large $CORE_{HSP}$ maximizes the agency's political autonomy and minimizes the influence of the president and Congress on agency policymaking. A configuration of actor preferences that creates a small $CORE_{HSP}$ minimizes agency autonomy and maximizes the joint impact of the president and Congress on agency policymaking.

We can summarize our overall arguments as follows:[2]

Observation 1: The larger $CORE_{HSP}$ is, the more political autonomy the agency has.

Observation 2: Agency heads have little ability to bring about policy change when:

(a) $CORE_{HSP}$ is small;

(b) $CORE_{HSP}$ is large, A lies outside $CORE_{HSP}$, SQ lies inside $CORE_{HSP}$ and close to A;

(c) $CORE_{HSP}$ is large, A lies inside $CORE_{HSP}$, SQ lies inside $CORE_{HSP}$ and close to A.

Observation 3: Agency heads have greater ability to bring about policy change when:
(a) $CORE_{HSP}$ is large, A lies outside $CORE_{HSP}$, SQ lies inside $CORE_{HSP}$ but far from A;
(b) $CORE_{HSP}$ is large, A lies inside $CORE_{HSP}$, SQ lies inside $CORE_{HSP}$ but far from A.

Observation 4: For an agency head's ideal point, A, which is located outside $CORE_{HSP}$, the most constraining part of the agency head's political environment will be the boundary of $CORE_{HSP}$ which is closest to A.

Observation 5: Changes in the size, shape, or location of $CORE_{HSP}$ will not necessarily force the agency head to change policy. Whether policy changes will result from a change in $CORE_{HSP}$ depends on an interaction among the following five variables: (a) the location of the initial status quo, which is SQ; (b) the location of the agency head's ideal point, which is A; (c) the location of the agency head's best choice in $CORE_{HSP}$, which is SQ*; (d) the initial size, shape, and location of $CORE_{HSP}$; and (e) the final size, shape, and location of $CORE_{HSP}$.

In other words, preference change by the president, House, and Senate can have a wide range of possible impacts on the agency head's choice of policy, including no change at all, a change in policy that benefits the agency head, and a change in policy that hurts the agency head.

Do Agency Heads Have an Advantage if They Move First?

In their study of success stories of public managers, Levin and Sanger (1994, 160–62) emphasized the importance of what they called "a bias for action." It was found that not waiting for others but instead boldly setting a course on their own was a common characteristic of successful managers. Kaufman (1981, 136) similarly stressed the costs for federal bureau chiefs if they passively react to events rather than seizing the initiative: "If administrative leaders are inactive, the opportunities to influence the course of events, circumscribed as these are, will fall to others. To be passive, then, is merely to make it easier for other people to have their way, to the extent that anyone can have his way." This general phenomenon—that passivity can have policy costs—emerges from our model as well. Following a period in which one or more of the ideal points of the president, House, and Senate have changed, the agency head can gain an advantage by preemptively changing agency policy first, rather than by passively allowing

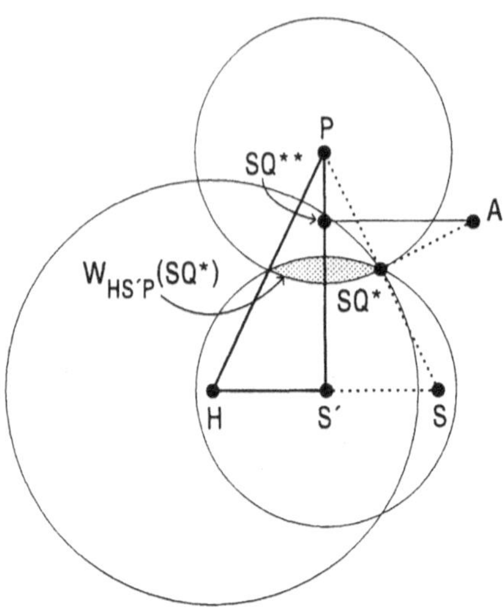

Figure 2. Preemptive Policymaking by the Agency Head

the president, House, and Senate to force a change in agency policy via the legislative process.

To illustrate, consider Figure 2. Initially, the agency head's ideal point, A, lies outside $CORE_{HSP}$, as defined by the larger P-H-S triangle (including the dotted lines), and his best policy in $CORE_{HSP}$ is at SQ*. Now assume that the Senate's ideal point moves leftward from S to S′, creating the $CORE_{HS'P}$ shown in Figure 2 by the solid triangle. The agency head's best policy in the new $CORE_{HS'P}$ is at SQ**, and if he moves expeditiously following the change in the Senate's ideal point from S to S′, he can thereby ensure that SQ** becomes the new policy.

However, this location for SQ** has an interesting property: given SQ* as the initial status quo policy and given the shift of S to S′, *no* coalition of the House, Senate, and president would have agreed on SQ** as their new policy. To see this, examine the indifference curves of P, H, and S′ through SQ*. The region where all three of these indifference curves intersect is shaded in Figure 2; this shaded region is the win set of SQ*, or $W_{HS'P}(SQ^*)$. These three actors would find it in their mutual interest to choose some policy inside $W_{HS'P}(SQ^*)$, and they would not all agree on the policy at SQ** since SQ** lies outside $W_{HS'P}$; in particular, SQ** is worse for the Senator at S′ than any policy in $W_{HS'P}(SQ^*)$. Nonetheless, the president prefers SQ** to anything in $W_{HS'P}(SQ^*)$ and so would protect SQ**, perhaps with his veto, from attempts by the House and Senate to upset it. Hence, we advance:

Observation 6: Following a change in $CORE_{HSP}$, the agency head may have an incentive to change agency policy preemptively, before Congress and the president have an opportunity to force a change in agency policy through the legislative process.

The Relationship between Autonomy and Goal Conflict

So far we have conceptualized agency autonomy as involving a large $CORE_{HSP}$, and we have treated this autonomy as if it were unambiguously desirable for the agency. However, the autonomy that stems from a large $CORE_{HSP}$ may be a mixed blessing for the agency head: A large $CORE_{HSP}$ means that, even when his ideal point lies inside $CORE_{HSP}$, at least one major institutional actor, and possibly the other two as well, will be unhappy with what the agency is doing. With a large $CORE_{HSP}$ and an A inside it, the resulting SQ* will invariably lie relatively far from at least the House's ideal point, or the Senate's, or the president's, and possibly from all three. Hence, the most "distant" actor (or actors) will be dissatisfied with agency policy and so will always be trying to get the agency to move policy in its (or their) direction. This may in turn mean that life for the agency head is full of conflict, with a resulting substantial level of unpleasantness. In contrast, despite the lack of autonomy that a small $CORE_{HSP}$ means for the agency, the benefit is that the other actors will be relatively happy with the policy that the agency will have to adopt. Hence, life for the agency head may be somewhat more serene, though at the definite cost of a loss of flexibility and at the possible cost of a policy that the agency head may not particularly like.

Persuasion and Policy Change

We now turn our attention to how the agency head might try to loosen the constraints of the political environment. Here we will discuss some conditions under which political executives may find it useful to try to *persuade* other actors to change their views of what constitutes good public policy. While our model cannot tell us whether a political executive's efforts at persuading other actors will succeed, it can tell us about *which* other actors it would be most important to persuade and in *what direction* he should try to move their ideal points.

There are two fundamentally different situations in which an agency head might find himself: his ideal point can lie *inside* or *outside* $CORE_{HSP}$. When the agency head's ideal point lies inside $CORE_{HSP}$, he can select an SQ* that is identical to his own ideal point. In this case, his prime strategy would be primarily *defensive,* aimed at simply keeping $CORE_{HSP}$ located so that A continues to lie inside it. If successful, the agency head could continue to select a policy, SQ*, at his own ideal point.

In contrast, the agency head is disadvantaged by a situation in which his ideal point lies outside $CORE_{HSP}$. In this case, his best choice in $CORE_{HSP}$ will always be different from his ideal point, and the farther away his ideal point is from $CORE_{HSP}$, the worse SQ* will be for him. If there is any potential for him to persuade others to change their preferences, his goal would be to select his target or targets so that the nearest border of $CORE_{HSP}$ is moved closer to his own ideal point, which in turn would allow him to select a better SQ*. Obviously, the best outcome would be for this nearest border of $CORE_{HSP}$ to be moved so much that his own ideal point falls inside this new $CORE_{HSP}$; he could then adopt his own ideal point as agency policy.

There are at least two different strategies he might adopt to move a border of $CORE_{HSP}$ toward his ideal point. In Figure 3, the agency head's ideal point, A, lies outside the original $CORE_{HSP}$, defined by the H-S-P triangle. His best choice is the SQ* inside $CORE_{HSP}$. He can try either of two approaches to move the nearest border, P-S, closer to A. First, he can try to persuade the Senate to change its ideal point from S to S′, which is so far to the right that the P-S′ border now reaches A. His best choice could thus be an SQ**, which is identical to A. For this strategy to work, however, the Senate's ideal point would have to undergo a considerable change. Second, the agency head can attempt to persuade *both* the president and Senate to change their ideal points—for example, from P to P′ and from S to S′, respectively—so that the new P′-S′ border reaches A. The virtue of this strategy is that, while the views of two different institutions would have to be changed rather than just one, the changes required for the president and for the Senate, are each smaller than the change required for the Senate, alone.

These examples suggest some generalizations about whom the agency head might wish to select as targets for persuasion. In general, the agency head should target that institutional actor whose ideal point is closest to A. If A is roughly equidistant from two of the other

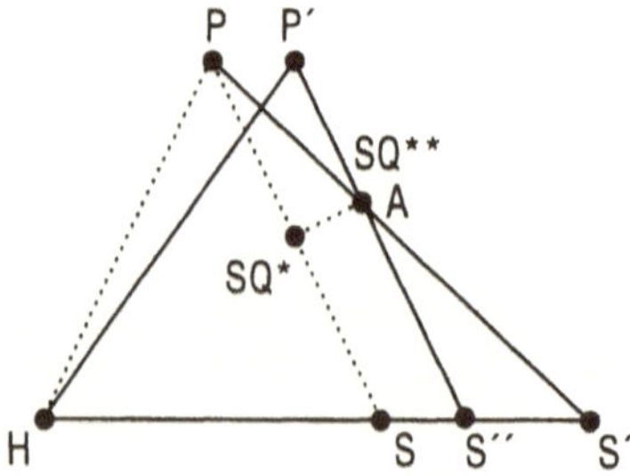

Figure 3. Policy Improvement Due to Persuasion of One or Two Other Actors

actors (as in Fig. 3), then the agency head will have to choose between trying to make a large change in one institution's preferences or trying to make smaller changes in two institutions' preferences. Overall, then, we would simply state:

> Observation 7: For the agency head whose ideal point lies outside $CORE_{HSP}$, efforts at persuasion should be aimed at the closest actor or actors.

Transformational Leadership and Policy Change

In his discussion of the strategies of political executives, Wilson (1989, 213) argues that "The decision makers who succeed are those who manage to combine a clear vision of what they want the agency to do with the ability to communicate that vision effectively and to motivate the key civil servants to act on it." In their book on public management strategies Bozeman and Straussman (1990) give some insight into why political executives may sometimes be able to have the impact that Wilson describes: it is almost always the case that multiple definitions of a policy problem are possible. They refer to a selection of one of these multiple definitions as "framing the issue" and they maintain (1990, 38) that "The issue frame circumscribes the public manager's discretion." For this reason, they emphasize (1990, 37) that "Framing the issue—determining types and levels of managerial discretion and relation to objectives—is, thus, crucial to strategic public management." Other studies of effective administrative leadership (e.g., Behn 1991, Caro 1974, Doig and Hargrove 1987, and Lewis 1980) likewise suggest that at least some leaders were capable of "framing the issues," "defining the problem," "setting the agenda," or engaging in "heresthetic" activities (Riker 1986). Indeed, De Pree (1989, 11) suggested that "The first responsibility of a leader is to define reality."

In sum, then, an effective political executive is capable of getting others to look at the world in a way that is politically useful to the executive. This is a rather different process than simply persuading others to move their ideal points (as described in the previous section). To help think about such issue-framing activities in the context of our multi-institutional policymaking model we will focus on three aspects of our model which have been important in our story so far but to which we have given little explicit attention.

First, we have not given much consideration to *the number of issue dimensions* involved in some problem area. Our diagrams, for example, simply assume without any argument that there are two issue dimensions. But the number of issue dimensions thought to characterize some problem area is not inherently generic to the problem area; instead, the number of issue dimensions is a function of the participants' beliefs and perceptions. As such, the number of these dimensions may be *politically manipulable.* That is, in some cases a political executive may find it useful to *augment* the number of dimensions currently under consideration (e.g., arguing that "there is an additional critical factor we need to consider, which is . . . "), while in other cases he may find it politically useful to *reduce* the number of dimensions currently under consideration (e.g., arguing that "there is just one overriding issue, which is . . . ").

Second, we have not given explicit consideration to *what the issue dimensions are,* and in particular, how they are related to each other. So far we have assumed that the two dimensions are orthogonal to each other; that is, the issue preferences on each dimension are separable and not statistically correlated. But this assumption begs the question as to why there is not instead a pair of dimensions in which the issue preferences are nonseparable and thus correlated with each other. In spatial terms, the vectors for each dimension would no longer be orthogonal to each other but would form an oblique angle. In effect, since the nature of the correlation among the issue dimensions is variable, it may be politically manipulable as well.

Third, we have not given explicit consideration to *the relative importance, or salience, of the issue dimensions* perceived to be involved in some problem area. For our figures so far we have assumed that each actor's indifference curves are circular; that is, each actor is assumed to consider the two issue dimensions to be of equal importance. However, it seems unlikely that any two issue dimensions will be considered of *equal* importance by *any* particular individual. Instead, it is more plausible to assume (a) that the issue dimensions are not equally important to any one individual, which means that each individual's indifference curves are elliptical in shape, and (b) that for any pair of issue dimensions, different individuals will have differently shaped elliptical indifference curves. Of course, if the salience of the issue dimensions is variable and not fixed, then the salience too is likely to be politically manipulable.

There are thus three variables which are politically manipulable for issue-framing: the number of issue dimensions, what the issue dimensions are, and the salience to each individual of the relevant issue dimensions. With three variables there are many possible strategies of manipulation, and we will focus on just one. We will begin with the assumption that the president, House, and Senate initially think about public policies in terms of *two* issue dimensions. We will then assume that the agency head is capable of changing the salience of these two initial issue dimensions to the other actors. This can presumably be done through public and private speechmaking (see, e.g., Doig and Hargrove 1987 on David Lilienthal at the TVA), through various rhetorical and heresthetical tools (as described by Riker 1986), through taking advantage of accidents and other unplanned events (e.g., the widely publicized cases of food and pharmaceutical poisoning which ultimately enhanced the powers of the Food and Drug Administration—see Quirk 1980, 192–96), and through a variety of other techniques.

In fact, we will further assume here that the agency head is capable of so enhancing the salience of one issue dimension, relative to the second, that the first *completely* structures the policymaking process. In other words, one dimension is simply eliminated or the two dimensions become so closely linked that they are perfectly correlated with each other. In either case, the dimensionality of the problem area drops from two down to just one.[3] Finally, we will assume that the agency head is capable of defining what that single dominant issue dimension is.

With these three assumptions, the question we address is this: Given the policy SQ* in $CORE_{HSP}$, which the agency head could initially adopt when policymaking takes place in a two-dimensional issue space structured by the X- and Y-dimensions, is there some single alternative issue dimension—either just X, or just Y, or something which is oblique to X and Y—which would allow him to choose a policy closer to his own ideal point?

The answer to this question depends on two variables. First, is A located *inside* $CORE_{HSP}$ or does it lie *outside* $CORE_{HSP}$? Second, what is the initial configuration of institutional preferences? That is, do the ideal points of the House, Senate, and president form a straight line or do they form a triangle? We will consider these possible cases in turn.

An Agency Ideal Point Inside a Straight-Line $CORE_{HSP}$

Consider Figure 4, in which the ideal points of the House, Senate, and president form a straight line, which means that $CORE_{HSP}$ is the dotted line connecting H and S. Since A lies inside $CORE_{HSP}$, the agency head could choose his own ideal point as SQ*. If A is inside $CORE_{HSP}$, condensing policymaking onto a single dimension cannot yield an improvement for the agency head: with A inside $CORE_{HSP}$, he is already able to select an SQ* that is identical to A. Indeed, when A lies inside $CORE_{HSP}$, condensing policymaking onto a single dimension (other than that defined by the H-S line) may even serve to reduce A's autonomy.

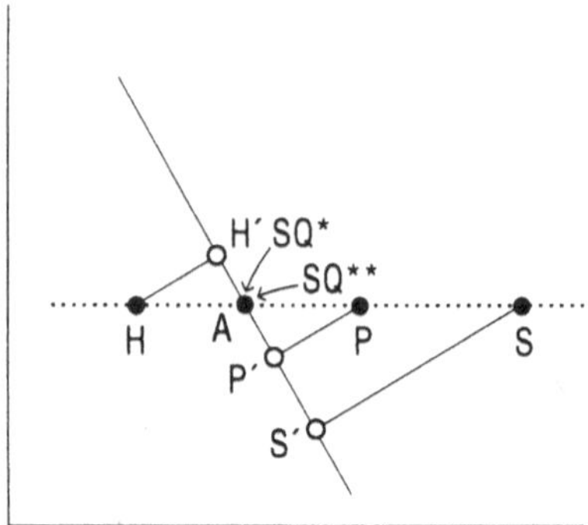

Figure 4. Choosing a Dimension When A Is Inside a Straight-Line $CORE_{HSP}$

To demonstrate these points, it is convenient to use A as the center of a straight line which pivots around A. In Figure 4, for example, a line is drawn through A, running in a northwest/southeast direction. Taking this diagonal line as the potential issue dimension along which policymaking might take place, we need to determine for each actor the point on this diagonal dimension which gives the actor the most utility. That is, we need to determine where each actor's ideal point would be if it were projected onto this diagonal line (i.e., onto the new issue dimension). When the original indifference curves are circular (in the two-dimensional space), the projected points on the single new issue dimension are found simply by drawing a perpendicular from the original ideal point to the new dimension line. For each individual, the point at which the perpendicular strikes the new dimension line is the actor's *induced ideal point* on the line. Thus, given the ideal point, H, of the House member in the two-dimensional space, the induced ideal point on the new dimension line is H′, the induced ideal point of the Senator is S′, and the induced ideal point of the president is P′. Since the new dimension line is drawn through A, A is its own projection on the line. Note in Figure 4 and the following figures that the induced ideal points on the new dimension line will be indicated by the open dots to distinguish them from the original two-dimensional ideal points.

On this new issue dimension in Figure 4, there is a set of points in equilibrium, which we label $CORE_{H'S'P'}$; these points lie along this issue dimension from H′ to S′ and include all points in between. Since A lies inside this new $CORE_{H'S'P'}$, the agency head has the freedom to choose a policy at his own ideal point, just as he would when A lies inside the two-dimensional $CORE_{HSP}$ on the dotted line. Hence, the agency head can now choose a policy, SQ**, which is located at his own ideal point. Since the initial SQ* was also at the agency head's ideal point, the agency head gains nothing here from condensing policymaking onto one issue dimension. In fact, as long as A lies inside the original CORE_{HSP} (along the dotted line), the result will always be that the agency head can choose a new policy at his own ideal point, no matter what new issue-dimension line is drawn through A; that is, SQ* and SQ** will always be identical. Hence, for this class of cases we would advance:

> Observation 8: When CORE_{HSP} is a straight line and A lies inside CORE_{HSP}, the agency head will be able to select a policy at his own ideal point. Selecting an alternative dimension can produce no improvement in the final policy for the agency head.

Moreover, selecting an alternative dimension may have a negative impact on the autonomy available to A. The reason is that, with each alternative dimension, both ends of $\text{CORE}_{H'S'P'}$ are closer to A than on the original dimension. For example, in Figure 4 the line segment H-S is a measure of the autonomy initially available to the agency head, while the line segment H′-S′ is a measure of the autonomy available to the agency head on the new dimension line. Notice that the H-S line is longer than the H′-S′ line; hence, the agency head has more autonomy with the former dimension than with the latter. For this reason we advance:

> Observation 9: When CORE_{HSP} is a straight line and A lies inside CORE_{HSP}, any dimension other than the original will reduce agency autonomy.

Next, consider a case in which CORE_{HSP} is again a straight line and A lies on the straight line though outside this CORE_{HSP} (see Fig. 5). Let us describe a single-dimension strategy as a *pivot* measured in terms of the number of degrees of counter-clockwise rotation from a horizontal line. In Figure 5, for example, a 120° pivot through A induces a $\text{CORE}_{H'S'P'}$ which does not include A. With this pivot the best the agency head could do is an SQ** located at H′ on the issue dimension; this is an improvement over the original SQ* (SQ** is closer to A than is SQ*) but it is still not optimal. Examination of other possible rotations reveals that the best pivot for the agency head is 90°, i.e., the optimal dimension is a vertical line. With this 90° pivot the induced ideal points on the line—P′, H′, and S′—are all identical to A, which means that this $\text{CORE}_{H'S'P'}$ is a single point. This means in turn that the agency head could pick an SQ** located at his own ideal point. In fact, this 90° strategy is the *only* pivot that allows the agency

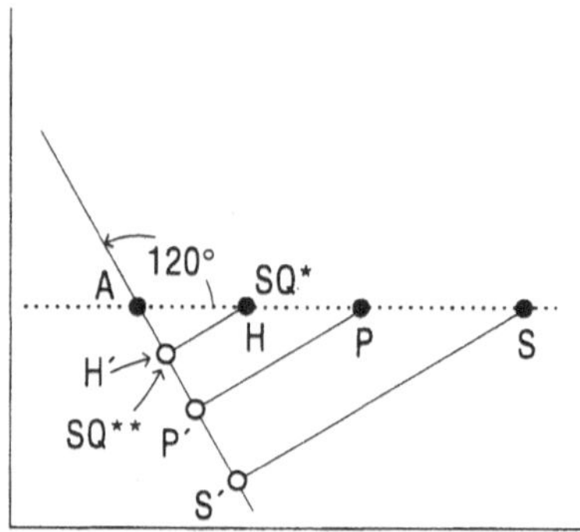

Figure 5. Choosing an Optimal Pivot When A Is to the Left of a Straight-Line $CORE_{HSP}$

head to choose a policy at his own ideal point. Note, however, that the agency head would have no autonomy at all with this solution. Thus we have:

> Observation 10: When $CORE_{HSP}$ is a straight line and A lies on this line but outside $CORE_{HSP}$, the optimal pivot for the agency head is always at a 90° angle to the line.

An Agency Ideal Point Outside a Straight-Line $CORE_{HSP}$

Next we turn to a more complicated case, shown in Figure 6. As before, H, P, and S lie in a straight line, thereby forming a $CORE_{HSP}$, which is the dotted line connecting H to S. In this case, though, A lies above the $CORE_{HSP}$ line; the agency head's best policy is thus the SQ* point on the $CORE_{HSP}$ line; see Figure 6a.

Now let us consider the issue dimensions which pivot around A. Figure 6a shows a pivot of 15°; the induced $CORE_{H'S'P'}$ includes A, which allows the agency head to choose an SQ* at his own ideal point. Figure 6b shows a pivot of 47°; in this case, $CORE_{H'S'P'}$ includes A at the upper end (at S′), which again allows the agency head to choose an SQ** at his own ideal point. In the 100° pivot shown in Figure 6c, $CORE_{H'S'P'}$ does not include A, which means that the SQ** cannot be located at A. We can summarize these results as follows:

> Observation 11: When $CORE_{HSP}$ is a straight line and A lies off this line, there is a set of pivots which allow the agency head to pick a policy at his own ideal point and a complementary set of pivots which do not allow him to pick a policy at his own ideal point.

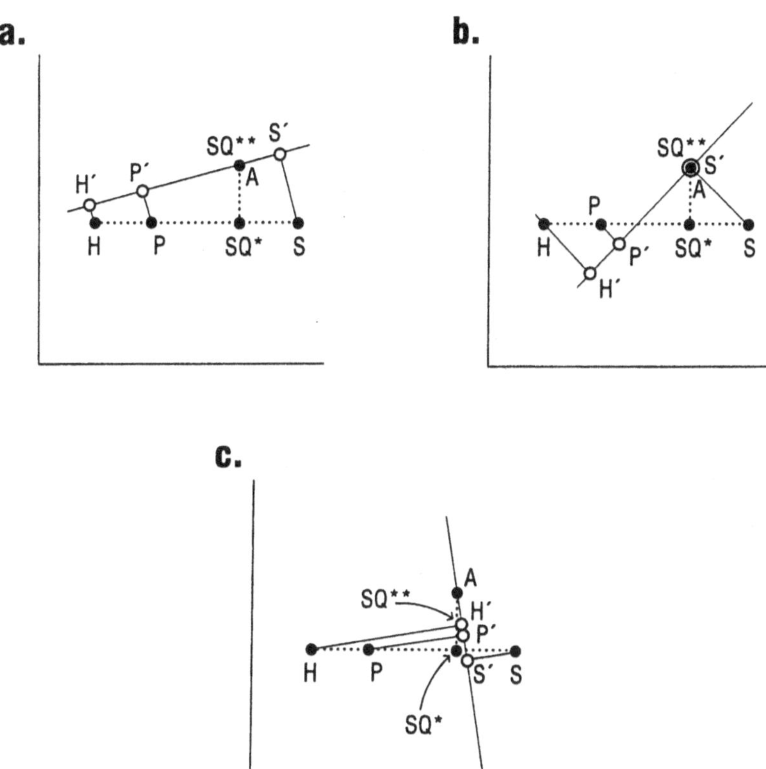

Figure 6. Choosing an Optimal Pivot When A Lies Above a Straight-Line CORE_{HSP}

We can graphically display the entire set of pivots which produce an improvement for the agency head and the corresponding set of pivots which do not. Using the ideal points from Figure 6, Figure 7a shows all the optimal and sub-optimal pivots. Any pivot that falls in the Optimal Strategies region will allow the agency head to select an SQ**, which is identical to A, and this SQ** will be better for him than the original SQ*. A pivot that falls in the Not Optimal Strategies region will not allow the agency head to select an SQ**, which is identical to A (though some of the SQ**s produced here may be better than the original SQ*).

Note that with the original two dimensions, the agency's ideal point can be at a variable distance from CORE_{HSP}. As A's distance from CORE_{HSP} increases, the agency head has a decreasing range of pivots that would allow him to select a policy at his own ideal point; that is, there are fewer and fewer pivots which he considers optimal. As

a.

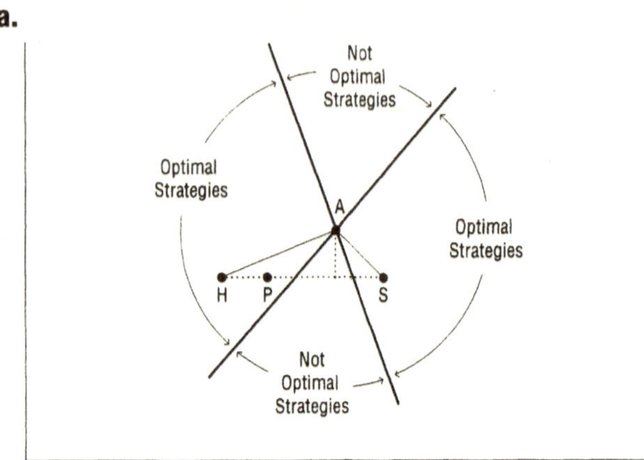

b.

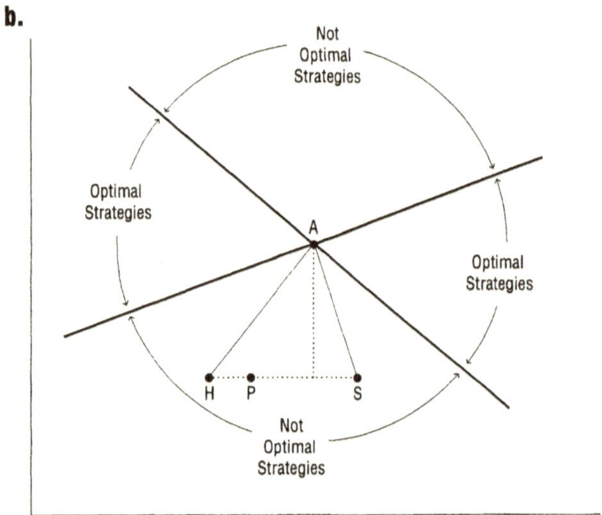

Figure 7. Sets of Optimal and Non-Optimal Pivots for a Straight-Line $CORE_{HSP}$

illustrated in Figure 7b, A is farther from $CORE_{HSP}$ (which is the H-P-S line), so the range of the Optimal Strategies shrinks and the range of the Not Optimal Strategies expands. A very distant location of A would leave the agency head with only a very small range of optimal pivots. Hence we suggest:

> Observation 12: When $CORE_{HSP}$ is a straight line and A lies off this line, the farther A is from $CORE_{HSP}$, the smaller the range of pivots which will allow the agency head to pick a policy at his own ideal point.

An Agency Ideal Point Inside a Triangular $CORE_{HSP}$

We now turn to the case in which $CORE_{HSP}$ is a triangle and not a straight line. In the first case, shown in Figure 8, we assume that the agency head's ideal point lies *inside* the $CORE_{HSP}$, which is the dotted-line triangle here. When A lies inside $CORE_{HSP}$, the agency head can always select an SQ* which is identical to A; hence, condensing policymaking onto a single dimension can never yield a better outcome for the agency head. As can also be seen in Figure 8 this new dimension induces a $CORE_{H'S'P'}$ that includes A, thus allowing the agency head to choose an SQ** at his own ideal point. Hence we make this note:

> Observation 13: When $CORE_{HSP}$ forms a triangle and A lies inside this triangle, the agency head will be able to select a policy at his own ideal point, whether policymaking takes place on two dimensions or on a single dimension chosen by the agency head. This means that condensing policymaking onto a single dimension can produce no improvement in the final policy for the agency head.

What happens to agency autonomy here is more complex than in the Figure 4 case (see Observation 9). For essentially the same reasons as before, A will be closer to H′ than to H, closer to S′ than S, and closer to P′ than P. Hence, in this sense, the agency head's autonomy is reduced. However, note in Figure 8 that A is closer to the P-S and P-H *boundaries* of the original $CORE_{HSP}$, for example, than it is to either of the endpoints of $CORE_{H'S'P'}$. Indeed, A can move *farther* back and forth along the induced $CORE_{H'S'P'}$ than it could move back and forth within the underlying $CORE_{HSP}$. In this sense, then, while the

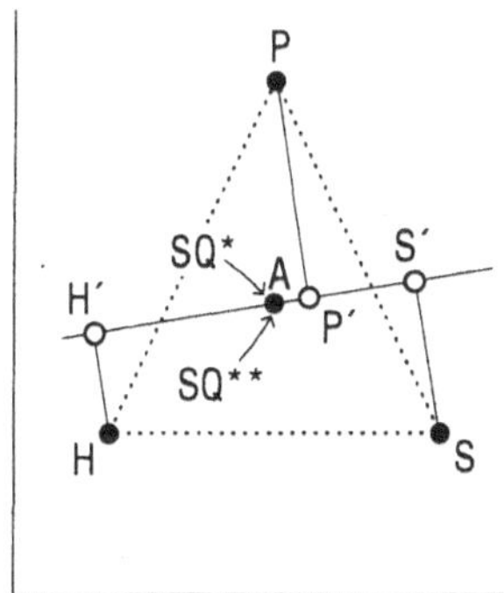

Figure 8. Choosing an Optimal Pivot When A Lies Inside a Triangular $CORE_{HSP}$

agency head does not get an improved outcome from condensing policymaking onto a single dimension (because SQ** = SQ*), his autonomy may in some ways be *increased* by such a condensation.

An Agency Ideal Point Outside a Triangular $CORE_{HSP}$

Finally, we assume that the agency head's ideal point lies *outside* $CORE_{HSP}$ (see Fig. 9). The agency head's best policy in this $CORE_{HSP}$ is the SQ* which is shown. As with the case where $CORE_{HSP}$ was a straight line (see Fig. 6), there are some pivots for which the induced $CORE_{H'S'P'}$ includes the agency head's ideal point and other pivots for which $CORE_{H'S'P'}$ does not include the agency head's ideal point.

For example, Figure 9a shows a pivot of 8°, and this $CORE_{H'S'P'}$ includes A, which means that the agency head can select an SQ** at his own ideal point. Figure 9b shows a pivot of 80°, a strategy yielding an SQ** that is not identical to his ideal point, though SQ** is closer to A than the original SQ*. We can summarize these observations in the following way:

> Observation 14. When $CORE_{HSP}$ is a triangle and A lies outside the triangle, there will be a set of pivots that allow the agency head to pick a policy at his own ideal point and a complementary set of pivots that do not allow him to pick a policy at his ideal point.

For an A that lies outside a triangular $CORE_{HSP}$, Figure 10a shows the set of pivots that improve the agency head's outcome and the set of pivots that do not. Any pivot through A falling in the Optimal Strategies region allows the agency head to select an SQ** that is identical to A, and this SQ** is better than the original SQ*. A pivot

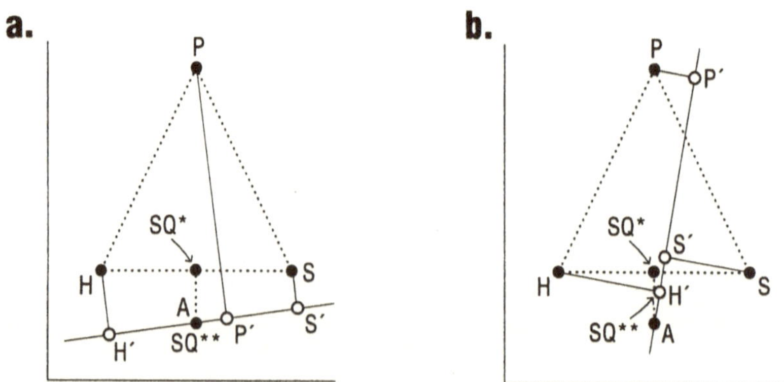

Figure 9. Choosing an Optimal Pivot When A Lies Outside a Triangular $CORE_{HSP}$

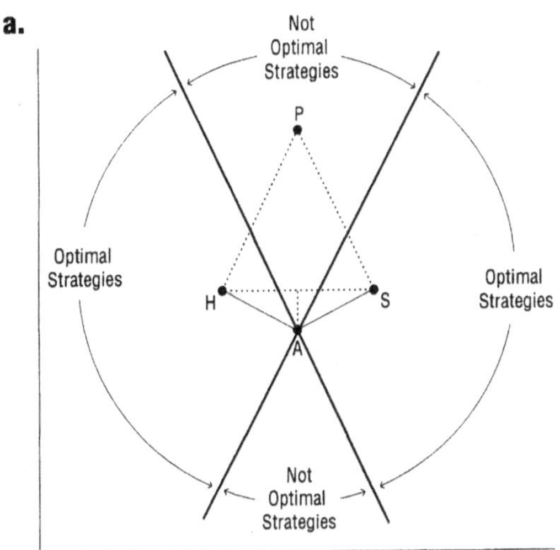

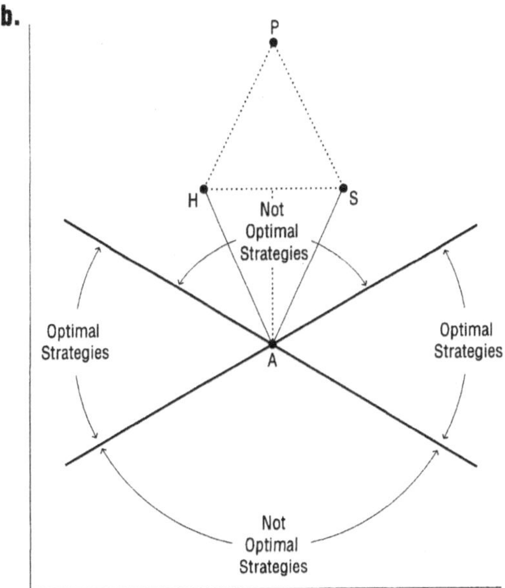

Figure 10. Sets of Optimal and Non-Optimal Pivots for a Triangular $CORE_{HSP}$

that falls in the Not Optimal Strategies region will not allow him to select an SQ** which is identical to A (though at least some of the SQ**s which are produced here may be better than the original SQ*).

As when $CORE_{HSP}$ is a straight line, the farther A is from a triangular $CORE_{HSP}$, the smaller the range of pivots which will allow the agency head to select a policy at his own ideal point. Figure 10b illustrates this argument. Compared to the set of Optimal Strategies in Figure 10a, the more distant A in Figure 10b produces a considerably smaller set of Optimal Strategies. Hence we suggest:

> Observation 15. When $CORE_{HSP}$ is a triangle and A lies outside this triangle, the farther A is from the triangle, the smaller the range of pivots which will allow the agency head to pick a policy at his own ideal point.

In general, it is worth noting that even with non-optimal pivot strategies, the SQ** that is produced can never be worse for the agency head than the original SQ* (at least in the case of circular indifference curves). Hence we would assert the following:

> Observation 16: Condensing policymaking from two dimensions down to one may improve the policy choice for the agency head and at least will never make the policy choice worse.

When there exist several optimal pivots for the agency head our last question involves which of these optimal pivots he should select. One plausible selection rule is for him to choose a pivot that places A exactly in the middle of the induced $CORE_{H'S'P'}$. This would ensure that A is as far as possible from each end of $CORE_{H'S'P'}$, thereby maximizing the distance the agency head's ideal point could move in either direction in the future without leaving $CORE_{H'S'P'}$.

We end this section with two qualifications. First, since presidents and legislators are presumably as sophisticated as the agency head, they may not be vulnerable to the agency head's issue-framing strategies. For this reason, an agency head's issue-framing strategy may often be aimed more at the *general public* because the public is (presumably) less sophisticated, and thus more susceptible to manipulation, than the president and legislators. While the ultimate goal would be to gain the support of the president and Congress, the strategy would be to gain this support via issue-framing appeals to the president's and legislators' *constituents.*[4] Second, in presuming that the agency head can successfully impose a single issue dimension when it is convenient, we are presuming not only that he is capable of doing so but also that other potential competitors—such as the president, legislators, or interest groups—do not advance their own dimensions. In fact, these other competitors may have both an incentive to combat the agency's issue dimension and the capability to advance their own most preferred issue dimensions.

For these reasons, then, the most appropriate model might not be our decision-analytic model (i.e., what is optimal for an agency head without strategic competitors?) but a game-theoretic model in which the agency head and his competitors vie for the support of Congress and the president via different kinds of appeals (i.e., via different issue-dimension pivots) to the general public. A much more complex model would be required to analyze this characterization of the agency head's problem. Such a model would allow us to answer two questions: (a) Does there exist a set of Nash equilibrium strategies (i.e., a strategy for each actor such that if one actor does not change a pivot, the other actors will not change their pivots either)?, and (b) If a set of Nash equilibrium strategies does exist, which actors will be most successful at getting their ideal policies adopted, and which actors will be less successful?

Conclusion

We have focused our analysis on the management of the agency's political environment, which many students of public management see as critical to administrative leadership. In general, our analysis confirms key assertions of the public management literature, but we believe that our analysis also improves understanding of agency political environments in three important ways. First, it provides a more systematic understanding of the conditions under which appointed political executives have or can gain some political autonomy. Second, it highlights the importance of some variables in political environments which are not usually treated explicitly in the public management literature. And third, it reveals the importance of political leadership. Let us summarize our findings for each topic.

First, the analysis confirms the argument by Bozeman and Straussman (1990, 5) that "strategic management is context dependent": there are conditions under which a political executive has some political autonomy of which he can take advantage, but there are also conditions under which he will have little or no autonomy at all. The analysis also reinforces their argument (1990, 36) that political executives need to "find the correct managerial space for action." In our terms, the effective executive needs to identify the relevant policy space so that he can take advantage of what autonomy is available.

Our analysis suggests that the primary factor influencing the agency's political autonomy is the size of $CORE_{HSP}$. The concept of $CORE_{HSP}$, moreover, introduces into the public management literature the analytical tool of equilibrium analysis, which clarifies when policies can be changed and when they cannot, given the configuration of actor preferences. When the external actors hold divergent preferences, thereby producing a large $CORE_{HSP}$, the agency head has the potential for exercising substantial influence over policy choice. When these powerful actors have convergent preferences, thereby reducing the size of $CORE_{HSP}$, the agency head will have less room to maneuver. Thus, the configuration of preferences of the critical actors in the agency's environment plays a key role in setting the limits of agency influence over policy.

Second, our analysis highlights factors in the environment that the agency head should consider. To realize the potential for influence when the external actors' preferences diverge, the agency head needs to take into account the location of the status quo policy, the location of his own ideal policy, and the location of the ideal policies of the other critical actors. An important aspect of administrative leadership, therefore, is concerned with recognizing and then developing a strategy for taking advantage of whatever opportunities the external environment does offer the agency head for moving current policy closer to his own ideal point.

Third, traditional political science views bureaucracy in such a way that, as Ellwood (1996, 61) put it, the "mission, structure, tasks, and politics matter more than leadership, particularly transformational leadership." Our analysis highlights some of the specific political skills which are required for the exercise of leadership in even the most routine situations as well as in situations where persuasion or even transformation may be possible. In particular, there are four skills relevant to an agency head's ability to gain a policy closer to his ideal.

Identification

Our analysis of the agency head's choices has presumed that the agency head actually knows the size, shape, and location of $CORE_{HSP}$ as well as the location of the initial status quo, SQ. However, these various pieces of knowledge are not *automatically* available to a real-world agency head; instead, they are something he has to discover on his own. Thus, even the routine politics described early in the chapter require skill in the identification of the boundaries of $CORE_{HSP}$ and the location of SQ in relation to it. Accurately estimating what is politically possible and what is not requires no small amount of perceptive observation and artful guesswork.

Anticipation

We also examined cases in which $CORE_{HSP}$ moves in one direction or the other, thereby forcing a change in the agency's policy. In some cases, the agency head could benefit from preemptively moving first, thereby influencing—or even deterring—the subsequent moves of the other actors. In other kinds of situations, some degree of prescience about future movements of the political environment—that is, movements of $CORE_{HSP}$—may offer the agency head similar opportunities to influence the ultimate choice of policy.

Persuasion

If the size of $CORE_{HSP}$ defines the nature of the agency head's political autonomy, then the capacity to change the size, shape, and location of $CORE_{HSP}$ increases the possibilities for the exercise of influence. We have demonstrated that there are situations in which the ability to persuade just one external actor to move his ideal point in one particular direction can reshape $CORE_{HSP}$. By taking such action, the agency head improves prospects for moving the status quo policy toward his own ideal point.

Issue Framing

The essence of transformational leadership involves the definition of reality by a political executive in such a way that other actors in the political environment perceive their interests as served by considering policymaking along the dimension selected by the executive. We have considered variations on how a policy issue might be redefined, via the collapse of policymaking onto a single dimension, so that the agency head can gain his ideal policy via the choice of an optimal dimension. In each case where the agency head's ideal point lies outside $CORE_{HSP}$, there are some circumstances under which the agency head could create a more favorable set of equilibrium policies—i.e., the induced $CORE_{H'S'P'}$—in support of his ideal point. It appears, then, that transformational leadership requires a leader who can not only identify a favorable dimension but who also has the rhetorical skill to impose this dimension on how other policymakers, or, more broadly, the general public, think about the issue.

In sum, political executives need to assess the configuration of the preferences of the powerful actors in their political environments and adopt policies that not only benefit their agencies but that also satisfy the concerns of powerful external actors. Moving the status quo policy while staying within the bounds of these constraints constitutes the primary responsibility of effective executives. Altering the boundaries of these constraints through persuasion requires additional managerial skill. Taking advantage of the rare opportunity to redefine the policy issue space in a beneficial way requires strategic and rhetorical skills of the highest order.

Notes

1. In Hammond and Knott (1996) we show how to model "line" agencies where the agency head can be fired by the president.
2. The detailed formal analysis from which these observations are derived can be found in Hammond and Knott (1999), which also contains several additional illustrations for these general arguments.
3. See Hill (1985) for an analysis of just the opposite strategy, one in which the agency head *increases* the dimensionality of the issue space from one to two.
4. See Hammond and Humes (1993) for a formal model of how electoral candidates can use these single-dimension issue-framing strategies to appeal to voters.

Part II

Methodological Frontiers in Understanding Public Management

Chapter 5

*Optimal Performance versus Risk Aversion: An Application of Substantively Weighted Analytical Techniques**

Kenneth J. Meier Texas A&M University
Jeff Gill California Polytechnic State University
George A. Waller University of Wisconsin–Milwaukee

The research literature on bureaucracy generally assumes that bureaucrats are risk averse, and some work goes further to characterize bureaucrats as risk-avoiding and conservative (LaPiere 1965; Sjoberg, Brymer, and Farris 1966; Wolman 1971; Boyer 1973; Kaufman 1981). At the same time the prescriptive literature, the most recent being the reinventing government movement (Osborne and Gaebler 1992; see also Barzelay 1992; Johnston 1993; Report of the National Performance Review 1993), requires bureaucrats to be entrepreneurs, individuals who take major risks in an effort to achieve major performance breakthroughs. Although diametrically opposed in terms of objectives (scholarship versus practical advice), both stress a concern with individuals and agencies that deviate from the norm (i.e., those that fail and those that succeed beyond expectations).

In situations such as these Meier and Keiser (1996) argue that traditional regression methods serve public administration and thus public management poorly. Regression-based techniques seek to generalize to the average case, a situation that neither the performance-optimizing nor the risk-averse literature sees as crucial. Perhaps the most critical comment in regard to the methodological development of public administration is Meier and Keiser's contention that as scholars of public management become better schooled in the more advanced techniques of regression, they will be progressing down the

*All data and documentation necessary to replicate this analysis are available from the authors (kmeier@polisci.tamu.edu). The S-Plus code to run GSRLS and other SWAT papers can be obtained from Jeff Gill (http://www.calpoly.edu/~jgill/).

wrong road. Meier and Keiser present a technique, substantively weighted least squares (SWLS), that is designed to infuse values into analysis by weighting cases of concern more heavily. This technique has been related to well-known statistical distributions and generalized (Gill 1997) such that the weighting parameter selection is flexible: Generalized Substantively Reweighted Least Squares (GSRLS). Together these techniques form the core of the Substantively Weighted Analytical Techniques (SWAT).

This paper extends the work on SWAT using a data set of 534 school districts in Texas. Specifically, it contrasts the differences between risk-averse bureaucracies and performance-optimizing bureaucracies. First, a brief primer on SWLS will be presented. Second, the data set and general model of organizational performance will be introduced for large Texas school districts. Third, risk-averse and performance-optimizing bureaucracies will be compared. Fourth, the results from the SWLS analysis will be compared to the results from GSRLS analysis. Because our goal is to illustrate an important methodological technique for public management rather than contribute to the substantive literature (in this case education reform), we will downplay the substantive findings and focus on the process of analysis.

SWLS: A Primer

The intuition behind SWAT is that not all public management cases are of equal interest to either scholars or practitioners.[1] Practitioners might be interested in agencies that perform better than average given the constraints the agency faces (e.g., the best performing urban school district) or in agencies that avoid failure in the face of complex tasks and uncooperative environments (avoiding bank failures or space shuttles that fall apart—see Romzek and Dubnick, 1987, and Heimann 1993 on the Challenger disaster). The way to incorporate these practitioner concerns into academic research is to focus on the residuals from an Ordinary Least Squares (OLS) regression that has agency performance as the outcome variable and agency inputs and policies as the explanatory variables. In their illustration Meier and Keiser (1996) were only interested in optimal performance, so they suggested dealing with those cases a given distance above the regression line (in this case those with an external studentized residual greater than 0.7, see Gill 1997 on generalizing this parameter). Rather than down weighting these "extreme" cases as a traditional regression analysis might do, they suggest that these cases should be overweighted (or the other cases down weighted) to determine how high-performing agencies differ from the average agency. Meier and Keiser down weight the average agencies in a series of regression by increments of 0.1 until the average cases are counted as equal to only 0.1 of a high-performing case. In the changes found in these regressions, they contend, are the unique management elements that distinguish an excellent agency from a mediocre one.

From a statistical point of view, SWAT assumes that the regression coefficients vary across agencies. One of the differences between an excellent agency and a poor agency is that the excellent one gets far more output for a given level of input. That difference will show up in the weighted regressions when compared to the OLS regressions. SWAT is not intended to estimate population parameters; it is designed to isolate cases of exceptional performance for prescriptive purposes.

Meier and Keiser (1996) contended that their technique was general enough to deal with most values that concern public administration, although their analysis only dealt with optimal performance. Meier, Wrinkle, and Polinard (1999a; 1999b) took the approach one step further and looked at agency performance but added the constraint that the performance must be equitable on racial grounds (see also Waller 1998). The current paper takes a third step by dealing with both the successes and the failures of public management.

Model and Data

The Data Set

The only restriction on the application of SWAT is that one needs measures of agency performance.[2] Our data set is 534 Texas school districts, essentially the universe of Texas school districts with more than 500 students and at least 10 percent minority population. All data were gathered by the Texas Education Agency and are for the 1990–91 school year.

The Outcome Variable

In 1991 all Texas students in the third, fifth, seventh, ninth, and eleventh grades had to take a standardized achievement test, thus creating uniform measures of student achievement and district performance.[3] Our outcome variable is the percentage of students in each district who passed this exam; the mean for all districts was 55.9.

Explanatory Variables

Resources and policies are traditionally linked to educational performance with an education production function (Burtless 1996).[4]

School district performance should be a function of environmental constraints, resources applied to the process, and district policies designed to improve performance. All performance models of public bureaucracy need to control for the type of inputs the bureaucracy receives.

In the context of educational policy, poverty is a serious constraint on the educational performance of students (Necochea and Cune 1996; Fuller et al. 1996). Our measure of poverty is the percentage of students from low income families.[5] Poverty is, of course, highly correlated with race and ethnicity. This study will also include the percentage of black and the percentage of Latino students as additional measures of educational constraints (Fernandez and Velez 1985; Kickbusch 1985; Moore and Smith 1986; Meier and Stewart 1991; Rong and Grant 1992). The relationships to performance should be negative.

The relationship between expenditures and educational outcomes is one of the most contested relationships in educational policy (Hanushek 1986;1989;1996; Hedges and Greenwald 1996; Murray 1995; Murray, Evans, and Schwab 1995; Smith and Meier 1994). Three "expenditure" variables are included in the analysis: per pupil expenditures for instruction, the average teacher salary, and the percentage of money from state funds. Per pupil expenditures for instruction are used in preference to total per pupil spending because many Texas districts spend lavishly on extracurricular events. Higher salaries are perceived in economic theory as a way to attract better qualified persons to a profession (Hanushek and Pace 1995). Finally, state aid can be used to compensate for inequities in local tax bases (*San Antonio Independent School District* v. *Rodriguez* 1973; *Edgewood Independent School District* v. *Kirby* 1989; See also Texas Research League 1986; Accountable Cost Advisory Committee 1986; Weiher 1988). All relationships should be positive.

Education policies are adopted with the intent to influence student performance. Three such policies deal with the learning environment. Many districts have adopted policies to encourage and even to compel students to attend classes. The measure we use is the average percentage of students who attend school.[6] Class size is also linked to student performance (see Pate-Bain et al. 1992; Nye et al. 1992; Hedges and Greenwald 1996; Hanushek 1996, 54). The measure is the number of students per teacher in the district. Finally, gifted classes are generally conceded to be the best education that a school system offers (see DeHaan 1963 for an early exposition of accelerated learning programs for gifted students). Attendance and gifted classes should be positively related to performance, and class size should be negatively related.

Teacher-based reforms are a key element in many efforts to improve performance. Two teacher measures are included—experience and certification. Experience is measured as the average number of years of experience teachers have, and certification is measured as the percentage of teachers who have a temporary certification as a subject specialist.

SWLS Findings

The Ordinary Least Squares results for all districts (no weights) are shown in Table 1. This will be considered our base regression and all other results will be viewed in comparison to it. The OLS results are fairly predictable. In terms of environment, average student performance drops as the student body has relatively more low-income students, black students, and Latino students. Money seems to matter only marginally. Teacher salaries are positively associated with student pass rates, but moneys spent on instruction and state aid are unrelated to performance. The non-teacher policies are all in the predicted direction, with positive relationships between performance

Table 1. *Determinants of Student Pass Rates—OLS*

Outcome Variable = Exam Pass Rate			
Explanatory Variable	Coefficient	Standard Error	95% Confidence Interval
Intercept	−35.7455	29.2202	[−93.0167:21.5257]
Environment			
Percent Low Income	−0.2931	0.0374	[−0.3664:−0.2198]
Percent Black	−0.2307	0.0346	[−0.2985:−0.1629]
Percent Latino	−0.1146	0.0262	[−0.1660:−0.0633]
Financial			
Instruction Funds	0.0004	0.0018	[−0.0032:0.0039]
Teacher's Salary	0.0012	0.0004	[0.0005:0.0020]
Percent State Aid	0.0303	0.0246	[−0.0179:0.0786]
Policy			
Attendance	0.9187	0.2934	[0.3437:1.4938]
Gifted Classes	0.1985	0.0996	[0.0032:0.3937]
Class Size	−0.9083	0.3370	[−1.5689:−0.2478]
Teachers			
Noncertified	−0.1256	0.0699	[−0.2626:0.0114]
Experience	−0.0006	0.2267	[−0.4450:0.4437]

Residual Standard Error: 7.153 on 522 degrees of freedom.

Multiple R-Squared: 0.59.

F statistic: 69.33 on 11 and 522 degrees of freedom, p value is 0.

and both attendance and gifted classes and a negative relationship for class size. Neither teacher noncertification nor experience appear to affect student performance.

The first type of district we look at is the performance optimizer; these are all districts that perform better than average when the explanatory variables are considered. The selection criterion is all districts with studentized residuals greater than 0.7 in the OLS regression.[7] To determine how these high performers differ from the other districts, we run 20 regressions setting the weight equal to 1 for high performers and decreasing the weight for other districts in increments of 0.05 until the final weight is 0.05.[8] Table 2 shows the final weighted results (that is, weights of 1 and 0.05) for these organizations that perform better than expected. The first apparent difference is that money matters for these districts, not just teachers' salaries but per capita instructional money and state aid as well. Unlike the average districts, high-performing districts get more out of their instructional money and more out of the discretionary money that comes from state government. Only two other statistical differences exist: gifted classes are not related to student performance in these

Table 2. *Performance Optimizers, SWLS*

Outcome Variable = Exam Pass Rate			
Explanatory Variable	Coefficient	Standard Error	95% Confidence Interval
Intercept	−17.3815	18.8670	[−54.3609:19.5978]
Environment			
Percent Low Income	−0.3793	0.0324	[−0.4428:−0.3159]
Percent Black	−0.2232	0.0287	[−0.2795:−0.1670]
Percent Latino	−0.0661	0.0235	[−0.1123:−0.0200]
Financial			
Instruction Funds	0.0042	0.0016	[0.0011:0.0073]
Teacher's Salary	0.0009	0.0003	[0.0003:0.0015]
Percent State Aid	0.0611	0.0205	[0.0209:0.1013]
Policy			
Attendance	0.8377	0.1807	[0.4836:1.1918]
Gifted Classes	0.1624	0.0932	[−0.0202:0.345]
Class Size	−1.1259	0.2843	[−1.6832:−0.5686]
Teachers			
Noncertified	−0.1686	0.0544	[−0.2751:−0.062]
Experience	0.1270	0.1781	[−0.222:0.476]

Residual Standard Error: 3.041 on 522 degrees of freedom.

Multiple R-Squared: 0.72.

F-statistic: 123.78 on 11 and 522 degrees of freedom, p value is 0.

optimizing districts, and noncertified teachers are negatively related to performance.

A simple comparison of significance or confidence interval coverage often is misleading because the individual slopes can change dramatically. For example, the coefficient for Latino students is only half the size of that for the average districts suggesting that Latino students in high-performing districts do not have as negative an impact on student scores. The logical inference is that these districts might well be using more effective instructional methods for Latino students (more on this relationship below).

One learns about administrative systems not just from studying how they succeed but also from studying how they fail. In fact, failures might be more informative than successes about how a system works (Simon 1957). Our second example involves "failures," defined as districts with an external studentized residual of less than −0.7 from the OLS regression, that is, districts that perform less well than expected given constraints and inputs. Again we ran 20 weighted regressions. The final weighted regression for the "failures" districts is shown in Table 3. The coefficients differ from both the average

Table 3. *The Failures—SWLS*

Outcome Variable = Exam Pass Rate			
Explanatory Variable	Coefficient	Standard Error	95% Confidence Interval
Intercept	−89.4017	29.9271	[−148.0589:−30.7447]
Environment			
Percent Low Income	−0.1942	0.0256	[−0.2444:−0.1441]
Percent Black	−0.2464	0.0273	[−0.2999:−0.1930]
Percent Latino	−0.1771	0.0175	[−0.2113:−0.1429]
Financial			
Instruction Funds	0.0017	0.0015	[−0.0013:0.0047]
Teacher's Salary	0.0012	0.0003	[0.0007:0.0018]
Percent State Aid	0.0309	0.0190	[−0.0063:0.0681]
Policy			
Attendance	1.2404	0.2971	[0.6582:1.8226]
Gifted Classes	0.2341	0.0862	[0.0651:0.4032]
Class Size	−0.2893	0.2895	[−0.8566:0.2781]
Teachers			
Noncertified	−0.1412	0.0616	[−0.2619:−0.0205]
Experience	0.0885	0.1840	[−0.2722:0.4492]

Residual standard error: 3.008 on 522 degrees of freedom.

Multiple R-Squared: 0.66.

F-statistic: 90.49 on 11 and 522 degrees of freedom, the p value is 0.

districts and the performance-optimizing districts. In terms of money, only teacher salaries appear related to student performance. The policy implication is that these districts will not be helped simply by a greater influx of money for instruction or money from the state. Some districts might be helped; but in general these "failure" districts will not. Attendance and gifted classes remain important, but class size drops from the list. Again, this suggests that these districts will be unable to take advantage of improvements in class size.

A risk-averse bureaucracy seeks to avoid failures; it seeks to satisfice (Simon 1947) rather than take large risks that might generate serious problems for the organization. The notion of a risk-averse bureaucracy is one that treats failing (bad performance relative to inputs) as the most serious problem. Within SWLS this can be operationalized as the reverse of the failures' regression. That is, one should gradually down weight the failures and leave the average-performing bureaucracies at the starting weight of 1.0. Our third example presents results for these risk-averse districts. Again, we ran twenty weighted regressions. Quite clearly being risk-averse is not a bad situation since the risk-averse districts are not all that different from the performance optimizers (see Table 4). They do not get any

Table 4. *Risk Averse, SWLS*

Outcome Variable = Exam Pass Rate			
Explanatory Variable	**Coefficient**	**Standard Error**	**95% Confidence Interval**
Intercept	−4.2609	20.6067	[−44.6501:36.1282]
Environment			
Percent Low Income	−0.3724	0.0306	[−0.4323:−0.3124]
Percent Black	−0.2109	0.0267	[−0.2632:−0.1587]
Percent Latino	−0.0687	0.0218	[−0.1115:−0.0259]
Financial			
Instruction Funds	0.0003	0.0013	[−0.0023:0.0028]
Teacher's Salary	0.0013	0.0003	[0.0007:0.0018]
Percent State Aid	0.0433	0.0190	[0.0062:0.0805]
Policy			
Attendance	0.7269	0.2078	[0.3197:1.1341]
Gifted Classes	0.1155	0.0732	[−0.028:0.2589]
Class Size	−1.4706	0.2489	[−1.9585:−0.9828]
Teachers			
Noncertified	−0.1234	0.0510	[−0.2234:−0.0234]
Experience	−0.0260	0.1711	[−0.3615:0.3094]

Residual standard error: 4.697 on 522 degrees of freedom.

Multiple R-Squared: 0.75.

F-statistic: 141.45 on 11 and 522 degrees of freedom, the p value is 0.

positive benefits from more instructional money, but other than that the same relationships are significant for risk-averse and performance-optimizing bureaucracies. These slopes are at times different, and that provides additional information valuable to the organization.

Perhaps the best way to examine four separate regressions at the same time is with a Multi-Regression Barplot. The individual bars of the barplot are drawn to reflect the size of the coefficients with the shading of the bars indicating statistical significance and confidence interval coverage. We think that confidence intervals are more appropriate to public management situations than significance levels and so do not report p values.[9] Figure 1 shows at a quick glance the major differences between performance-optimizing agencies, failures, and risk-averse agencies.

Tables 2, 3, and 4 were only the final weighted regressions. Those results are the most useful in SWLS, but the intermediate regressions also can reveal interesting patterns. One major difference between the performance optimizers and the failures is the relationship between Latino students and test scores. If we treat the OLS regression coefficients as equal to one and then plot the optimizing and the failure coefficients from each regression on a graph, as in Figure 2, the pattern of relationships becomes quickly obvious. For the failures, the size of the Latino student coefficient gradually increases until it is 54% *larger* than the OLS coefficient. In contrast, the optimizer's coefficient shrinks until it is only 60% of the OLS coefficient. What this means substantively is that a one percent increase in Latino students has less than one-third the negative impact in the optimizing districts as in the failures. This does not result because the optimizing districts have fewer Latino students; in fact, they have slightly more (32.2% compared with 30.0%; the average districts have 31.3%). This suggests that examining the programs targeted at Latino students in the optimizing districts could well provide important technical knowledge toward improving the performance of Latino students statewide.

GSRLS Results

SWLS was developed with the limitations of the technical base of public administration in mind. It can generally be performed with any statistical package that can do weighted least squares (that is, virtually all of them). The intuitive appeal of the technique, however, should not blind one to the fact that several criteria in the process are essentially arbitrary. Using a studentized residual of 0.7 was proposed by Meier and Keiser (1996) to designate enough cases as high performing so that the results would not reflect the idiosyncracies of

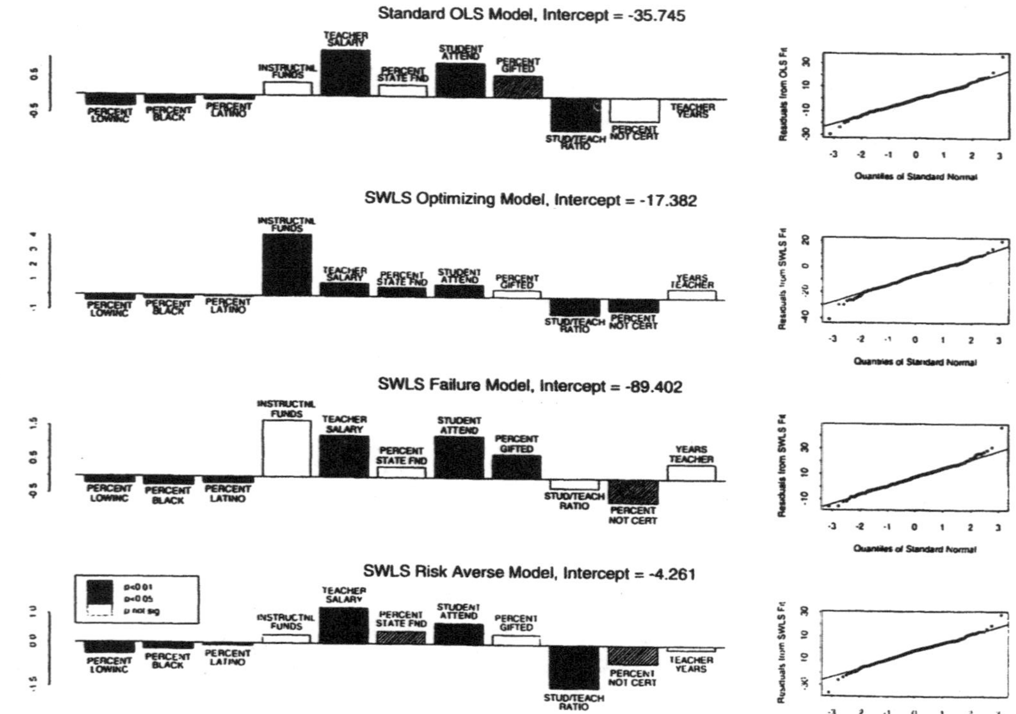

Figure 1. SWLS Multi-Regression Bar Plots

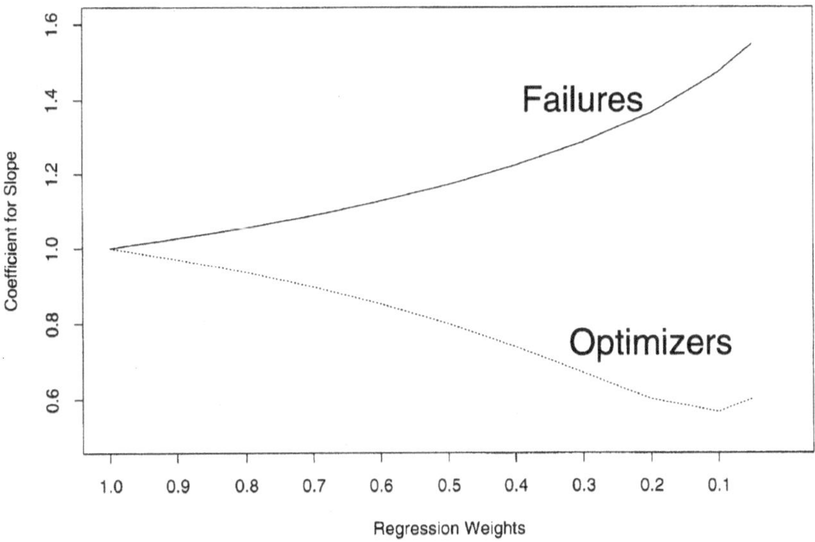

Figure 2. Change in Slopes for Latino Students, Failures versus Optimizers

a single agency or two (their data set had only 50 cases). With larger data sets, a studentized residual of 0.7 is not especially exclusive. In our current example it selects more than 120 districts. Some analysts might well want to be more selective (see Gill and Meier 1998 for an illustration).

The weighting criteria—gradually decreasing by 0.1—was proposed simply because it was tractable. This paper goes a step further to down weight in increments of .05. Different weighting concerns could be used in appropriate situations. Finally, SWLS does not reexamine the external studentized residuals after the first regression; that is, it does not reweight subsequent regressions based on the residuals of the previous regression. While this has the advantage of reducing the number of steps, it has the disadvantage that one case will remain weighted highly when it may be only marginally better than the average case. A general approach (Gill 1997) to substantive weighted least squares that permits the analyst to set the value of these parameters and recalculate the studentized residual after each regression can address some of these limitations.

Differences between SWLS and GSRLS

To keep the GSRLS results as similar as possible in structure to the SWLS results, we will use the same studentized residual and the same weighting scheme. The only difference is that GSRLS will recalculate studentized residuals after every regression and base its weight assignments on these new studentized residuals. In general the reweighting algorithm (GSRLS) did not give radically different results from the constant weight algorithm (SWLS) for these data. This generalization applies to the applications where unsuccessful and typical cases were down weighted (optimizing model), where successful and typical cases were down weighted (failure model), and where failure only cases were down weighted (risk-averse model). The comparison yields no dramatic cases such as the switching of signs on variable coefficients where the coefficients are significant.

There are some important differences between the SWLS and GSRLS approaches. However, the primary observable implication is that it seems to be harder to get substantively interpretable coefficient values with GSRLS, that is, confidence intervals that do not include zero. This is because the studentized residual threshold is reevaluated at each of the intermediate model weighting specifications. A weak relationship between the explanatory variables and the outcome variable, therefore, tends to become further down weighted unless it is particularly prominent in the featured (final unweighted) group. Since the entire SWAT process is designed to facilitate this type of qualitative selection process, any change which increases the probability that cases become down weighted will result in further selectivity of effects.

Figures 1 and 3 highlight the model differences by graphically comparing model coefficients while simultaneously indicating statistical significance (i.e., confidence levels for intervals in the corresponding tables). These Multi-Regression Barplots allow (vertical) comparison of coefficients under different modeling procedures. Note, however, that (horizontally) comparing effect magnitudes within models is inappropriate as the magnitude of each effect is expressed in its own units of measurement.

Four variables differed in interesting ways. Teacher Salary and Percent State Funding had 99% confidence intervals bounded away from zero in the SWLS Optimizing Model, but both 99% and 95% confidence intervals from the GSRLS Optimizing Model included zero.[10] So we can infer that high-performing cases can use salaries and levels of state funding as policy tools to improve learning outcomes. If the higher standard of GSRLS is imposed, meaning the case selection is more restrictive, then the data do not provide any evidence to suggest that these variables can be used as effective policy instruments. It is interesting to note that this observed model difference exists for the Optimizing Model only. The Failure Model and the Risk-Averse Model do not differ for these variables. The Percent Latino variable behaves the same way (the confidence intervals in-

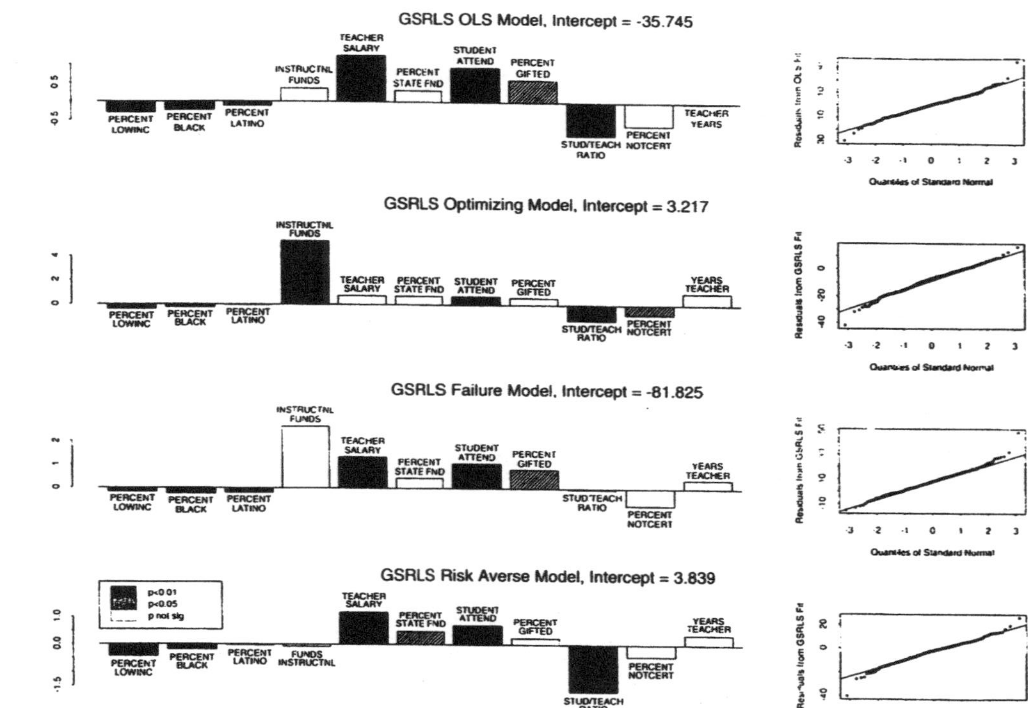

Figure 3. GSRLS Multi-Regression Bar Plots

clude zero in GSRLS, but the 99% confidence interval in SWLS is bounded away from zero), but this is not a variable that is controllable in the same way by policymakers.[11] The variable Percent Noncertified Teachers provides weaker conclusions in the GSRLS Model versus the SWLS Model for every construct: Optimizing, Failure, and Risk-Averse. In the Optimizing Model, GSRLS shows a 99% confidence interval bounded away from zero, whereas the SWLS shows a 95% confidence interval bounded away from zero. For the other two models, Failure and Risk-Averse, SWLS shows a 95% confidence interval bounded away from zero and GSRLS shows no inferential ability from the data. This comparative analysis shows the increased selectivity of GSRLS (notice the decrease in selected cases in Tables 5, 6, and 7), indicating that the smaller groups showed a weakening of the relationship between the percentage of teachers working without a certificate and educational outcomes. We must be cautious, however, since the GSRLS confidence intervals for Percent Noncertified in the Failure Model and the Risk-Averse Model are not bounded away from zero, indicating that the data along with these models provide no

Table 5. *Performance Optimizers, GSRLS*

Outcome Variable = Exam Pass Rate			
Explanatory Variable	**Coefficient**	**Standard Error**	**95% Confidence Interval**
Intercept	3.2174	24.7320	[−45.2574:51.6921]
Environment			
Percent Low Income	−0.3943	0.0460	[−0.4844:−0.3041]
Percent Black	−0.2409	0.0399	[−0.3191:−0.1627]
Percent Latino	−0.0610	0.0320	[−0.1237:0.0016]
Financial			
Instruction Funds	0.0053	0.0020	[0.0013:0.0093]
Teacher's Salary	0.0007	0.0004	[−0.0003:0.0015]
Percent State Aid	0.0700	0.0257	[−0.2897:0.12044]
Policy			
Attendance	0.6698	0.2315	[0.2160:1.1237]
Gifted Classes	0.1909	0.1264	[−0.0569:0.4387]
Class Size	−1.3100	0.3688	[−0.0003:−0.5871]
Teachers			
Noncertified	−0.1585	0.0701	[−2.0329:−0.0211]
Experience	0.1964	0.2480	[−0.2959:0.6825]

Residual standard error: 2.955 on 522 degrees of freedom.

Multiple R-Squared: 0.57.

F-statistic: 62.51 on 11 and 522 degrees of freedom, the p value is 0.

Unweighted Cases on First Iteration = 125.

Unweighted Cases on Last Iteration = 58.

Table 6. *The Failures, GSRLS*

	Outcome Variable = Exam Pass Rate		
Explanatory Variable	Coefficient	Standard Error	95% Confidence Interval
Intercept	−81.246	38.8950	[−158.0588:−5.5904]
Environment			
Percent Low Income	−0.1627	0.0307	[−0.2228:−0.1027]
Percent Black	−0.2478	0.0326	[−0.3117:−0.1839]
Percent Latino	−0.1999	0.0213	[−0.2416:−0.1582]
Financial			
Instruction Funds	0.0027	0.0022	[−0.0017:0.0070]
Teacher's Salary	0.0013	0.0004	[0.0005:0.0021]
Percent State Aid	0.0428	0.0241	[−0.0043:0.0900]
Policy			
Attendance	1.0576	0.3954	[0.2826:1.8326]
Gifted Classes	0.2678	0.1147	[0.0430:0.4925]
Class Size	−0.0463	0.3959	[−0.8222:0.7297]
Teachers			
Noncertified	−0.1462	0.0917	[−0.3259:0.0335]
Experience	0.0758	0.2592	[−0.4322:0.5838]

Residual standard error: 2.943 on 522 degrees of freedom.

Multiple R-Squared: 0.55.

F-statistics: 57.53 on 11 and 522 degrees of freedom, the p value is 0.

Unweighted Cases on First Iteration = 126.

Unweighted Cases on Last Iteration = 58.

evidence of a relationship (which is *not* the same as a denial of the relationship). The final notable difference is that the variable Percent Gifted declined in inferential quality from SWLS to GSRLS for the Failure Model only: 99% confidence interval bounded away from zero versus a 95% confidence interval bounded away from zero. In the other three models no reasonably defined confidence interval is bounded away from zero. So the proportion of students that high-performing districts place in gifted classes affects the examination pass rates, and this finding is reasonably robust across different modeling processes. Conversely, there is no evidence from these data to infer the same relationship for school districts that are poor performers or satisficers.

A central question of this part of the analysis is: what does it mean when there are changing levels of confidence interval coverage (99%, 95%, or inferior coverage) between two comparison models (i.e., optimizing versus risk-averse or failure) and what does this mean with regard to concurrently changing coefficient values? For instance, percent noncertified teachers is not significant in the OLS

Table 7. *Risk-Averse, GSRLS*

Outcome Variable = Exam Pass Rate			
Explanatory Variable	Coefficient	Standard Error	95% Confidence Interval
Intercept	3.8388	21.4250	[−38.1541:45.8318]
Environment			
Percent Low Income	−0.4276	0.0325	[−0.4913:−0.3640]
Percent Black	−0.1917	0.0280	[−0.2465:−0.1369]
Percent Latino	−0.0250	0.0231	[−0.0704:0.0203]
Financial			
Instruction Funds	−0.0001	0.0013	[−0.0027:0.0025]
Teacher's Salary	0.0012	0.0003	[0.0006:0.0017]
Percent State Aid	0.0481	0.0196	[0.0098:0.0865]
Policy			
Attendance	0.6985	0.2142	[0.2786:1.1184]
Gifted Classes	0.0814	0.0808	[−0.0769:0.2398]
Class Size	−1.6884	0.2535	[−2.1852:−1.1915]
Teachers			
Noncertified	−0.0860	0.0540	[−0.1918:0.0198]
Experience	0.0738	0.1813	[−0.2816:0.4292]

Residual standard error: 4.771 on 522 degrees of freedom.
Multiple R-Squared: 0.73.
F-statistic: 126.718 on 11 and 522 degrees of freedom, the p value is 0.
Unweighted cases on first iteration = 408.
Unweighted cases on last iteration = 379.

model but is significant for every other model (SWLS and GSRLS). This is because the effects are masked when all types of districts are considered with equal weights. This is evidence that the SWAT approach enables researchers to understand the prescriptive impact of explanatory variables in a more *substantive* way. The OLS model would have provided administrators at poor-performing schools the wrong advice as to how to improve their future results.

In all models there are statistically significant variables that policy makers have little control over: percent low income, percent black students, and percent Latino students. They are all significant at alpha = 0.01. Since administrators cannot manipulate these levels, prescriptive guidance should generally be focused elsewhere. At the same time, the impact of these variables does vary across the different types of districts. This variance likely results from specific educational processes that are not in our model. For example, a district with an excellent bilingual education program could well generate a smaller regression coefficient for percent Latino students.

The variable percent enrolled in gifted classes is significant (alpha < 0.05) for the OLS model, but is not significant for the optimizing or risk-averse model (SWLS and GSRLS). This effect is analogous to spurious controlled variables in that the effect disappears when the control is implemented. Since the GSRLS models are in effect controlling for specified phenomena, residuals' behavior, the analogy is appropriate. The central question about the percent enrolled in gifted classes variable may be one of causality. If a school is under performing, then the effect of increasing the availability of gifted classes is more dramatic. This chain of causality can be considered a partial explanation for the spurious effect: low-performing schools can improve the percent passing through increased emphasis on gifted classes if they have potentially gifted students to fill them. Conversely, high-performing schools may have already determined the correct proportion of gifted classes to offer.[12]

Conclusion

SWAT is a set of flexible tools that needs to be included in every public management scholar's repertoire of skills. It is a general way to add substantive values into statistical analysis. It focuses attention on key cases designated by the analyst, performance optimizers, failures, equitable agencies, or any other value that can be measured. By its emphasis on key cases, it can bridge the academic-practitioner gap. When coupled with in-depth case studies of selected key programs/agencies, it offers the potential for significant gains in the efficiency of process analyses by specifying what cases and what variables to examine.

An important benefit of using SWAT tools is that effects which are masked or distorted in standard linear models for specific types of cases (high-performing, low-performing, risk-averse) can be revealed. This paper showed several cases where the prescriptive recommendation from OLS regression would have provided *exactly the wrong recipe* for improvement for some type of school system. Thus SWAT techniques are a powerful addition to any public manager's toolkit.

A substantial portion of this paper compared SWLS with GSRLS. In general the results were similar, suggesting that the use of SWLS, the less demanding option in terms of technique, will serve public management adequately. At the same time, we need to stress that GSRLS is the more conservative technique statistically and, therefore, is to be preferred. The solution quite clearly is to get GSRLS software included in the widely available software packages (visit http://www.calpoly.edu/~jgill/).

This paper has not exhausted the potential of the SWAT approach. In a series of papers we adapt the approach to several additional questions. By varying the studentized residual parameter, we will ask how do exceptional agencies differ from those that are simply better than average (see Gill and Meier 1998). By developing a pooled time-series version, we will investigate the difference between consistently good performers and those that are often good but erratic (Smith, Meier, and Gill 1998). We also plan to investigate how SWAT is affected by sample size. Many new and exciting developments for public management lie ahead.

Notes

1. An extended discussion of the philosophy of science that underlies SWAT can be found in Meier and Gill (2000). That manuscript should be the starting point for any SWAT analysis because the philosophy and assumptions undergirding SWAT are dramatically different from those of classical statistics.
2. This is not actually a statistical restriction but a substantive one. The technique can be used in any regression; what makes the technique useful for public management is that it is used in performance models.
3. Student test scores are not the only possible measure of organizational performance in education. Graduation rates, skills imparted, successful employment, or placement in higher education are other possible output indicators. Because much of the education policy literature and the policy debate focus on standardized test scores, we are comfortable with this measure.
4. This literature is far too large to cite comprehensively. See the extended bibliography in Burtless (1996).
5. Median family income in the district, when included in Table 1, is unrelated to educational performance. Our measure of low income is the percentage of students who are eligible for free or reduced-price meals in the school lunch program.
6. This might also be an environmental variable measuring commitment to education by students and/or their families.
7. Pindyck and Rubinfeld (1991, 170) state that it is a useful diagnostic tool "... to consider the residual that is obtained for each observation *when the regression line is estimated with that particular observation omitted.*" The residual is omitted so that any bias created by an extreme value does not affect the line from which the deviation is calculated. Externally studentized residuals are obtained by dividing the residual, $\in (i) = y_i - \beta(i)x_i$, from an OLS regression by the estimated standard error of the regression, $s_i(i)$, in which the ith observation has been omitted. The *externally studentized residual* is thus found by: $\in {}^*(i) = [y_i - \beta(i)x_i]/s_i(i)$. This standardizes the

residuals such that the studentized residuals fit the student t distribution. External studentized residuals with values greater than 1.96 in absolute value are regarded as outliers worthy of particular attention in standard OLS regression diagnostics. In this example of SWLS application, we are choosing to examine those cases with external studentized residuals greater than 0.7 (optimizers) and those with external studentized residuals less than −0.7 (failures). Most standard regression packages including SPSS and SAS will calculate studentized residuals.

8. The easiest way to run these equations is to create a new variable equal to 1 if the studentized residual is >0.7 and equal to 0.95 otherwise. This variable is then used as the weight factor in the regression (again, most statistics packages include a weight option in their regression programs). For the next regression the weights are 1 (if the studentized residual is >0.7) and 0.9 otherwise. Weights are 1 and 0.85 in the third regression and so on. We run 20 total regressions, with the last regression having weights of 1.0 and 0.05. The size of weighting increments is a matter of choice; with many cases one can run the process to end up with a smaller final weight.
9. A 1-alpha confidence interval is functionally equivalent to rejection of the null hypothesis at the alpha (e.g. 0.05) level in standard null hypothesis significance testing. However, the NHST (null hypothesis significance testing) paradigm has been shown to be deeply flawed, albeit pervasive, in the social sciences (Gill 1999). We therefore present tabular results with 95% confidence intervals and remind the reader that these can be interpreted as designating significance at the alpha=0.05 level if the more problematic, but common, language is preferred.
10. While we believe the concept of statistical significance is inappropriate or incorrectly applied in most social science research (see Gill 1999), the reader might be more comfortable thinking of these relationships as "significant" or "not significant" at the .01 and .05 levels.
11. Substantively, this finding could be important since it underscores our discussion of how high-performing districts teach Latino students.
12. This assumes the size of gifted programs is equal to the district's supply of students capable of performing at that high level. An average district with fewer classes than needed could be detrimentally affected. Some literature assumes most students would benefit from gifted classes (see Meier and Stewart 1991). That assumption currently lacks empirical support.

Chapter 6

The Art of Partnering across Sectors: The Influence of Centrality Strategies of State R & D Projects

Gordon Kingsley Georgia Institute of Technology
Julia Melkers Georgia State University

One of the fine arts of public management is figuring out ways to influence the behavior of networks of organizations. In this study we examine instances where the public agency's position vis-à-vis the network is relatively weak. The agency may not be recognized as a member of the network; it may not have the authority or means to coerce the desired behavior; and it may not have a large amount of resources.

This is precisely the situation confronting most state science and technology (S&T) agencies. The most common solution is to use grants as leverage for stimulating cooperative research and development (R&D) projects between the state agency and organizations associated with a targeted industry (Coburn 1995). The state agency goal almost always includes disseminating the outcomes of the R&D project throughout its jurisdiction. The use of such projects means that one route by which public agencies achieve influence is partnering with organizations that have stronger ties to the targeted industry. However, there is some evidence that agencies play important direct roles in encouraging the use of technology (Kingsley, Bozeman, and Coker 1996; Moon and Bretschneider 1997; Melkers and Cozzens 1997). Unfortunately, the links between state-sponsored projects, technology adoption, and use are not well understood. In most evaluations, the agency and the project are used synonymously without differentiating the channels of communication that flow from each project participant (Kingsley and Bozeman 1997).

In this study we examine the importance of centrality as a strategy pursued during R&D projects. Centrality is a concept drawn from social network analysis that examines the number and importance of ties one actor has with other actors in a network. Central organizations have been found to have greater influence upon the behaviors of network members (Boje and Whetten 1981; Provan and Milward 1995; Galaskiewicz 1979). However, the evidence supporting this relationship with regard to technological innovations is mixed (Valente 1995).

Our interest is understanding whether agencies pursue a strategy of using or creating relatively central organizations through R&D projects. The focus upon agency strategies poses certain design challenges in terms of the unit of analysis and the selection of methods. We employ concepts drawn from social network analysis which offer a great deal of information on relationships within the network targeted by an R&D project. But the formalism of this approach is less useful in examining the strategies and relationships of a non-network member, in this case a state agency, to network behaviors. Since this is our unit of analysis, we employ an embedded case study design for exploring the impacts of agency strategy upon the targeted network.

We explore this topic through case studies drawn from two large multicase evaluations of state S&T agencies in Alaska and New York: (1) the Alaska Science and Technology Foundation (ASTF), and (2) the New York State Energy Research and Development Authority (Energy Authority). The authors were principals and participants in these studies. The cases follow R&D projects from inception to impacts through interviews and surveys of project participants and members of the targeted networks.

A Framework for Analyzing Centrality

The case studies are organized using a model (see Figure 1) adapted from social network studies of centrality (Boje and Whetten 1981; Provan and Milward 1995). *Attributed influence,* the dependent variable, is the importance of the communications that network members received concerning the outputs of the R&D project in their decision to adopt a technology. *Centrality* refers to the proportion of information exchanges that involve a specific network member. Case studies are examined for both local and global forms of this concept. The local form is evident in the contacts that organizations have among peers within the network. Global centrality examines the power relationships that set the terms of exchange among network members. As was noted earlier, the greater the centrality of a communication source, the more likely it is to be attributed as a source of influence. The technology transfer *strategies* pursued in the R&D project may attempt to use centrality to their advantage in two ways (Mandell 1990). First, R&D projects may actively recruit an organization that

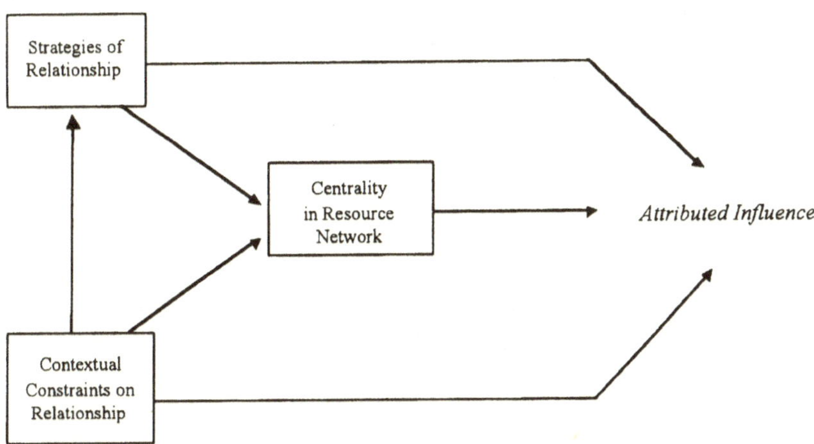

Figure 1. A Causal Model of Centrality and Attributed Influence in an Interorganizational Network (adapted from Boje and Whetten 1981).

plays a central role in the targeted network. Second, R&D projects may try to increase the centrality of a project participant by making it more attractive to a targeted audience. As can be seen in Figure 1, it is also possible for strategies to have a direct influence upon *attributed influence*. This means that weak ties are used and the centrality hypothesis fails. *Contextual constraints* act as a control on the capacity of participants to pursue strategies, achieve centrality, or attribute influence. These include (1) the requirements for acquiring and operating a technology; (2) the number and location of the project participants; (3) the number and type of services offered by the sponsoring agency; and (4) the market and regulatory influences.

The case studies were not organized or written with this centrality model in mind. There is sufficient evidence to address the four elements of the model. However, the match is not a perfect one. The evidence in the case studies is particularly limited for linking *centrality* and *attributed influence*. However, our interest is primarily in the links between *contextual constraints, strategy,* and *centrality*. These topics were explicitly explored in the case studies.

Funding Technology Development and Influencing Networks: Selected Examples

The case studies are drawn from large-scale evaluations conducted in the early 1990s (Bozeman et al. 1992; Kingsley, Bozeman, and Coker 1996; Melkers and Bugler 1994, 1995). Both studies were designed to determine the effectiveness of agency projects in terms of commercialization and technology transfer. The methods of the Energy Authority evaluation were adapted in the ASTF study. Consequently, both consist of case studies of "successful projects" and mail surveys of grantees and constituents. ASTF and the Energy Authority represent the "bookends" among the population of state S&T agencies. ASTF is relatively young and small and serves a largely rural state. The Energy Authority is older and larger and serves a state with a mature, diversified industrial base.

We draw upon six case studies of R&D projects from the ASTF and the Energy Authority. These are only a fraction of the thirty-nine case studies compiled between the two projects. Two criteria led to the selection of these cases. First, the write-up of the case studies had to cover the four elements of the model. Case authors are selective in their presentation of the evidence. As a consequence, evidence relevant to this study that was covered in the research protocols did not always make it into the final case report. This was aggravated by the fact that there were multiple authors producing these case studies. The second criteria was that the cases had to be representative of the range of impacts reported in the complete set of studies—from widespread technology transfer to limited technology adoption.

The Case of Alaska

The Alaska Science and Technology Foundation (ASTF) is relatively young, having been established in 1988, with a $100 million endowment, where the earnings cover the cost of operations for the Foundation. The staff of the agency has remained small, with fewer than ten employees. The mission of the agency, as defined by the statute, is to use basic and applied research to enhance economic development and technological innovation in Alaska. By 1996, it had funded 124 grants ranging from $20 thousand to $1.1 million.

From a network perspective, ASTF pursues a strategy of placing *itself* as a central resource for small businesses and technology developers by enlisting the aid of others to act as their representative in the provision of services (ASTF 1995). One method for doing this is a "circuit rider" program where individual consultants are employed by ASTF to provide one-on-one technical assistance to grantees. ASTF also does this through a technical assistance program that includes workshops, business assistance networks, additional funding assistance, and university participation. However, there is a limit to the central role ASTF is willing to play. Early in the life of a project, ASTF is usually the major promoter of information about the research. But projects are expected to become self sufficient and self-promoting by procuring additional funds to continue with their activities or business development. In fact, such funding is viewed as an important indicator of project success.

In describing the ASTF projects (as well as the Energy Authority projects), we also present contextual constraints (Table 1). In the first case, Orthopedic Regeneration Hardware, the goal of the project was to develop and commercialize a bone regenerator. This device was designed to augment and improve an existing technology. The grantee was a start-up company which had close ties with the University of Alaska (which provided access to university laboratories). While the firm experienced sales and FDA approval within three years of the grant, it also suffered through a major reorganization due to poor forecasts of the market demand for the technology.

The second case, the Electric Generator Protection System, involved three engineers who were to evaluate and refine a highly sophisticated protective instrument for use in the electric utility industry. Here again, the grantee was a start-up company using the talents of the three partners who had first worked together in an engineering firm in Seattle. While they had significant experience with the electric utility industry, their resources as a company were limited.

The third case, Research and Development of a Birch Sap Products Industry, involved the development, compilation, and exchange of essential information concerning birch tree physiology relating to the properties of birch sap. The companies working in this industry are typically quite small. Both the ASTF and grantee roles were critical to the outcomes of the project. The birch syrup process was refined, the association in Alaska was established, and the grantee's business has developed a national market for its products. Further, the product has been adopted by other food processors in the development of their own unique products.

The Case of New York

The Energy Authority was created in 1975 in the wake of the energy crisis and charged with securing safe and economic energy resources for the state of New York. This mission reflects a broader concern with energy in which economic and environmental values are often inseparable. As energy crises have ebbed, greater emphasis has been given to these other missions in response to legislative, executive, and constituent pressures.

The primary business of the Energy Authority is sponsoring R&D projects. Over five fiscal years (from 1988 to 1993) the Energy Authority provided, on average, $15 million per year for R&D contracts. More than one-half of the ninety or so full-time employees of the Energy Authority are project managers charged with the disburse-

Table 1. *Alaska and New York Case Studies*

Alaska Case Studies (ASTF)				
Cases	**Context**	**Strategies**	**Centrality**	**Attributed Influence**
Automatic Control System for Ilazarov Orthopedic Regeneration Hardware	Targets: global medical community Regulatory issues Market acceptance	Agency: provide funding stability; provide access to business and technical advice through workshops Grantee: gain financial support through investors; get FDA approval	Global centrality from vertical channels with federal regulator Local centrality from horizontal channels of partners and researchers	Commercialization; reorganization of firm
Electric Generator Protection System	Targets: global utilities market Distance of partners Establishment of new major partner Influx of large global marketing and processing budget	Agency: provide access to business and technical advice through workshops Grantee: repetitive testing of product; outsourcing of production; division of expertise Partner: dissemination of product information; global marketing and promotion; establishing manufacturing and shipping capabilities; user involvement in product testing	Global centrality from vertical channels with large industry partners and utilities Local centrality from horizontal channels of partners and researchers	Demonstration of technology; global marketing and promotion efforts
Research and Development of a Birch Sap Products Industry	Targets: retail trade and specialized food industry Cottage industry Little business development knowledge Seasonal New process, new product	Agency: teambuilding and providing access to business and technical advice Grantee: develop network; establish cottage industry with supportive components; encourage business development; national marketing campaign and distribution network; develop users of products	Global centrality from establishment of vertical channels in new professional association Local centrality from horizontal channels of suppliers and other grantee	Commercialization; establishment of professional association

Table 1. *Alaska and New York Case Studies* **(Continued)**

New York Case Studies (Energy Authority)				
Cases	**Context**	**Strategies**	**Centrality**	**Attributed Influence**
Low Income Weatherization	Targets: local housing agencies High regulatory demand	Agency: team building Co-Funder: field testing to demonstrate viability; issue regulation requiring procedure Contractor: distribute results of field tests to local agencies	Global centrality from vertical channels of state regulator (contractor) Local centrality from horizontal channels of test site agencies (sub-contractors)	Technology adopted as a standard for state and local agencies by state regulator
Radon Monitoring	Targets: schools, housing industry High regulatory demand High market demand Small-scale producer Diverse consumers	Agency: advisory board, growth of firm Contractor: market demonstration and marketing activities	Global centrality from vertical channels of advisory board and the contracting firm Limited local centrality from the horizontal channels of the school test sites	Commercialization
Wood Waste Power Plant	Targets: utilities, wood waste processors Low market demand Low regulatory demand Large-scale consumers, small-scale producers	Agency: demonstration site and distributing final reports Contractor: making plant and personnel available for tours/presentations	No global centrality Limited local centrality from the horizontal channels of the contracting firm and Energy Authority	Demonstration of the technology but no transfer

ment and oversight of R&D funds. The Energy Authority has sponsored more than 1,500 projects during its lifetime. The size of awards ranges from just a few thousand dollars to more than $1 million. The typical project is fairly large, averaging about $200,000. The Energy Authority leverages funds by requiring co-funders for R&D projects.

All projects are subject to the same procedures for encouraging technology transfer. This game plan has been used throughout the Energy Authority's history, regardless of the stage of development, type of objective, or size of the project. The fundamental premise driving managers is that project success comes from selecting "good" projects, i.e., those that produce outcomes that are useful to someone. While network centrality is not a criterion in Energy Authority deliberations, the quest for the good project can lead to the participation of such an actor. The Energy Authority cases summarized here were selected because they represent a range of possible outcomes from projects in terms of technology use by the targeted network.

The product in the Low Income Weatherization case was designed as a field test of a new diagnostic technique for identifying infiltration heat loss in single and multifamily structures (see Table 1.) The technology combines the use of blower doors, which pressurize and seal structures, with handheld infrared scanners for monitoring air leaks. The New York Department of State (NYDOS) was responsible for the implementation of this program, which was funded through the U.S. Department of Energy and the U.S. Department of Health and Human Services and provided by local agencies. The targeted organizations were local agencies responsible for weatherizing low-income housing.

The objective in the Radon Monitoring case was the development of a low-cost, easy-to-use radon monitor that could be marketed to the housing industry and to schools. The project produced a passive monitor that required no power to operate and could be used on both a long- and short-term basis. The primary markets for the monitor were real estate professionals and radon monitoring firms. It could also be adapted for use in schools and other buildings where an accurate and quick measurement of radon emissions might be required. In fact, a respresentative of the New York State Department of Health ordered twenty monitors to be used in testing radon in the schools.

In the Wood Waste Power Plant case the objective was to demonstrate the use of urban wood waste to produce electric power as a means of attracting wood waste processors to the power generation business. The demand for this type of private sector power generation was supported by regulations that specified the price that utilities had to pay from alternative sources. The strategies pursued by the Energy Authority and the firm were very passive. While the technology is still in use by the firm, it has not been transferred elsewhere.

The Influence of Centrality Strategies

The model presented in this chapter provides a useful framework for assessing the strategy employed by state technology development organizations and the subsequent outcomes of their efforts. Table 1 provides a summary of the application of the centrality framework to these cases.

In both the ASTF and the Energy Authority cases, there was evidence of strategies designed to use centrality as a mechanism to achieve success in the form of technological innovation with commercial applications. However, there are some important differences in the success of the centrality strategies pursued in these sample cases. In most cases both local and global centrality were pursued and achieved. There were some notable exceptions.

The Birch Sap Products Industry case was perhaps the most successful of the Alaska cases, in part because the target industry is quite small. Here, ASTF's strategy involved team-building using local ties among birch sap producers and the informal partnering of two ASTF grantees. Local centrality was pursued further with the invitation to these grantees to participate in ASTF workshops on small business management. Through the life of the project, the grantee played an increasingly important role. First, she clearly pursued a local centrality strategy in engaging peers and support for the industry from suppliers and other processors by establishing a communications network for herself. Second, a global strategy was pursued among birch sap producers with the formation of the professional association that would serve as a communications network for the industry in Alaska. This association was created and has become an important resource among producers of birch sap. Producers cite the association and the training programs as important influences in their business and technology decisions.

The Electric Generator case was dramatically helped in its pursuit of global centrality as a result of a major corporate buyout. The participants in this case pursued a mix of strategies, each focusing on the ultimate goal of successful commercialization of the product. The grantee strategy involved refining the technology, assessing the market, and informing the market of the technology. The large industry partner (who was not part of the grantee's initial strategy) pursued a strategy of global market acceptance. Once the grantees demonstrated their link with this larger network, ASTF provided some guidance but otherwise stepped back to allow the grantee to interact with that network. The utility industry now identifies the corporate buy-out partner as the major source of this technology.

Conversely the Orthopedic Regeneration Hardware case had limited success in achieving global centrality. This strategy was especially evident in its pursuit of FDA approval. Local centrality was also a goal as the grantee brought on new engineers and partners as well as additional investors who were to play a part in firm management. The role of ASTF was to support these activities, and in some situations, to provide introduction or support for a relationship pursued by the grantee. While the company has sought global and local centrality, it has been unsuccessful in achieving either status within the medical community.

Only one of the New York cases (Low Income Weatherization) accomplished both local and global centrality with approximately equal success. The Energy Authority assembled a team in the project that had both global ties (through the state's primary regulatory agency) and local ties to the targeted network of low-income housing providers. This is not a particularly large or diverse network of organizations. Here, the Energy Authority activities were focused on providing financial resources and building a team of organizations that could produce quality field tests. This meant bringing in an independent contractor to administer the different demonstration sites for the technology. The practical consequence of these strategies was to position the findings of the project in a highly central set of organizations. Both global and local centralization are in evidence. The global centrality stems from the regulatory role (i.e., vertical communication) played by NYDOS in diffusing the audit procedure. The local centrality comes from the local agencies that tested the technology communicating with their peers as well as from the consultant who managed the project. The role of the Energy Authority was devoted primarily to team building.

For the Radon Monitor case, the market for the product was established prior to the project. None of the actors in the project had a particularly central relationship with the housing industry. Thus, the goal was to increase the company's technological capabilities so that it would be sufficiently attractive to a more centrally positioned firm to arrange a partnership. The project sought to appeal to global centrality by creating a vertical communication channel between suppliers and consumers of the technology that could overcome existing impediments to success. For example, the housing industry, while providing the basis of a network, generally has a low level of diversity. Furthermore, the project involved the launch of a new business that had few existing ties to industry because it consisted only of the new firm and the Energy Authority. One strategy for addressing these problems was the appointment of an Advisory Board to oversee both the technological and business development of the project. By developing the radon monitor, it was hoped that the start-up firm would be more attractive to firms already supplying the housing industry. In addition, the firm initiated a series of associations with established firms that would provide the corporate resources for creating and marketing the product. The Advisory Board also proved useful in providing early demonstration sites. In the end, however, the housing development and real estate industries attributed their adoption only to the company advertising and promotion efforts.

Finally, the firm in the third Energy Authority case (Wood Waste Power Plant) did seek a degree of local centrality. The Energy Authority issued the findings from the project in a final report, in news releases, and through presentations to trade associations. The firm participated in these presentations and has allowed visitors to examine the workings of the facility. However, neither the agency nor the firm held a position of global or local centrality with respect to other wood processors. Their efforts did not prove sufficient to influence this targeted network.

Conclusion

The cases represent a mix of different strategies pursued by state agencies to encourage technology and economic development. As evidenced in the case discussion above, the agencies operate under different contextual factors, which in turn affect their strategic direction. The Alaska cases illustrate the importance of networks in project success. The agency aggressively pursues a strategy to place itself and its projects in a more central position in regard to the targeted networks. They accomplish this goal in a variety of ways, including team-building, the construction of networks, and attempts to bolster the grantee. ASTF pursues a strategy of network centrality early in the life of the project and expects that the grantee will assume such a role later: The centralization strategy changes over the life of the project. Further, strategies are individualized somewhat by project and individual grantee needs, both technological and economic.

The New York cases, on the other hand, illustrate more of a "hands off" approach where the emphasis is limited to growth strategies and team-building strategies through projects. There is limited effort to position the agency as a central actor in the targeted network. In both team-building and growth strategies the emphasis is on vertical communication patterns rather than horizontal. In terms of centrality, this means the agencies are pursuing a strategy of global rather than local centrality. From the agency perspective, this strategy appears to be the most effective because it fits with agencies' existing communication networks. Agency managers tend to communicate with other agencies and large firms more than with smaller contractors. By professional temperament and context, this is an easier group for them to access.

A large portion of the communication, however, is informal. Public managers in both Alaska and New York (as well as other state S & T programs) interact regularly with a range of professionals, including individuals from industry and suppliers and customers. While a portion of this interaction may be part of the formal activity involved in the management of projects, there is a great deal of activity that occurs which is not part of the formal structure of the program. In fact, public managers will often communicate with a variety of groups. Though they view the connections they make as value added, they do not necessarily consider this as part of their job. This is the case in New York State, where the agency priority is to develop "good projects" and they find themselves gravitating towards things that make effective connections and networks. They do not focus on a game plan that concentrates on centrality. Instead, they pursue a variety of channels where centrality is not a conscious objective. In Alaska, this type of communication is facilitated through the circuit rider interaction as well as through grantee workshops and conferences. Here, the priority is not only to develop "good projects" but also to create networks and to improve the community of business in the state. In 1995 ASTF revised its funding process by involving the customer or beneficiary of the science or technology in all projects, which is expected to enhance ASTF's impact on Alaska (ASTF 1995). Although ASTF sponsors more formalized processes, both agency-to-grantee and grantee-to-grantee communication channels remain an important informal interaction. For example, both agencies emphasize team building, but in doing so managers do not appear to think purposefully about centralization.

This study cannot answer the question of how critical centrality is to technology adoption. Though there are indications that this relationship is important, this question must await further research. But it does tell us a good deal about the ways in which centrality is used in the strategies of project participants. We also have developed a preliminary understanding of the relationship between contextual and environmental factors and strategy. Future research should address priorities and perspectives about centralization strategies from the different players' perspectives. It is unclear how deliberate public managers' actions are and how the perspectives on those actions differ among day-to-day project managers, agency heads, and the grantees themselves. Future research could help to develop a better understanding of the link between centrality and project/agency outcomes.

Chapter 7

*Stories from the Front Lines of Public Management: Street-Level Workers as Responsible Actors**

Steven Maynard-Moody The University of Kansas
Suzanne Leland Kansas State University

Public management research and theory are preoccupied with top-level managers (Kettl 1993a, 58). This exclusive attention on top management limits our understanding of governance because leadership and policymaking also occur at other levels, including the street level (Vinzant and Crothers 1999). Police officers, teachers, caseworkers, rehabilitation counselors—the entire range of street level workers—make discretionary decisions about the amount and character of services provided to citizens.[1] Their choices and oversights alter the distribution of government services and, for better or worse, the way government programs are delivered to and perceived by citizens (Meyers and Dillon 1999, 6; and Tyler 1990, 174). In the long chain of policy actors, street-level workers are the last, yet we know very little about the norms and beliefs that guide their judgment. What makes a client or citizen worthy of extraordinary help or of minimal, at times rude, treatment? Imbedded in this simple question are issues of the nature of justice, social policymaking, and street-level work.

Most of the literature on street-level workers examines front-line staff, such as caseworkers and police officers, who use their considerable discretion to make their difficult work lives easier and safer. The prevailing picture shows street-level workers using discretion to serve their, not their clients', needs, but street-level workers are not monolithic. Rehabilitation counselors present at times an alternative view in which street-level workers provide more and often extraordinary services to chosen clients, often at considerable personal cost and risk.

*This research was supported by the National Science Foundation, grant number SBR-9511169.

Methods

Setting

The observations in this paper are based on one fieldwork setting from a larger, multisite research project. The overall project involves five research sites in two states, one in the Southwest and one in the Midwest, and a range of street-level workers: teachers, police officers, and disability counselors. The current findings are based on fieldwork in a vocational rehabilitation office in a large, impoverished midwestern urban area. All of the counselors and their direct supervisor participated in our research.

Vocational Rehabilitation, or in social service jargon, "Voc Rehab" or "VR," is part of the state social service system. Voc Rehab reports to the State Commissioner of Disabilities and Rehabilitation, who reports in turn to the Secretary of Social and Rehabilitation Services, the largest state agency. Eighty percent of Voc Rehab's budget comes from the federal government.

Voc Rehab differs from most welfare agencies in that the organization has a legal obligation to provide client-approved, individualized services. They serve, in Handler and Hollingsworth's (1971) term, the "deserving poor," or those who become poor or needy not because of a moral failing, such as substance abuse or sloth, but because of a medical disability. To receive services from Voc Rehab, a client must be disabled and in need of some service in order to return to work. Voc Rehab serves the visually and hearing impaired, those injured at work, the mentally retarded, and the wheelchair bound—individuals who, for the most part, are not blamed for their condition. Handler and Hollingsworth (1971, 211) observed that services for such clients are "characterized by the absence of discretionary official controls." VR counselors cannot refuse clients who meet criteria for services. Nonetheless, they retain far-reaching discretion regarding the manner in which these services are provided.

Counselor after counselor in our sample observed that, in contrast to other social services, they have more, not less, discretion. Contradicting Handler and Hollingsworth's (1971) observation that caseworkers were locked in often discriminatory discretionary relationship with the "undeserving poor," many VR counselors started their careers in social casework and left these people-processing jobs because they felt they had no authority to decide what was best for the client. One observed, "Now in our profession the VR counselor probably has the most authority. . . . The VR counselor has . . . the most discretion, the most judgment."

The setting for this research is an impoverished urban community with the highest crime rate, highest murder rate, lowest median income, highest percentage of minorities, and lowest educational level in the state. While all of the clients had some physical or mental disability, most were also poor. Even those who were injured on the job were predominantly the working poor. Clients typically received welfare as well as disability benefits. As one counselor described his cases, "A lot of folks have been incarcerated, have not finished high school, can't read. They have lots of needs and face a lot of real barriers to employment."

Stories

The research process involved extensive on-site observation over the ten-month research period, in-depth entry and exit interviews, a discretionary questionnaire, and archival research. Voc Rehab counselor work stories are the primary source for observations about decision norms. In our research protocol, we do not consider "story" synonymous with "interview" or "case study," even though both are a form of narrative. Our stories are closer to the traditional, everyday definition. We encourage street-level workers to tell stories that have a plot or story line with a beginning, middle, and end; have characters; explain the relationship among characters; describe the feelings of characters toward each other and events; and include a description of the setting and circumstances in which the events occurred. These stories do not necessarily report historical events and the storyteller does not need to be the main character, although this is often the case. We do ask the street-level worker to tell stories about fairness but are open to stories about working with clients or life in their agency.

Like all methods, story-based research has strengths and weaknesses. Stories reveal information that is rarely found in interviews or especially in other quantitative forms of social scientific information (Bellow and Minow 1996). Stories allow the simultaneous expression of multiple points of view because they sustain and suspend multiple voices and conflicting perspectives. They can also present highly textured depictions of practices and institutions. Rather than merely repeating the rules or beliefs, a story can show what situations call for certain routines and how the specifics of a case fit or do not fit standard practices. They illustrate the consequences of following, bending, or ignoring rules and practices. They bring institutions to life by giving us a glimpse of what it is like working in a state bureaucracy or cruising a tough neighborhood in a patrol car.

Stories give prominence to human agency as central to understanding governing, and this is perhaps their greatest contribution as a public management research tool. Stories offer insights into how actors make choices, understand their own actions, and experience frustrations and satisfactions. They give research a pungency and vitality because they give prominence to individual actions and motives. Like other interpretive approaches, story-based research "shifts the focus from discovering a set of universal laws about objective, sense based facts to the human capacity for making and communicating meaning. . . . Our social institutions, our policies, our agencies are human creations, not objects independent of us" (Yanow 1996, 5).

Although their value is in revealing interpretations and meaning, stories are objective in the sense that they can be reproduced as a text that can be transcribed, read, argued over, and interpreted by researchers and research subjects alike. No single story text is definitive, but a single rendition can provide a common starting place and a reference point for interpretation. Accepting the hermeneutic tradition's central insight that "no interpretation, no reading, can be made in a wholly neutral or disinterested fashion" (Dienstag 1997, 7), a text starting place provides a discipline to interpretations that at least offers the potential for reliable and shared interpretations so essential to the intellectual tradition of social science. These stories, however, are not objective in the sense that they represent the factual retelling of events. The stories are the textual embodiments of the storytellers', in this case the street-level workers', perspectives. These perspectives are at times inconsistent and conflicting; they are self-referential and often invoke self-justification for actions that may, in retrospect, be questionable. This element of circularity and rationalization limits our ability to say what happened in a narrow factual sense but, at the same time, strengthens our ability to interpret the fairness and justice norms evoked by street-level workers, which is the purpose of this research program.

Fieldwork

We selected the site by looking for a natural working group consisting of ten to fifteen individuals. In the case of Voc Rehab, we chose one regional office that included service counselors to the blind to increase the diversity of workers and clients. After describing the research protocol and receiving consent, we begin with an entry interview and general instructions.

Story collection begins with the counselor telling an uninterrupted rendition of his or her story. When finished, we probed to get each storyteller to render the story more fully. The stories and probes were tape-recorded and later transcribed verbatim. These transcribed stories were then reviewed by the storyteller for accuracy. This process was repeated for each storyteller. During interviews and fieldwork we were also told stories that were labeled "incidental stories" and transcribed but not revised. Fieldwork ended with exit interviews.

We collected fifty-one stories from the VR counselors. Thirty-four discussed issues with specific clients, such as efforts to help the client beat the system, their own overinvestment in certain clients, and deciding who did and did not deserve service. Twenty-three stories dealt with organizational issues, such as working with other agencies, working within their own agency, and dealing with reform efforts. Eight stories dealt with client and organizational issues. This paper focuses on client issues.

It is important to stress that our observations do not assume that the stories are historically accurate accounts; our research examines norms and beliefs, not events. Moreover, our stories cannot help us understand the prevalence of a problem. Stories are biased toward the memorable and, therefore, the non-routine and dramatic; they exaggerate the good and egregious and downplay the everyday. The observations reported here are inductively derived from the stories as told by our street-level workers.

The Nature of Street-Level Decisions

Making Judgments

"This whole job is judgment," one counselor summarized, and the counselors' stories say a great deal about how they understand and confront difficult decisions. The rules regarding eligibility for Vocational Rehabilitation services are clear and have changed little since the agency was founded in 1918: (1) there must be a documented disability; (2) the disability must present a barrier to employment; and (3) the person must need Voc Rehab services to prepare for, obtain, or maintain employment. VR counselors have little discretion over who qualifies for services. Nevertheless, VR counselors have and exercise broad discretion over the nature and quality of services provided—a point missed by many who advocate clear and precise rules as the antidote to abuses of discretion.

Once a client is deemed eligible, VR counselors respond in one of three basic modes of services. First, they can respond in a normal, routine, bureaucratic way. This involves following the standard procedures of medical and occupational testing, developing a treatment plan with the client, placing in an appropriate service or providing the needed prosthesis, job training and placement, and case closure with all of the normal delays, waiting, and paperwork. This normal response is often positive, professional, and cost effective; normal treatment is "good" treatment.

Not all clients get this standard treatment, however. Some clients, to the extent possible without a clear violation of eligibility rules, are given less: they are discouraged, delayed, and, as soon as possible, dismissed. In this second mode of response, appointments are postponed and made inconvenient. Paperwork becomes a barrier, not a gateway, to service. Testing and evaluation is overdone since many of the tests can be difficult and discouraging, and only the minimum required services are provided. "That is all that is allowed, period," as the counselor stated in her story. Job placements are often premature and either doomed to failure or do not fit the client's aspirations. Sometimes counselors will even warn other counselors and agencies that a particular client is a troublemaker, thus hampering any future efforts for her or him to obtain services. These cases are closed as quickly as possible, with the ironic effect of increasing the counselor's "success" rate. As in most social services, success is measured by case closures, or what the counselors call "twenty-sixes," the computer code for "case closed."

But, as their stories testify, street-level workers also use their considerable discretion to provide extraordinary service to some clients, the third mode of response. At times they use their discretion to make their jobs more difficult and demanding. For the chosen clients, VR counselors expedite all procedures, often stretching, and at times breaking, the rules. They will advocate for the client's interests to the point of confronting supervisors and other agencies. For these clients, the street-level workers work unpaid overtime, ignore other cases, and become personal chauffeurs. They craft diagnoses and treatment plans to authorize all available services and keep cases open long after they could be closed, postponing the administratively valued twenty-sixes. Counselors will spend their own money, check in on weekends, and generally overinvest—indeed, step beyond the normal bounds of professional distance between counselor and client—to help these clients proceed. "I spent so much time with him, [my supervisor] was ready to send me packing, but he was desperate," as one counselor described her relationship with one client. "He was so depressed he could not function. I would take him out to lunch." Another counselor kept his over-committed relationship with a client a secret from his supervisor, "This is one of those that poor [supervisor] would probably just faint dead away. This is one she does not want to know about. She always says, 'I don't think I want to know.'"

These three modes of response, from reluctant to routine to extraodinary treatment, exist on a continuum but represent fundamentally different forms of service. How counselors decide who gets which form of treatment defines, in large measure, the meaning of justice and fairness in the delivery of social services. Street-level workers make an initial judgment of client worthiness which foreordains the nature of services. Judgments by counselors about client worthiness are a "values switch" that turns on and off various levels of service. This judgment is not one- or even two-dimensional but based on richly nuanced norms (see also Scott 1997).

Who Are the Worthy?

When asked to tell stories of fairness and justice, the Voc Rehab storytellers in our sample told of clients who were fairly denied or were fairly given extraordinary service. To these street-level workers, fairness had little to do with the bureaucratic norm of treating everyone the same or even fairly implementing the laws and regulations. To our storytellers, fairness and justice meant providing the client services based on his or her worth.

At first glance, this observation reinforces the negative portrait of out-of-control street-level bureaucrats who replace the rule of law with their own moral judgments and stereotypes, but as the stories accumulate, a more complex, multidimensional portrait of street-level judgment emerges. Street-level definitions of "worthiness" involve a complex balancing of client needs, the ability to respond to service, and concern for the husbanding of public resources. Indeed, the manner in which VR counselors make complex decisions about service provision is close to what we as citizens may reasonably ask of a responsible actor. Unlike other actors in the policy process, street-level workers do not see clients as abstractions—the "disabled," "the poor"—but as individuals, as people with flaws and strengths, who rarely fit the one-size-fits-all approach of the policies they struggle to implement. What, then, are the dimensions of worthiness described in these stories that guide street-level judgment and discretion? The various dimensions of worthiness that emerged from the stories are not discrete; they bleed and blend into each other, just as the world of street-level workers is not one of simple categories or hard-and-fast rules and definitions.

Worthy Because of Real Need

Worthy clients have a genuine need that extends beyond qualifying for services. Our field research site was in a low-income, urban community, and real need usually included poverty. Certainly .the middle class or wealthy disabled—a rare occurrence in our agency—received appropriate, routine service, but the VR counselors reserve their extraordinary care for those who lack the resources to help themselves. Worthiness begins as socioeconomic triage.

Themes often emerge from the stories by negative example. Even though VR counselors cannot dismiss out of hand the unworthy client—their discretion is more in the nature and extent of service delivery, not in terms of intake—they feel their work is demeaned by the client with a superficial and one-dimensional need.

Worthy of Investing Effort and Attention

Neither the easy nor the impossible clients are, in the view of the VR counselors, worthy of investing extraordinary care. VR counselors do not consider the normal client as warranting extra attention: they are effectively but routinely handled. Contrary to most research on street-level bureaucrats, our counselors were drawn to the hardest cases, those that made their work more difficult. One counselor, who works with disabled high schoolers, acknowledges that she gets overinvested in the hard cases: "The kids I get really attracted to . . . are really vulnerable; the ones who don't have a lot of support. I probably get more involved in their lives than I should."

But challenge is not enough; to be worthy of extra investment the client must be able to respond to treatment. In one story, a counselor overinvested in a client he knew was unlikely to change. The result of this experiment in overinvestment in an unworthy client was the punishment of the counselor, not by the agency but by the client himself—the alcohol-abusing, wheelchair-bound client slammed his newly outfitted, hand-controlled car into the counselor's own van. Moreover, the storyteller ends by saying that "People love to tell that story" because it reinforces by the negative (and humorous) outcome the importance of making careful judgments of worth.

Clients who can respond to treatment are realistic. Unrealistic clients make the counselor's job impossible: if they try to achieve the unrealistic goals, they fail; if they do achieve more realistic goals, the clients are not satisfied. Most counselors assume a "father knows best" attitude toward the client. While ostensibly there to meet the client's needs, they believe, from repeated experience and with considerable justification, that they are better suited to determine what is realistic for the client. A worthy client is therefore realistic: someone who "doesn't want to be a nuclear physicist, just community college." Unworthy clients are "Like someone who is mentally retarded and wants to become a computer analyst." Unrealistic clients are helped but do not solicit the kind of engagement as the realistic clients who work closely with the counselor and reinforce the counselor's sense of his or her own expertise.

Clients who cannot respond to treatment are deemed unworthy. Foremost among the unlikely to respond are those with personality disorders. These are individuals who are out of touch with reality; their lack of realism is pathological, and they repeat destructive behaviors, never learning from mistakes because of endless rationalizations and blaming others. Clients with personality disorders are often smart and manipulative. They are often difficult and unpleasant to work with, real "pains in the neck." A personality disorder can negate other dimensions of worth. Such clients are avoided if possible, put up with if necessary, but never considered worthy.

For the VR counselor, this dimension of worthiness is complicated when the client is a minor or an adult in the care of others. VR counselors told several stories of a client clearly worthy but with an uncooperative parent or guardian who made it impossible to achieve treatment goals. In these cases the counselors reluctantly pulled back. Several counselors told stories of parents who blocked efforts to help their child gain independence. These parents had come to rely on the Supplemental Security Income check the child added to the household income or on the live-in baby sitting their disabled family member provided younger siblings. Everything about the kids called out to the counselor, but their inability to help justified deeming the case unworthy of all but routine treatment. The counselors could not make a difference so they turned their scarce attention to others. Judgments about worthiness are often judgments about allocating scarce government resources, especially counselor time and effort.[2]

Morally Worthy

The client's moral worth is closely related to, and perhaps indistinguishable from, their realism. To the street-level worker, client motivation is the primary dimension of moral worth. Motivated clients are good clients; they are the truly deserving poor. The second, and clearly secondary, dimension of moral worth is the reason for their disability. If the client is responsible for his or her own disability—a drunk driving accident, for example—he or she is less worthy than someone who is disabled by birth, disease, or accident. But the client's motivation to improve or learn to cope is far more important in judgments of worth than the cause of the disability. If someone is disabled because of years of heavy drinking, the motivation to improve transforms that person into a worthy client. Conversely, if someone is disabled through no fault of character but is not motivated, he or she is unworthy of extraordinary service in the eyes of the

VR counselor. Motivation makes a client easier to handle since motivation is often defined in terms of cooperation with treatment. The motivated client is, nonetheless, deemed morally superior and worthy of investment: "The most difficult ones are the ones who don't try and I just cut them off after a while." In this way, the street-level worker is reflecting a deeply held American value in the moral standing of effort (Hochschild 1995).

The motivated clients are not destroyed by their disability. They are examples of strength and dignity despite hardship.[3] As one VR counselor describes this dimension of worthiness: "If someone is really trying, I will bend over backwards for them. I'll do whatever I can to help them out. I wish I could do it for everyone but I can't. . . . I think it transcends categories. . . . Then you get someone in here who has all the potential in the world, and they choose to blow it all and it makes me angry."

Moral worth has a second dimension: morally worthy clients do not try to con or scam the system. VR counselors see their work as virtuous. Even clients with profound and genuine needs who are trying to manipulate the counselor and the system for undue advantage get labeled troublemakers. Some try—usually unsuccessfully—to con the counselor by being helpless: "She's real whiny and real dependent, and she is going to try to hook you and suck you in, 'poor me, I need all this help, you're the only person who can help me.'" Others are more demanding. In either case, legitimate and justified services are not withheld, but the counselors do not go out of their way to help. Gossip and rumors about demanding and manipulative clients spread across the agency as counselors warn others to watch out for the client's scams. When con artists appear, they receive proper but perfunctory treatment, and they are often assigned to counselors with reputations for taking the least guff from clients.

Worthy of Investing Resources

Client worthiness also has a material dimension that is tightly entwined with the other three aspects of worthiness. Like other street-level workers, VR counselors do not see themselves as working for the state or ultimately accountable to elected officials; they insist that they work for citizens, not supervisors, agencies, and top officials.

In defining their jobs as working for the taxpayers of the state, these street-level workers take their fiduciary responsibility seriously: "these are our tax monies too," as one counselor put it. Worthy clients are good investments. Counselors are ready to invest in long-term and costly training if they feel that it will end in a secure and adequately paying job. They resist recent efforts spurred by welfare reform to push clients into low-paying, dead-end jobs if they feel such clients are worthy of a public investment in education. They are willing to spend money to meet client needs, and to spend more than legislators and top officials may want, but only on those clients who, in their judgment, will repay the investment. VR counselors spend more on some clients than on others, even when the clients have superficially the same disabilities and circumstances.

This material dimension of worth is a summative judgment of the other three: If clients have genuine needs, can respond to treatment, and are of good character, then they are likely to repay society for the investment of time, effort and money. It is also the most tangible expression of how judgments about worth alter the distribution of government services. It means the difference between a few weeks of training and referral to a minimum wage service job—the counselors generically refer to these as "working at McDonald's"—and several years of tuition and support at a community college and the possibility of a well-paying job with a future.

Response to Worthy Clients

These dimensions of client worthiness do not provide easy, unambiguous criteria to street-level workers: they are complex and subtle; grey, not black and white. Although experienced street-level workers learn to make these nuanced judgments, distinguishing the worthy from the unworthy is neither simple nor straightforward. In dealing with this uncertainty, VR counselors develop a norm of suspending judgment. Often they begin contact by providing routine treatment, but if they see the elements of worth described above, they start testing the client.

In many ways, the judgment of worth is based on a courtship of counselor and client, but it is a courtship of unequals. Counselors do not make snap judgments—experienced counselors have been burned too often. Instead, as one counselor put it, they give the client "little pearls" and see how he or she responds. As clients pass or fail these little tests, counselors either elevate them to the status of the worthy, demote them to the rank of unworthy, or leave them in the vast middle ground of normal or standard treatment.

As an example, one counselor told the story of a thirty-year-old man who dropped in the office just before lunch. He was scheduled to start community college the next week but had just learned that his financial aid (a Pell Grant) was held up because he had failed to register for the military draft when he was eighteen. The counselor recalled,

> "Well, you know the system normally would say that I can't talk to you right now, I got to make an appointment for you to come in 'cause it is about 11:30. Besides school starts next week and there is no way, we legally have sixty days to determine eligibility, and so I'm sorry we can't do this."

In other words, he should respond as "the system" would require by following the standards procedures. But to do so would not help the client. Moreover, as the story unfolds, the client had many strikes against him: "He never worked and was pushing thirty. He had been incarcerated more than he had been out." As details were added by the storyteller, the client became more than just an aging loser: he was clearly disabled, had the ability to succeed in community college, and he admitted both his problems and had already tried to turn his life around.

The story, like much street-level work, presented contradictions and dilemmas with the client simultaneously having traits of worthiness and unworthiness. The counselor responded by testing. He gave the walk-in a doctor's form to document the disability and said he needed to get it back by 3:00. The client returned by 3:00 with the form completed. In a short four hours the client proved his worth, and the counselor responded by cutting through all the red tape so that he could start college.

Like the walk-in, once deemed worthy, clients receive extraordinary service and attention from these street-level workers. Their cases are kept open long after the rules would permit—and the supervisors would prefer—postponing the bureaucratic measure of success, the much-valued "twenty-sixes," the code for file closed. To achieve success for the client, the VR counselors reduce their own measure of success, a situation that can put the agency and agency director at some risk if they collectively fail to meet their monthly quota of case closures. Reviewing the status of case closures is the number one agenda item at the monthly staff meetings, and the agency and counselors are under constant and, with welfare reform, increasing pressure to increase the closure rate.

Street-level workers will work overtime for the worthy client. The stories show that they will let other cases slide and postpone the all-important paperwork. They drop what they are doing. They come in on weekends to a help a client move to a better apartment. They spend their own money, provide a shoulder to cry on, and battle the bureaucracy on behalf of clients they deem worthy. In one story, the VR counselor sued her own agency to get the needed services for a worthy client, an action that eventually helped the client, but risked the unforgiving ire of the state bureaucracy.

In all the worthy client stories that we collected, the investment pays off. The clients are profoundly and permanently helped. These stories have similar endings: years later the client continues to work, perhaps has a problem now and then, but remains a productive member of society. Although worthy clients may not quickly meet the bureaucratically defined measure of success, a rapid case closure, both the street-level worker and the citizen win. Stories of the services given to worthy clients show how street-level workers can make lasting differences in the lives of some clients. They describe their work as a calling, and these few clients are the ones that call out to them and make their difficult and often unrewarding work worthwhile. The worthy clients make the street-level worker feel worthy as well. The citizens also benefit because these clients are the genuine success stories. They are the clients who deserve help, receive help, and are now productive, nondependent members of the community.

Comments

Street-level judgment and discretion are ever present; they cannot be reformed out nor managed away. Street-level workers feel they are on their own with little support and guidance. They rely on their experience, skills, expertise, and values as they implement public policy one client at a time. Our stories are likely biased in favor of street-level workers since the observations reported here are from their perspective. Nonetheless, our research suggests that the dominant view of street-level workers—that they use their discretion to make their work lives easier, more pleasant, and safer—tells only part of the story. Our street-level VR counselors made choices and decisions that often made their work harder, more stressful, and more threatening; if not for their lives, at least for their careers.

But, more importantly, the counselors' judgments about the worth of the client and the nature of the services provided underscore the profound responsibility these street-level workers take for their work. Here, on the front lines of governing, there are none of the gambits and ploys that so characterize the decision making of elected representatives and high-level officials. Principal-agent theories portray street-level workers as the agents of upper-level officials (Garvey 1993; Wilson 1989), but the street-level workers in our field research were not strongly committed to their agency—although there was a strong bond to co-workers, including the supervisor—or to the state agency or government. They did not express allegiance to policy actors or feel any devotion to implementing every detail of the laws and regulations that circumscribe their work. Their sense of responsibility was to the clients and community, and their judgments and decision norms were derived from experience with clients—both first hand and passed on from other counselors—that forced them to temper idealism with realistic assessments of what is possible. They invert principal-agent ideas by defining the client—not the supervisor, agency, or elected official—as the principal. These street-level workers are, in Brehm and Gates's phrase, "principled agents" (1997, 202).

Our research also underscores Brodkin's (1997, 24) telling observation: "But neither formal policy nor caseworker ideology is sufficient to account for the interpretation of welfare policy at the street level. Caseworkers, like other lower-level bureaucrats, do not do just what they want or just what they are told to want. They do what they can." In doing "what they can"—not what they want, what supervisors and elected officials want, or even what the clients always want—street-level workers have to make painful choices about the distribution of time, effort, and agency funding. As Lipsky (1980) pointed out, they are responsible for rationing services and resources and this responsibility pervades all aspects of their work.

The VR counselors did not, as Wilson (1989) suggests, shirk this burden but struggled mightily to meet needs and handle the caseload. Like all service agencies, Voc Rehab caseloads often double the sixty or seventy the counselors consider manageable. The large loads increase the counselor's feeling of detachment. The heavy caseloads do not diminish the deep sense of responsibility to the clients, however. The caseloads do force counselors to make vexing and, at times, agonizing choices: "So, I take it very seriously," one counselor told us. "The more people I get the more frustrating it is because I can't meet all of their needs. . . . You cannot provide the comprehensive services that are really needed. . . . Instead, you go from the top of the list." As our research shows, these choices about who gets minimal, routine, and extraordinary services—in essence, who gets what services from government—are guided primarily not by rules, policies, wishes, and demands of lawmakers, but by street-level judgment of client worthiness.

Notes

1. Although the term "street-level bureaucrat" is more commonly used in the research literature, our "workers" did not like the term; they found it demeaning. In deference, we replaced it with the less offensive "street-level worker."
2. Services to disabled children have always been problematic because of the potential for abuse, with the families, not the child, receiving the cash award. In 1990, in *Sullivan v. Zebley*, the U.S. Supreme Court

found that children should receive the same benefit as similarly disabled adults. This has been a costly and, in the eyes of critics, an often abused extension of disability rights. In response to these critics, the 1996 Welfare Reform Law reduced cash benefits to as many as 95,180 disabled children (*New York Times*, 15 August 1997, p. A1.)

3. The image of the "Super Crip" is a double-edged sword for the disabled. As Joseph Shapiro writes (1993, 332), "But the change in their [the disabled] mindset is powerful enough to win rights and perhaps eventually convince a nation and the world that people with disabilities want neither pity-ridden paternalism nor overblown admiration. They insist simply on common respect and the opportunity to build bonds to their communities as fully accepted participants in everyday life."

Part III

Reform, Reinvention, Innovation, and Change

Chapter 8

*Making Sense of Change**

Eugene B. McGregor, Jr. Indiana University

Making Sense of Change

The global pace of reinventing, regenerating, and transforming public enterprise has quickened. At this writing, myriad change initiatives defy intellectual comprehension,[1] let alone practical application. A complex vocabulary only adds to the confusion, to wit the following:

- Banishing bureaucracy (Osborne and Plastrik 1997)
- Competitiveness and competitive advantage (Porter 1980, 1985, 1990)
- Conversion (e.g., defense conversion)
- Deregulation (DiIulio 1994) and reregulation
- Devolution revolution (Kost 1996; Donahue 1997; Liner 1989)
- Downsizing and creative destruction (Nolan and Croson 1995)
- Excellence (Kettl and Ingraham 1992; Fountain et al., 1994)
- National performance reviews (Clinton and Gore 1997; Gore 1996)
- Next Steps (Morley 1993; Kemp 1990)—United Kingdom
- Privatization (Savas 1987)
- Realignment
- Rebuilding (Lappe and Du Bois 1994)
- Reconfiguration (Venkatraman 1991, 122)
- Redesigning of organizations and work systems
- Reengineering (Davenport 1993; Hammer and Champy 1993; Linden 1994)
- Reforming the state (Chevallier 1996)—France

*This paper has benefited from the comments of colleagues in the SPEA Workshop in Public Policy and Management; special thanks are owed Larry Schroeder, Jose Alfredo Gomez, Derek Kauneckis, Christine Martell, and Kathleen Weber. In addition, the author is indebted to Hal Rainey, Jeff Brudney, Larry O'Toole, and other reviewers of this paper whose contributions do not absolve me of responsibility for errors, weak argument, or bad judgment.

- Reinventing corporations and agencies (Osborne and Gaebler 1992; Naisbitt and Aburdene 1985; Thompson and Jones 1994)
- Remaking (Lappé and Du Bois 1994)
- Renewing (Kiel 1974; National Academy 1994)
- Reorganizing (Galbraith 1995; Lawler, Lawler, and Associates 1993)
- Restructuring (Lodge 1990)
- Rethinking (Smith 1995)
- Retrenchment (Schwartz 1997)
- Revitalizing and reviving (Rivlin 1992)
- Revolution (*Harvard Business Review* 1991)
- Rightsizing
- Industrial transformation (Hamel and Prahalad 1994)
- Organizational transformation (Hamel and Prahalad 1994)

Thus a casual inventory easily generates *at least* eighteen r-words, one b-word, two c-words, three d-words, an e-word, one p-word, and—most powerful—two versions of the t-word. Cumulative summaries depict a global rush toward "seamless" (Linden 1994), "virtual" (Davidow and Malone 1992; Rheingold 1993), and "excellent" corporations, governments, and even communities. In addition, an extensive "best practices" literature announces or anticipates imminent and discontinuous transformations, paradigm shifts, and other administrative silver bullets (Drucker 1968; Nayak and Ketteringham 1986; Osborne and Gaebler 1992; Tapscott 1993; Pierce and Guskind 1993; Handy 1989, 1994; Hamel and Prahalad 1994). It is the cacophony of change terminology combined with the seeming absence of navigational aids that launches this paper.

The Problem

This paper presents a framework for making sense of change. It does so by offering a simplified scheme for understanding myriad change options and choosing from among available change strategies. The argument unfolds in five sections. First, the paper confronts the problem of simplifying complexity on terms useful to practitioners. Second, a definition of change and its underlying notion of innovation are offered as a means of understanding the direction and pace of the current confusion. Third, the concept of a "change strategy" is presented as two simplifying heuristics—one characterizing the value-added calculus confronting all managers, and a second clarifying the choices available to managers who would emphasize numerator-based change strategies. Fourth, the notion of a "change strategy" is subjected to practical examination about how and under what conditions organizational change can be made to occur. Finally, summary conclusions further test the strength and practical utility of the argument.

How can one make sense of the change cacophony cited above? Classic social science thinking is overwhelmingly descriptive. It seeks empirical generalization and analytic models that help explain and predict what is "really going on" Three approaches have well-developed literatures (Galaskiewicz and Bielefeld 1998, chap. 1). The first, the selection approach, seeks to understand organizational ecology and the impact of environmental change on organizational change and institutional survival. The second, the adaption approach, attributes change to the contingency actions of managers who design organization instruments, structures, and resource portfolios to achieve strategic goals. The third approach, the structural embeddedness approach, seeks to understand how social networks affect organizational tactics, strategy formulation, and outcomes. All three approaches are insightful and present credible claims of being "applicable" to public and nonprofit management literatures (Galaskiewicz and Bielefeld, 1998).

The practical managerial problem, however, is that descriptive understanding and insight are, by themselves, insufficient guides to complex problem solving. The enduring public management dilemma is that an action-forcing environment demands that practicing managers achieve an "instrumental understanding" by which "messy realities" are handled decisively in order to influence future events and achieve results (Lynn 1996, 100). By the instrumental test, descriptive theory does only part of the job, that of fitting general statements to hard managerial realities in order to understand the change story.

The remaining task is to distill the lessons that might inform future action. However, recitation of best practices surrounding the eighteen r-words, one b-word, two c-words, three d-words, an e-word, one p-word, and two t-words is not a lesson-distilling exercise. It is an invitation to further confusion. Use of heuristics, by contrast, is one possible way to reduce complexity by creating analytic models descriptive of underlying realities that suggest action options. Useful heuristics have two characteristics (Lynn 1996, 100–101): first, they suggest testable propositions supporting general statements about what is true and not true about change. Second, heuristic insights help managers penetrate real-world complexity and lay bare underlying situations on which they can act. At the least, heuristics debunk myths and propose insights by which both scholars and practitioners can sort out competing claims about change "best practice" (Holzer and Callahan 1997). At the most, heuristics may provide useful new ideas for trial and evaluation.

Theoretically, public management practice in the U.S. should be a fertile test bed for heuristic development. Indeed, one would normally expect U.S. public management innovations and inventions to provide templates of change for the rest of the world. No other civilization idolizes inventiveness and innovation to the extent found in the "Republic of Technology."[2] The national fascination with invention and reinvention has spilled over into all areas of our national life.[3]

Yet, the current image of the U.S. public sector is fundamentally at odds with over two hundred years of national experience and romantic notions of American inventiveness and Yankee ingenuity as cultural norms. Currently dominant are images depicting a confused and stodgy public sector change taker (Bennett 1997), reluctantly reacting to change thrust upon it rather than anticipating and guiding change in the public interest.[4] The dominant thinking about current American practice attempts to explain why it is that significant government change is difficult or impossible to achieve.[5] Thus one recent assessment of Vice President Al Gore's National Performance Review (NPR)—now called National Partnership for Reinventing Government (NPRG)—finds that the NPR was, "deeply troubled by its split focus" and lack of intellectual coherence (Kettl 1997, 449). Other analysts conclude that the U.S. ought to imitate countries such as New Zealand for coherence, comprehensiveness, incentive alignment, clear performance specifications, and a convergence with private sector best practice (Scott, Ball, and Dale 1997, 374–79).

Change theory parallels recent depictions of American practice. For example, recent analyses depict public managers "groping along" in "swamps" and other murky and perturbed environments (Behn 1988; Schall and Feely 1992; Schall 1995; Golden 1997). The imagery reinforces early notions of incremental muddling (Lindblom 1959) and probing (Lindblom 1990) that have long persisted as realistic characterizations of public policy decision making. These notions have been joined most recently by images of "management by groping *along* [emphasis added]"[6] (Behn 1988; Golden 1997), "evolutionary tinkering" (Sanger and Levin 1992), and a tendentious "management of emergent issues"[6] (Bryson et al. 1996). Thus public management change discussions are currently dominated by procedural observations about *how* change is produced. Little is available in the form of end-state visions and broadly applicable principles by which public sector change practice can be guided (Lynn 1996).

By contrast, private sector management theory projects bold end-state heuristics and substantive definition. While public theory muddles, gropes, and tinkers, private management theory engages strategic issues of "*logical* incrementalism" (Quinn 1980), "competitive advantage" (Porter 1980, 1985), and "competing for the future" (Hamel and Prahalad 1994). For private sector management, the management of change and innovation is idolized. It is the highest skill informed by a substantial theoretical base (see also Rowe and Boise 1973; Nystrom and Starbuck 1981; Pennings and Buitendam 1987; Walton 1987; Tushman and Moore 1988; Van de Ven, Angle, and Poole 1989; Utterback 1994; Kantor 1995).

Private management infatuation with change is not accidental. Innovation is a naturally occurring result of the operation of free markets where entrepreneurs marshal resources in creative ways to capture the opportunities presented by constantly shifting markets (Drucker 1968, 1993; Schumpeter 1942). Thus entrepreneurs scramble out from under collapsing markets and seize the opportunities presented by new and expanding markets. Constant change results. No wonder Schumpeter could be cheerful about the gale forces of change that blow through whole societies and organizations.[7]

Is public management as sluggish as recent reports might suggest? Is it clear that the NPRG is a failure? Or even in trouble? How could one tell? It is notable that public management is not bereft of discussions about innovation and change. For example, there is a nascent theoretical literature on the substance of public management change (Ingraham, Romzek and Associates 1994; Linden 1994; Cohen and Eimicke 1995). There are also illustrations of innovative leadership. Robert Behn's account of the merger of welfare and employment and training programs in Massachusetts (Behn 1991) is one well-known example. Lee Friedman's analysis of the Manhattan Bail Project (Friedman 1997) and the Nancy Roberts and Paula King account of the development of public school choice in Minnesota (Roberts and King 1996) are two other recent examples. Yet, citing instances of successful change management establishes neither a heuristic nor a principle of successful action. Nor is it adequate to note that many studies of innovation and change in public and private bureaucracy simply do not support the conclusion that the U.S. public sector takes a backseat to the private sector in the change business (Roessner 1977; Wamsley and Wolf 1997; Holzer and Callahan 1997).

More convincing are substantial evidence and theory demonstrating that public sector change does in fact occur for understandable reasons. For example, the historical record clearly shows that U.S. government has managed to reinvent itself several times (L. D. White 1948, 1951, 1954, 1958; Mosher 1968; Stillman 1996). Change has been the leitmotif of American public administration. It was a recurring theme as the nation evolved from its founding era and occupied a continent; fought and rebuilt after a civil war;

managed and regulated the large-scale industrial bureaucracies of the progressive era; administered a colonial empire and prosecuted two world wars; and dealt with a succession of depressions, recessions, and cold wars. Indeed, one recent study of 141 U.S. reform initiatives undertaken during the period 1945–94 offers the judgment that: " . . . there is not too little management reform in government, but too much" (Light 1997, 1).

How could this be? Clearly wrong is the popular conclusion that public sector decision making is fatally flawed because public managers somehow lack an incentive to innovate. It is at odds with U.S. managerial history, noted above. It is also based on implicit, but refutable, notions such as: "Lacking the incentive of competitive private markets, public managers are immune to innovation and excellence. . . . "Nor are constitutionally weak civil servants shorn of opportunities to innovate. Such notions ignore the realities of political processes fully analogous to marketplace signals that alert public managers to the need for change (Moore 1995, chap. 4). Indeed, Louis Bragaw's scholarly assessment of Coast Guard management (1980, 11) indicates the existence of a "hidden stimulus" fully as powerful as private sector competitive market mechanisms in promoting public sector innovation and excellence. Finally, it is clear as a practical matter that the actual flow of innovation and change sometimes moves in a direction opposite the popular image.[8]

Definitions

How can a public manager make sense of change? What is needed is a general formulation of what public sector change means or how innovative management practice might be defined, judged, and promoted. Heuristics come from an examination of the underlying nature of public sector change.

This paper views *change* as a general class of phenomena in which previously known and certain arrangements for doing work give way to new and uncertain habits and patterns. Not all change is managerially interesting. This paper is interested in significant change, or *innovation,* roughly defined as the thoughtful (i.e., deliberate) introduction of new and better ways of making decisions, organizing actions, and designing processes that lead to improved organizational performance (Behn 1997, 7–9).

It is striking that the pace of *management* change since the mid-1980s has accelerated over the more leisurely first eight decades of the 20th century. To appreciate the recent frenetic pace of change, one need only recall that public administration reform efforts were typically cast in the form of Toynbeesque reform episodes initiated by major commissions designed to improve governmental performance in a "challenge and response" format. For example, there were ten general management reform efforts in the middle eight decades in the twentieth century, by Ronald Moe's count (1992), starting with the Keep Commission of 1905–09 and concluding with the Grace Commission of 1982–84, an average of one commission every eight years.[9] The performance of reform commissions was clearly mixed. The more successful commissions, such as the Brownlow Commission of 1936–37 and the Hoover Commissions of 1947–49 and 1953–55, found their efforts subsequently emulated by state and local government in the form of little Hoover commissions. By contrast, the less successful commissions—notably the Ash Council of 1969–71, the Carter reorganization project, and the Grace Commission—have been largely forgotten.

Sometime after the Grace Commission concluded its ill-fated attempt to extract massive economies and efficiencies from a deficit-racked federal budget, the pace of public management change accelerated. The precise date of the transition is difficult to fix, but the mid-1980s seem about right. Several instructive initiatives were launched:

- The Ford Foundation Innovations in American Government Program run by the Taubman Center at Harvard University's John F. Kennedy School of Government since 1986 (web page: *http://ksgwww.harvard.edu/~innovat/*);
- The Clinton-Gore reinvention labs (Gore 1996) number nearly 300 agency-based federal experimental "reinvention labs" that have grown steadily in number since 1992 (web page: *http://www.npr.gov*);
- The Alliance for Redesigning Government/National Academy of Public Administration network tracks state and local government innovation. The Public Innovator Learning Network URL is *http://www.alliance.napawash.org/alliance/index. html.*

This brief enumeration does not include the experimental activity surrounding attempts at reinventing nonprofit enterprise, schools, churches, and other organizations. For example, public schools in the nation's nearly 15,000 school districts are engaged in wide-ranging discussions about the transformation of public education in an experiment known as Goals 2000.[10]

As the change rhetoric has heated up in virtually all sectors of the American economy, public managers have clearly been experimenting. For example, mere perusal of the nearly 300 federal experiments—reinvention labs—launched under the *aegis* of NPR/NPRG reveals a diversity of labels, concepts, and initiatives. The following represents many of the most common themes:

- Customer-focused services
- Interagency cooperation
- One-stop shop centers
- Self-directed work teams
- Reengineering prompt payments
- Automated offices, records, and services
- Just-in-time service delivery
- Partnering with communities and states
- Flexible workplace
- Teleservice and electronic data interchange
- Benchmarking and customer service piloting
- Enhancing service delivery through decentralization
- Streamlining projects through partnerships

Where is the change parade headed? Among the most critical attributes of this new era are the following:

1. The basis for management depends less on the management of the physical resources of land, labor, and capital and derives instead from the management of knowledge and information embedded in smart products and complex production processes (Drucker 1968, 1993).
2. The foundation of human resource management has shifted. Of less interest is the traditional emphasis on managing the tasks, duties, and responsibilities of personnel whose operating costs must be minimized. More important is the management of a capital asset where the knowledge, skills, and abilities possessed by people defines what they are capable of doing (McGregor 1991).
3. Production standards have been redefined. Strategic applications of information technology (IT) destroy time and distance as barriers to human organization and production. The result is an expanded production frontier for customer service excellence, and *the customers know it* (Fountain et al. 1994).
4. Traditional organization charts are candidates for inversion (Mechling 1994). A strategic application of information technology further augments the role played by front-line workers who represent the human capital required to deliver services that are "fast, focused and flexible" (Sentell 1994).

5. The public environment has become highly competitive. Productivity occurs in a fishbowl environment of networked communications and interactions such that productivity standards are constantly changing and are globally benchmarked.
6. The above realities are executed under conditions of fiscal constraint and an atmosphere of suspicion about the productive potential of government. Thus the governance structure of public accountability is changing with fiscal shortfalls providing the license for changes that "produce more and cost less."

The reality is that public managers confront constant change of many kinds at all levels of the public sector. As the foregoing discussion has established, change is no longer the anomalous event.

Change Strategy

If public sector change has a thousand constantly changing faces, when should any particular change be tried? By whom? Why and when? Clearly, the answer cannot come from an enumeration of the endless possibilities. The answer must come instead from a sense of strategy that imposes an order and direction on the confusion. Strategy is the pattern of organizational activity that, " . . . integrates an organization's major goals, policies, and action sequences into a cohesive whole" (Quinn 1980, 7).

At its heart, public sector strategy represents a coherent view about how public value is best produced. Thus strategy is a "public value-added calculus" that endeavors to reduce the cost of production (the denominator) in relation to the value of the final product (the numerator) for a production process that converts resource inputs into some value-added organizational performance or result. This is shown in Figure 1. Strategically, public organization performance is defined by the production of services consumed and valued by some combination of customers, consumers, clients, and citizens (C^4) who lie outside the organization and who exercise the ability to make their preferences and views known to the producers of value.

The overriding idea of Figure 1 is that public organization performance has a "bottom line." The reader will note that consumption and production activities are placed at the same point of the conversion process because, unlike the goods-producing sector, consumption and production occur together and simultaneously (Fountain et al. 1994, 2). When viewed strategically and heuristically, public managers have only a few basic change choices (Moore 1995; Hamel and Prahalad 1994). For example, managers can:

VALUE-ADDED PRODUCT / RESOURCE INPUT COST	Consumption[a] / Conversion Process / Production	PERFORMANCE

Figure 1. Public Value-Added Calculus[a]

[a] Public sector consumption is loosely defined to refer to the act of accepting and using "products" by any or all of the following: customers or clients, consumers, and citizens (C^4).

- shrink the denominator by decreasing the cost of operations through automation, cutbacks, or other efficiency moves that reduce the total resource claim on money, people, space, and so forth;
- redeploy the denominator by improving the conversion processes by which resource inputs are converted into outputs. Examples might include improvements in an organization's capacity to respond to crisis and to innovate based on investments in training and development of front-line workers;
- grow the numerator by increasing the value or quality of *existing* public services, such as making them more responsive to citizen need or increasing fair and equitable;
- grow the numerator by creating some *new* value not currently produced. In effect, this option envisions the invention of a new industry.

Denominator management is clearly the easiest and the most tempting of the options. It is also the weakest option. Indeed mere denominator reduction, by itself, is not necessarily strategic even though resource cutbacks may make production processes appear faster and cheaper. Moreover, indiscriminate cutback management can lead to diminished numerators and anorexic organizations if resource cutbacks are not carefully assessed for the existence of false economies that not only reduce current performance, but undermine the other three strategic options in the bargain.

Stronger but more difficult strategies are numerator-based and aim to increase stocks and flows of value flowing from the sunk public investment. Indeed the most powerful change strategies are those that create new value within existing industries or even create new industries altogether. For example, Hamel and Prahalad provide a classic illustration (1994, 103) of the options widely available to private managers who must "compete for the future" on a global basis by meeting unserved and unarticulated customer needs in new and creative ways.[11] The result is a competition for "opportunity shares"—shares of industries yet to be established rather than market shares of well-established industries—used by such exemplars as Japan Victor Corporation, Swatch, and Electronic Data Systems to create, respectively, VCR machines, inexpensive fashion watches, and customized information technology management systems.

Is there a public sector analogue? We adapt the Hamel and Prahalad example to public service simply to illustrate the kind of thinking that is required by a strategic view of change and innovation. We accept as axiomatic that organizations survive by meeting the service needs of their recipients, who may be any combination of customers, consumers, clients, and citizens (C^4). By this logic, *recipients* may be either those presently served or those presently unserved but who might be served in the future. In addition, recipient *needs* are either fully known and articulated, or unknown and unarticulated. Thus, an "articulated" need is a condition in which recipients know they want something that can be supplied. An "unarticulated" condition exists because potential recipients either are not aware that they have a particular need or are unaware of the possibility of meeting a conceivable need (e.g., before phones existed, few people thought of making phone calls.).

A schematic representation of recipients and needs is shown in Figure 2 that suggests action options available to practitioners regardless of the original position of an organization. Conceptually then, the "strategic vision" of an organization can be placed at the center of the four choices as a means of recognizing that every public manager can move the numerator of his or her organization in one of four different directions or some combination of the four.

Clearly public managers have lots of ways to add value to the numerator of the strategic calculus outlined in Figure 1. The most basic available move is the "warrior" strategy of cell 1, defined as enhancing the value of services to those already served whose needs are well-known and well-articulated. This is the strategy that limits change and innovation to already defined and established markets. The term "warrior" also suggests the inevitability of competition in commodity service provision—such as prisons, schools, police and so forth—where warriors must search for change strategies that cut costs while enhancing service quality. The reader will note that existing services can almost always be enhanced with speed, responsiveness, quality, cost, and accessibility.

Alternatives to the warrior position are found by considering the two directions in which any public manager might contemplate change. One is to move in the direction of expanding the client base by reaching out to new customers, consumers, clients, and citizens or by eliminating work backlogs that effectively deny services to consumers. This would be the "globalization" move that aspires to

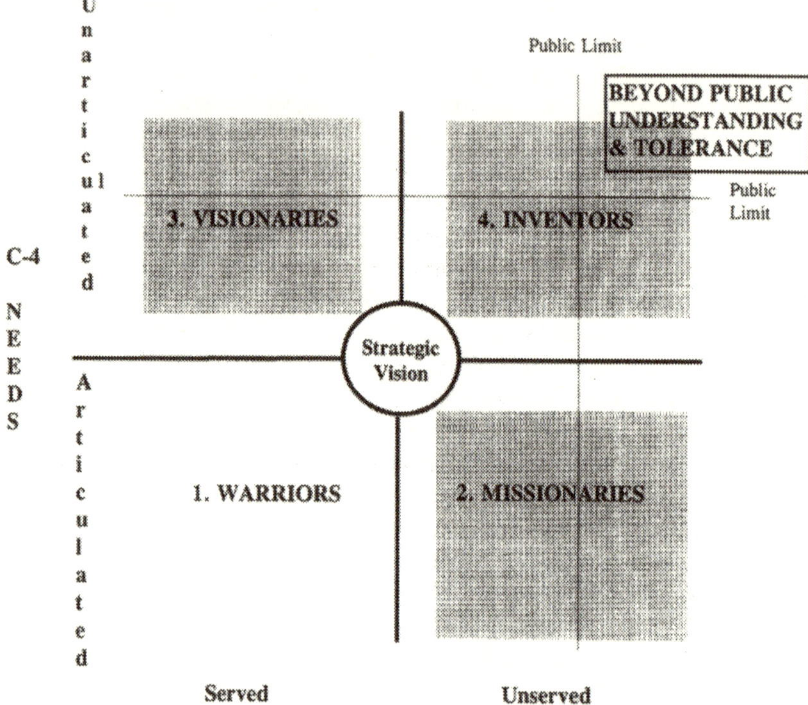

Figure 2. Strategic Directions Matrix (Adapted from Hamel and Prahalad, *Competing for the Future,* 1994, p. 103.)

serve all the clients in the catchment area. A second change direction is to fill unarticulated needs by meeting needs that a customer, consumer, client, or citizen may not realize can or should be met; this is a service enrichment strategy of which service customization might be an example.

In sum, public managers have three alternatives to the warrior position. What might be termed "missionary" strategies attempt to expand the customer base of a public agency without redefining the needs of the consumer. "Visionary" strategies, by contrast, seek to meet a richer set of needs of which recipients are only dimly aware. Third, "inventors" attempt to combine both expansion and enrichment strategies by creating values that do not presently exist for a customer base that does not yet exist because a felt and articulated need has not yet been defined. While the first two choices involve organizational transformations within the confines of a defined industry or product line, the third option requires an industrial transformation in the sense that managers are involved in the creation of whole industries that did not previously exist.

An Illustration: The utility of Figure 2 can be illustrated by a mind game. Simply think of some service or product and imagine how it could be both expanded and enriched. The case of Mark Moore's mythical head librarian in Belmont, Massachusetts provides a convenient illustration (Moore 1995, 13–16). Public libraries have a classic image, familiar to all, as quiet information warehouses administered by professionally trained librarians. In traditional systems librarians are guardians of the books, magazines, and other materials that can be browsed and borrowed by patrons. Public libraries serve a recognized client base with well-articulated needs. The "warrior" position in library change management involves deciding how to provide the core service with maximum speed, efficiency, and convenience to the client.

Figure 2 reminds us that there are the many other uses to which libraries might be put. For example, the library manager might enrich the line of educational programming, such as great books for latchkey children who need somewhere to go after school. Or the library could become a multi-media center for the world's digitized information made publicly available through the internet and other electronic means. It could also become an education and training facility for those requiring free and easy access to the information and knowledge pools necessary to productive economic and social life. It could serve as a community meeting place, a kind of public forum. Indeed the possibilities are endless and probably not fully articulated in even well-educated communities. Strategically, one would say that the "warrior" library strategy had been enriched by the "visionary" vision.

A second change strategy would consider the types of patrons served. In the library stereotype, those traditionally served are people who like to read and need a comfortable place to sit and read in peace and quiet. They are joined by community literati who eagerly use the library to sample the latest best-seller list, high school students researching term papers, and young parents seeking enrichment for children by introducing them to books and stories. There is, however, a large population of the unserved not typically reached by traditional library programming. They might include, for example, busy professionals, members of the elderly community unable to obtain transportation, the illiterate and marginally literati, people with special needs for information for which consultants might ordinarily be required at high cost, and single parents lacking educational day care for semi-independent school children. The above illustrations suggest examples of underserved and unserved populations that could be brought into the fold by a "missionary" strategy.

Finally, "inventers" might envision a combined strategy where citizen needs for customized information, knowledge, and training are flexibly and quickly met even in advance of community awareness of the need for information service. Hypothetically, one might imagine a globally networked information emporium complete with gourmet food, a kind of public combination of Borders Books & Music and Barnes and Noble bookstores, accessible to the entire community and complete with concierge service worthy of a Ritz-Carlton Hotel. Regardless of speculative illustration, the point of cell 4 of Figure 2 is that "inventors" aim to create product and service lines—whole industries, in effect—that did not exist before.

In sum, Figure 2 demonstrates that all public and private enterprises have before them large zones of unexploited value-creation opportunity denoted by the shaded areas outside the baseline warrior strategy. This conclusion obtains even though the public case appears bounded in the case of some agencies in two particular ways as indicated by dotted lines. First, inasmuch as public organizations are territorially bound to towns, cities, counties, states, and nations, it would appear that there are limits to public agency globalization as shown by the vertical dotted line. Thus town or county librarians do not ordinarily think of themselves as managers of multinational corporations who must design and operate global operations. The second limit is indicated by the horizontal dotted line that reminds us that the articulation of public needs is a bounded one, although bounds will vary with each agency.

Applications

Thus far all that has been demonstrated is that public managers have grounds to think deeply about strategic change. *How* can a manager move a strategic vision in one direction or another? The question has two possible meanings, only one of which concerns this discussion. The first meaning refers to the substantive end-state moves a manager must consider in order to produce the change options noted above. The second refers to the procedural recipe for launching successful change. Since the burden of this argument is that the latter question has little meaning until the former question is clearly framed, we deal with the former issue only.

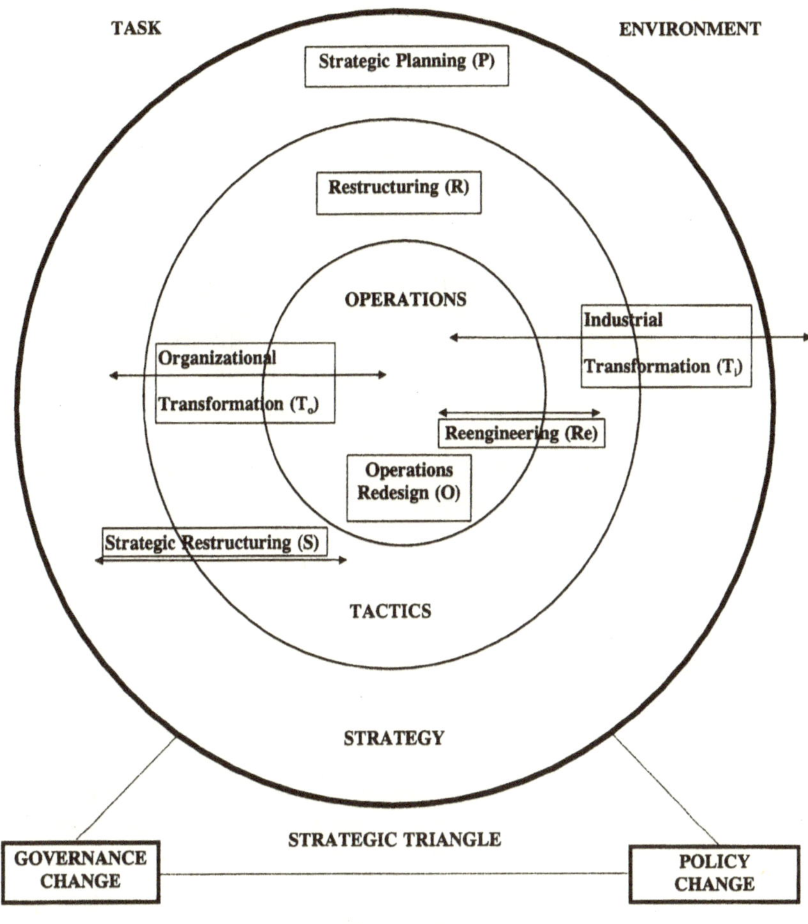

Figure 3. Management Change Modes and Levels

Clearly, multilevel thinking is required of those concerned with implementing change. This is diagrammed in Figure 3, where a basic vocabulary is needed to describe change options. At the broadest level, a trichotomy of issues dominates the *task environment* of public management (McGregor 1993; Moore 1995). The first, management operations, is the change-making domain of appointed public managers and is represented by the three concentric circles of management decision making encircled in a bold line and perched on a "strategic triangle" base. The second "corner" of the triangle is the governance cluster that involves politicians, oversight agencies, and governing bodies whose function it is to spend public authority on behalf of change. Governance change is positioned as the lower left rectangle of Figure 3. The third is the policy cluster that consists of the substantive problems to be solved on behalf of clients, customers, consumers, and citizens who are the recipients of public service.

The essence of change management is, then, that the public manager simultaneously manages down, up, and out in a "strategic triangle," although the relative positioning of governance and management operations has been reversed in Figure 3 for convenience, even though governance is "up" and operations is "down" (Moore 1995, 22–23). In reality all three clusters interact. For example, issues of governance and reform of the state deal with the structure of authority and patterns of accountability in government, whereas policy refers to problem solving action by public instruments (Peters 1996; Chevallier 1996). Thus, for example, to the extent that government is reformed to enhance marketplace principles, encourage civic participation, or authorize flexibility or deregulated government in the name of "customer service excellence" (Peters 1996, 19; Stillman 1996, chap. 7), then operations management will also be changed. Similarly, program innovations—management ops—that forge partnerships with citizens (e.g., neighborhood policing) or involve vigorous use of self-service mechanisms (e.g., information kiosks) also redefine civic engagement; the result is that governance and the prospects for problem solving are changed as well as management practice.

The key point that Figure 3 makes clear is that even when two parts of the strategic triangle—governance and policy—are held constant, public managers have lots of ways to change administrative operations. This can be seen by distinguishing three levels of management action. One is strategy that represents the organizational goals, visions, policies, and missions from which a strategic architecture is forged. The second is tactics, whose broad domain consists of deployment manipulations whereby middle managers design organizations, allocate resources, and monitor organizational performance. The third level is operations—the technical operating core of any organization—comprised of production processes, work systems, and standard operating procedures on which all productivity is based.

For purposes of simplicity, we reduce management change options to seven broad types of action, grouped in six categories below. The action types represent unique combinations of one or more *contiguous* management levels. What is striking is the extent to which middle management—the tactical layer of organization—is centrally involved in producing major change, a concept sometimes overlooked by strategists and political people attempting to move quickly and visibly and, in some cases, all too impatiently without middle management advice and assistance. There are no known cases of change that skip contiguous management levels as would be seen, for example, if a gopher tunnel were to tie strategic change to operational change, bypassing altogether the tactical interventions of middle management.

The first four groups focus largely on warrior strategies, whereas the last two operate in the shaded areas of Figure 2. All action groups involve numerator management in the sense that enhanced value to the customer, client, consumer, and citizen is the goal whatever the denominator reductions that might otherwise be envisioned.

1. Operations Redesign (O)

The most basic change strategy involves a redesign of core technologies, work systems, and production processes. The purpose of such a move is to enhance the efficiency and quality of an existing product line. Where operations redesign alone is employed, the basic final product remains the same, even when partial customization of product with respect to consumer and client needs is achieved. Some examples include:

- downsizing by automation
- cutbacks and load shedding
- self-managed teams
- work systems redesign
- concurrent engineering

As a general matter, the basic aim is to make service fast and flexible by making organizations "lean and mean." What changes is not the final product but the work system through which the product is produced.

2. Restructuring (R)

A second change option is reorganization that targets organizational designs, resource allocation processes and procedures, and performance monitoring systems as candidates for change. Where restructuring alone occurs, basic operations and final products and missions remain unchanged. What does change is the shape of the organizational architecture that links core operations to strategy. Some examples include:

- delayering
- decentralization
- recentralization
- contracting out
- shifts of organizational design (e.g., U-Form, M-Form), design (e.g., functional, matrix), or charter (e.g., charter schools)

Thus, restructuring might be used to produce a product line more efficiently or to make it richer and of higher quality. Contracting for public services is one way to do the former; chartering new arrangements—such as charter schools—may be a way to make a product richer or, at the least, to threaten an unproductive organizational arrangement with competition as a spur to productivity.

3. Strategic Planning (P)

A third single-level change involves strategic planning. Strictly defined, strategic planning does no work. It is largely a non-move, a temporizing step, from the standpoint of final product delivery. Its aims and purposes are the contemplation of major shifts of goals and missions, the instruments through which goals and missions are achieved, and the means by which resources can be acquired. Where "strategic planning" alone is pursued, what is produced are the organizational and institutional blueprints that identify "what we must be doing right now" to intercept the future (Hamel and Prahalad 1994, 110–11, 283). Some examples include:

- external scanning and forecasting
- internal scanning and forecasting
- mapping of problems, solutions, and stakeholders
- formal strategic planning process
- projecting a strategic architecture or an outline whereby resources are leveraged and stretched to cover new goals

4. Reengineering (Re)

Reengineering is multilevel change designed to enhance an organization's competitive position within an already established market. Reengineering envisions major organizational retooling of the production system facilitated by information technology, where the basic mission and product line remain unchanged. In essence, the same product is produced but in a manner that changes both core production processes *and* the relationships between middle management and frontline workers. Some examples include:

- process innovation, such as conversion of line operations to job shop production
- automation and integration of labor-intensive production processes, thus destroying functionally specialized bunkers that characterize traditional industrial bureaucracies.

The practical effect of such change is to force decisions downward in organizations. The application of information technology to core processes potentially enables the achievement of massive improvements in productive efficiencies by redefining core production processes and the work units on which production is built. One example involves shifting public services from a curative to a preventive posture (Linden 1994; Sparrow 1994). This is seen in community policing or in managed health care systems where work units become "problems to be solved" in advance of emergencies rather than response times (e.g., "you call, we'll come") to emergency situations (Moore, Sparrow, and Spelman 1997). Another example would consist of such innovations as electronic benefits distributed through ATMs, a "spin-in" technology already well developed by the private banking sector, that can replace the disbursement of paper checks to recipients. Electronic tax filing is yet another illustration of the reengineering notion where the final product remains the same (i.e., filing tax returns), but the core process used to produce the outcome is "reengineered."

5. Strategic Restructuring (S)

Strategic restructuring joins strategic and tactical levels of management without penetrating to the level of core operations. It often involves interorganizational designs, such as:

- strategic alliances
- partnerships
- consortia
- interorganizational configurations and webs
- wholesaling organizational functions previously retailed (e.g., home mortgages)

Strategic restructuring is used for many purposes, generally to redefine the competitive position of a service delivery agent vis-á-vis competitors. Thus consortia—such as Sematech—are used to marshal a critical mass of resources required to protect and extend some vital function or product line, such as domestic microprocessor manufacturing, by pooling risks and resources to deal with strong outside competition. Wholesaling strategies are also a useful means of achieving efficiencies by moving to the private marketplace the retail aspect (i.e., dealing with customers) of services such as mortgage financing. In nearly all cases, the final product remains the same, mortgage capital made available to borrowers, for instance. What changes is simply the organizational mechanism by which the product is produced. One can envision many missionary and visionary goals served by strategic restructuring that expands and customizes service delivery.

6. Transformation (T)

Sixth and finally, the most innovative of the management change options are the transformational moves that entail a multilevel change of the final product, the structures through which resources are allocated and work is organized, and the processes and work systems by which product lines are produced. At least two types of transformation exist:

- *organizational transformation* (t_o): simultaneous shifts of three management levels to accommodate either service enrichment or expansion initiative. Thus mass customization might be seen as an illustration of the mass production of case management services.
- *industrial transformation* (t_i): creation of new products and markets previously nonexistent. In essence, new industries are created.

In the t_o case, an organization produces a new product that is new to the organization but not the industry. Examples might include extensive use of public schools and libraries as day care and social service centers, thus expanding their traditional roles. In such cases, organization structure and process cannot remain untouched for new services and products require new designs. Organizational transformation occurs in cases where a bureau or agency creates and develops a new mission or pulls off a shift between or among different mission portfolios. Once again, missionary and visionary goals are served.

In the t_i case, a new industry is invented when bureaus or agencies invent products not yet produced by any organization. In this case, whole industries are created. Examples abound among public research and development agencies that have produced communications satellites, weather satellites, smart machines, synthetic material, software, aerospace vehicles, and genetic engineering discoveries. More than a few industries have been "spun-off" to the private sector from such public inventiveness.

Conclusions

The times clearly call for public sector change. The basis of this conclusion lies with the widespread view that a discontinuity exists between the evolving needs of society and the current operation of public bureaucracy. The preface of the Kennedy School of Government's Visions of Governance for the Twenty-First Century conveys one framing of the "change issue" (Nye et al. 1997, ix):

> What will effective government mean in the next century? We have been told that the era of big government is over, but no one has yet articulated what will take its place. Clearly change is needed. We are witnessing a widespread loss of confidence in and a dissatisfaction with government as it is currently functioning. While the possible reasons for this situation are many, the simple fact that the world itself is changing rapidly stands as the primary cause. Mid-twentieth-century visions of government must yield to new conceptions consistent with an information-based economy and society.

A further finding is that public sector managers are responding. As a collective venture, the American public sector is aggressively doing what perhaps it does best of all: imagine new ways of doing business, select promising experiments, try them out, and learn from the results. Evidence of general agreement about the need for change lies in the frenzy of innovation and change now apparent at all levels of U.S. government and throughout the world as well. The result is a chaotic literature and vocabulary that this paper tries to sort in a managerially intelligible way.

More specific findings derive from our use of three heuristics. The first heuristic was a value-added calculus that binds all managers, public and private, to a bottom-line standard of practice. Public managers will have to decide whether to pursue a numerator-based or a denominator-based strategy, or some combination of the two. Moreover, Figure 1 establishes the severe limitations of attempting to drive change through the device of denominator cutbacks alone and shows the availability of other more attractive options.

How can the difficult task of value-added change, the numerator enhancement option, be conceived? The second heuristic, the "strategic directions matrix" summarized in Figure 2, illustrates an infinity of strategic change choices available to public managers. Numerator growth is achieved in many ways. One way is to make existing services faster, more flexible, and more responsive to customer needs and requirements while either holding the line on cost or reducing resource requirements—the classic warrior strategy. Public managers can also choose to expand the customer base. Alternatively, they can respond to as yet unarticulated future needs and requirements of "customers." They can also create new products and services. Furthermore, since all organizations have the potential to explore any of the four quadrants simultaneously, managers can select a mix of options. It is not necessary to bet the public farm on one value-added initiative. In short, public managers have lots of ways to grow numerators.

The third heuristic enumerates the implementation options. Many basic management changes can be achieved without renegotiating the constitutional charter of civil servants and without radically altering the governance and policy roles of public managers. Indeed, even severely micromanaged and constitutionally humble public managers have both opportunity and a political mandate to create useful change. As in the second heuristic, there are lots of ways to get the change job done. Not only are there myriad action options broadly classified within each of the seven major groups, combinations and sequencing of the options multiply further the possibilities for change.

It bears emphasis that much of what is referred to as transformational change is mediated by information technology (IT), a general term that refers to both hardware and software components of computing, telecommunications, and related infrastructure that support client servers, networks, and consulting services required by modern IT use. As a general matter, it appears increasingly difficult to find successful change strategies that do *not* involve applications of IT (Borins 1998, chap. 7), for a host of innovations now in operation and on the drawing boards could not occur without a value-added application of information technology hardware, software, and infrastructure. Thus, IT is the centerpiece of such diverse experiments as (Milward and Snyder 1996; Fountain et al. 1994)

- Victor the Cyber Lawyer, "doc-in-the-box" health diagnostics, tax code advice
- Community voice mail
- TeleFile Touch Tone tax filing (Massachusetts)
- Electronic Federal Benefits (NPR) and state ATM welfare payments
- Intelligent transportation systems (ITS), including electronic toll roads and smart infrastructure collecting tolls, providing

downstream information about hazards and driving conditions, accident notification and clearance
- Information distribution through kiosks, web pages, 800 numbers

In sum, our basic conclusion is that the "what" and the "how" of change are intertwined. One cannot figure out how to achieve an innovation without also having a clear notion of how big the change is to be. For example, wise opinion about change converges on the conclusion that it is the series of small (yet important) innovations rather than big, sweeping change that marks effective change management (Savoie 1998). Furthermore, scholarship concludes that small, early successes create the political foundation for successful change management (Frederickson and Perry 1998). Clearly, knowing the difference between a "large" change and a "small" change is critical for the change management process.

The paradoxical aim of this paper was to contribute to the *practice* of change management by using simplifying concepts to reduce the complexity and confusion that characterize current public management discussions. The exercise was based on a premise that the pace of public sector change has accelerated to the point that growing confusion seems the only likely result if heuristics are not employed. It is a counterintuitive wisdom that simple schemes allow one to appreciate the nearly infinite opportunities managers have to make strategic contributions to change.

We defend the need for simplicity and clarity even as we recognize that astute managers can find strategic advantage in the absence of clarity, since confusion provides space in which clever managers can maneuver (Sanders and Thompson 1996). Yet even that political reality underscores our premise. Managers are astute and effective precisely when they, at least, are clear about what *they* are doing. It is also true that this paper has not dealt with the replication of change that is the means of sustaining innovation (Borins 1998; Light 1998). However, it seems unlikely that effective public sector change can be either replicated or sustained when people generally are not clear about what change really means, the strategic purposes served, and how innovation can be achieved.

Notes

1. See "Diffusion of Innovation Literature"; 1995. The Rogers volume alone claimed 3,900 publications in 1995 (p. 443) such that compilation of a bibliography of even a subset of the change discussion would itself constitute a very large volume.

2. Boorstin (1978). The conclusion of the Boorstin book is instructive of the American fascination with experimental change (p. 96): "We began as a land of the Otherwise. Nothing is more distinctive, nor has made us more *un*-European than our *dis*belief in the ancient well-documented impossibilities. Every day we receive invitations to try something new. And we still give the traditional, exuberant American answer: 'Why not!'"
3. One need only review the records of the annual recipients of the National Medal of Technology to be reminded of the extent to which Americans have enshrined inventiveness, innovation, and change as national traits. "The 1997 National Medal of Technology," *Scientific American*, Vol. 276, no. 6 (June 1997), 16–16c.
4. John J. DiIulio, Jr., writes (1994, 1): "The nation's federal, state, and local public service is in deep trouble. Many government agencies cannot attract and retain first-rate executives, managers, and line staff. Most do not operate in a way that inspires public confidence. In reaction, some observers say 'privatize everything,' others deny that serious problems exist, and still others chant 'run government like a business.' All three responses are misguided. The real challenge is to articulate and implement an effective strategy for improving government administration, and soon. So far, this challenge has gone unmet."
5. To illustrate from a notable assessment of the prospects for federal government change: "No one . . . should underestimate how hard it will be to change patterns of bureacratic operation, organizational forms, and structural constraints that have evolved over the course of a century. . . . In truth, the federal government as it functions today cannot be reinvented because it was not invented in the first place. The bureaucracy evolved through pragmatic, almost catch-as-catch-can responses to particular problems as they appeared. It is this development that warns of the need for an incremental, evolutionary, experimental approach to institutional reform." (DiIulio, Garvey and Kettl 1993, 6)
6. The Behn argument in defense of groping takes pains to point out that "MBGA is a sequential process of adaptation in pursuit of a goal" (p. 657). Thus, MBGA is to be distinguished from "muddling through" and "groping around," where the difference lies in the idea—still largely procedural—that managers who have MBGA compasses, "know in which azimuth they are headed," and learn along the way how to achieve the goals they have set (p. 649).
7. The classic Schumpeter argument (1942, 83) postulates the existence of "gales of creative destruction" that revolutionize economic structures from within, "incessantly destroying the old one, incessantly creating a new one"; (noted in Florida 1995, 315).

8. That public innovation feeds the private sector is a point also made on a cross-national basis in Peters (1996), citing Tellier (1990), Peters and Savoie (1994), and Derlien (1995).
9. Care must be exercised in such counts. For example, the Moe count includes only the highly publicized federal government-wide initiatives. It buries a number of relatively secretive study commissions such as President Johnson's Heineman Commission in a single category labelled "Study commissions on executive reorganization (1953–68)," and necessarily ignores significant sector-specific reforms, such as the Goldwater-Nichols Department of Defense Reorganization Act of 1986 or the Civil Service Reform Act of 1978. Not counted were periods of enormous legislative and legal activism such as occurred during the 1930s and 1960s. Still, the Moe count of reform initiatives does say something about the pace and process of *managerial* change.
10. Signed into law on March 31, 1994, as the *Goals 2000: Educate America Act,* designed to create a "world-class education for every child." The act grew out of the Bush administration's attempt "to reinvent our schools" McGregor (1994).
11. Gary Hamel and C. K. Prahalad, *Competing for the Future: Breakthrough Strategies for Seizing Control of Your Industry and Creating the Markets of Tomorrow* (Boston: Harvard Business School Press, 1994), p. 9: "In fact, the United States and Britain have produced an entire generation of denominator managers. They can downsize, declutter, delayer, and divest better than any managers in the world. Even before the current wave of downsizing, U. S. and British companies had, on average, the highest asset productivity ratios of any companies in the world. Denominator management is an accountant's shortcut to asset productivity."

Chapter 9

*Local Heroes? Reinvention Labs in the Department of Defense**

Mark T. Green The University of Colorado at Denver
Lawrence R. Jones Naval Postgraduate School
Fred Thompson Willamette University

The National Performance Review (NPR) is unique among federal management reform efforts. In the first place, it has been remarkably tenacious: now in its seventh year and under a new name, the National Partnership for Reinventing Government, it still shows no sign of abating. Second, the NPR relies on the initiative of front-line employees to an unprecedented degree. Most government reform efforts have taken the form of detailed guidance from the top, from the Congress or the president. In contrast, the NPR has merely asserted a set of principles: putting customers first, empowering public employees to acquire and manage resources, cutting red tape, and using common sense,[1] and left it to front-line employees to figure out how those principles should be implemented.

For example, according to the NPR, putting customers first means providing "customer services equal to the best in business." (Gore 1993, 44). Frontline employees have interpreted this to mean that they must identify their customers, listen to them, and give them what they want (see Barzelay 1992; Barzelay and Moukheibir 1997). In the same vein, the NPR also recommends reliance on market mechanisms wherever possible and the outsourcing of offices and bureaus

*We gratefully acknowledge that the research reported here was carried out under the sponsorship of the Office of Performance Improvement and Management Reengineering, of the Office of the Secretary of Defense (OSD). We would especially like to acknowledge the help given us by Rachel Kopperman Foster and John Raines of that office, who collected much of the data reported here. We would also like to acknowledge the contributions of our students: Colin Ray, Bradley Adams, Commander James Gosnell, and Captain Todd Jenkins, USMC, who conducted most of the interviews with the lab representatives. This work however, represents the views of the authors only.

performing noncore missions—purchasing, providing office space, printing, duplicating, accounting and financial services, personnel services, etc. (Gore 1993, 44).

NPR's grassroots reinvention efforts are concentrated in about 325 agency-designated Reinvention Laboratories. These are work units throughout the federal government that have volunteered to experiment with managerial innovation. Following authorization by their departments and the NPR, labs may demand waivers from administrative rules and regulations that inhibit organizational change. Indeed, it is frequently asserted that their freedom from rules and regulations is the lifeblood of reinvention. Moreover, the NPR claims that the labs are the chief means by which a new management culture will be inculcated throughout government, especially in agencies that have been slow to embrace wholesale managerial change.

Over a third of all Reinvention Labs in the federal government are located in the Department of Defense (DoD). These labs are working on all kinds of innovation: reengineering around information technology, empowering employees and customers, using the private sector to achieve public purposes, promoting internal and external competition, taking new approaches to internal management—delegation of authority to staff, continuous improvement, Total Quality Management (TQM), self-managed teams, participatory management, greater reliance on incentives, flatter organizations, cross-training, and geographic decentralization—all with the objective of improved consumer service and enhanced mission performance at lower cost.

While one can identify some amazing successes among the DoD's Reinvention Labs, not all have been equally successful; many have accomplished little or nothing.[2] This paper seeks to explain why some labs have been more successful and others less so. We explore two kinds of explanations, both endogenous to the labs themselves. First we look to lab characteristics that derive from their basic functions/missions—characteristics that cannot be changed without altering an organization's purpose or reason for being. Second we look at characteristics that can be managed or, at least, influenced by lab personnel. Finally, we identify some characteristics of the defense department that appear to be particularly inimical to managerial reform.

Having explained our purpose, we would like to stress our observation that reinvention is not easy for the reinventors. Many of DoD's reinventors claim that their efforts have been ignored or even punished. In well-run organizations, managers who find ways to increase productivity or performance are generally given greater responsibility and authority. Teams that increase their performance are rewarded and given new jobs. Managers who fail to increase productivity and performance are shunted aside or terminated. In an environment of constraint, the members of less-productive teams are shed—their jobs being reallocated to more productive employees.

A surprising number of lab representatives believed that they were much more likely to lose promotions or their jobs if they increased productivity than if they did nothing. Many said that their employees were at greater risk from increased productivity than from low productivity! Several talked about how their agencies punished success. A few noted that Reinvention Labs were the first units of their organizations to be "BRACked". (BRAC stands for Base Realignment and Closure; hence, to be "BRACked" means to be shutdown.)

The point is that many of DoD's Reinvention Lab representatives believed they had nothing personal to gain from their efforts, and some felt they had a lot to lose. They nevertheless persevered. In the end, what is remarkable is not that some labs were unsuccessful or that some successes were eventually undone, but that so many, nevertheless, pushed forward with changes that were both dramatic and effective.

An Overview

By definition, a Reinvention Lab is a place where experimentation takes place, where new practices, processes, and procedures are tried. Based on self-reports from the eighty-eight (of approximately 120) Reinvention Laboratories in the DoD that responded, some DoD Reinvention Laboratories are much more successful than are others. As seen in Table 1, about 40 percent believe they have been able to make significant changes in the way they do business; another 20 percent believe they have made some changes; while the rest report that they have not done much.

For the most part, it appears that these self-assessments closely track the reported accomplishments of the individual labs. All of those reporting significant success also claim measurable performance improvements. Most of those reporting some success can point to a well-formulated plan of action and, in some cases, initial positive results from their efforts.

Reinvention Laboratories verus Reinvention Success Stories

Table 2 cross-tabulates the 212 reinvention successes reported in *Reinventing the Department of Defense* and the success rates of Reinvention Labs by parent organizations (DoD 1996). Table 2 makes it abundantly clear that reinvention has also taken place in the DoD outside of formally designated reinvention labs. For example, all Air

Table 1. *Reinvention Laboratories Levels of Innovation*

Organization	Total	Not Significant	Some	Significant
Air Force	7	1	3	3
Army	22	11	3	8
Navy	14	8	5	1
Marine Corps	12	7	2	3
Central Imagery Office	1	0	0	1
Defense Finance and Accounting Service	4	3	0	1
Defense Investigative Service	1	1	0	0
Defense Logistics Agency	18	0	4	14
National Security Agency	6	3	0	3
DoD Science and Technology Labs	3	0	1	2
Totals	**88**	**34**	**18**	**36**

Force units use the Malcolm Baldridge criteria to prepare self-assessments for the Inspector General. The criteria have seven main categories: leadership, information and analysis, strategic planning, human resource development and management, process management, business results, and customer focus and satisfaction.

Nevertheless, although reinvention successes have been identified in many organizations not formally designated as Reinvention Laboratories, the labs play a distinct role in the reinvention effort. Moreover, it appears that organizations that report many reinvention successes also have a higher proportion of their labs reporting significant achievements.

Table 2. *DoD Lab (percent) and Reinvention Successes by Parent Organization*

Organization	Lab		Total Successes Reported
Air Force	43	(%)	37
Army	36		34
Navy	7		8
Marine Corps	25		5
Other Defense Agencies	42		39
Defense Logistics Agency	75		46
Corps of Engineers	NA[a]		37
DoD Science and Technology Labs	67		6
Totals			**212**

[a]NA, Not available.

Mission and Function

Some scholars attribute the inability of organizations to carry out widespread managerial reform to inherent qualities.[3] This argument comes in a variety of forms, but it has two main strains. The first is commonly associated with the work of James Q. Wilson (1989), although it is fairly widespread (Ingraham 1996; Mintzberg 1996e; Savoie 1995b; Hood 1983; see, however, Borins 1995a, 1995b, 1998). This view holds that government's most important functions are inherently unmanageable, otherwise they could be performed satisfactorily by the private sector. The second holds that execution of government's core missions necessarily gives rise to exceedingly large and complex organizations, which in turn leads to organizational inertia (Thompson, 1967; Roberts and Wargo 1994). It has been further suggested that in the absence of considerable organizational slack, organizational inertia will be very nearly complete in large, complex entities (Demchak 1995, 1996; Demchak and Rochlin 1991).

Is Function Destiny?

According to Wilson, public managers have impossible jobs because their organizations are inherently unmanageable (1989, 158–71). Wilson's argument goes something like this: to manage effectively one must measure *both* results and activities and, where government is concerned, it is rarely possible to measure both, and, as far as its most important functions are concerned, often, neither results or activities are measurable.[4]

Wilson identifies four kinds of organizations based upon the measurability of their jobs: production, craft, procedural, and coping organizations (see Fig. 1). If he is correct, it would seem to follow that labs in production organizations would be more likely to achieve significant managerial change than coping organizations would and that procedural and craft organizations should lie somewhere in between. Wilson further asserts that function is destiny. Combat units are craft organizations in war, procedural organizations in peace.

	Activities Can Be Observed	Activities Cannot Be Observed
Results Can Be Observed	**PRODUCTION ORG.**	**CRAFT ORGANIZATION**
Results Cannot Be Observed	**PROCEDURAL ORG.**	**COPING ORGANIZATION**

Figure 1. Types of Agencies

Table 3. *DoD Reinvention Laboratories by Functional Classification*

Function	Total	USA	USAF	USN	USMC	DLA	Other
Combat	3	2	0	0	1	0	0
Logistics	21	2	3	3	2	10	1
Contracting	5	0	0	0	0	4	1
Acquisition	5	3	0	2	0	0	0
Financial Management	2	0	0	0	0	0	2
Information Technology	4	0	2	0	0	2	0
RDT & E[a]	2	2	0	0	0	0	0
Human Resources	7	5	0	1	0	0	1
Education and Training	5	2	0	2	0	0	1
Administrative Support	34	6	2	6	9	2	9
Total	**88**	**22**	**7**	**14**	**12**	**18**	**15**

[a]Research and Development Testing and Evaluation.

Depot maintenance and supply management functions are performed by production organizations; research, development, testing and evaluation by craft organizations; most administrative support, acquisitions, contracting, financial and human resources management by procedural organizations; and most other overhead activities in DoD by coping organizations.

DoD Reinvention Laboratories perform a variety of functions (see Table 3). The greatest numbers of DoD Reinvention Labs are found in the Administrative Support area. This group includes thirty-four laboratories or 40 percent of the total. Next comes logistics organizations with twenty-one laboratories (24 percent), etc. Because DoD labs are classified by function, Wilson's claims can be tested merely by using the functional classifications to reclassify labs as production, craft, procedural, or coping organizations (see Table 4).

It was our presumption that production organizations would achieve the greatest success, coping organizations the least, and craft and procedural organizations would be somewhere in between. As

Table 4. *Type of Organization versus Likelihood of Success*

Type of Organization	No Success	Some Success	Significant Success	Total
Coping	5	3	4	12
Craft	4	0	5	9
Procedural	23	7	14	44
Production	2	8	13	23
Total	**34**	**18**	**36**	**88**

Table 4 shows, we discern no such relationship. As we explain later, however, it turns out that all successful labs define themselves as production organizations (in the sense that they try to measure both results and efforts), but then, so do many of the unsuccessful ones.

Is Size Destiny?

DoD Reinvention Labs range in scale and scope from small single-function offices to large multifunctional, multisite organizations, e.g., Army Forces Command. We counted multifacility/multi-installation Reinvention Laboratories as large; those that comprise a single facility or installation as medium; and those that comprise only a portion of a single facility as small.

If size and complexity make organizations unmanageable, then we might expect to find that large labs are less likely to make significant changes in the way they operate than small ones, with medium sized labs somewhere in between. Again, however, looking at Table 6, which cross tabulates size of lab against reported success, we see no such relationship. Small labs are evidently not more likely to make significant changes in the way they do business than are large ones.

This does not mean that Roberts and Wargo (1994) or even Demchak (1995, 1996) are wrong, any more than our previous finding means that Wilson (1989) was mistaken. To be designated a Reinvention Laboratory, an entity must submit a proposal laying out its objectives/purposes in seeking lab designation, matching those objectives/purposes with NPR principles. The proposal must also provide a plan of action identifying resource requirements, milestones, and performance measures and suggest a means of reporting per-

Table 5. *DoD Reinvention Laboratories by Size*

Organization	Total	Small	Medium	Large
Air Force	7	3	1	3
Army	22	11	4	7
Navy	14	3	8	3
Marine Corps	12	2	10	0
Central Imagery Office	1	0	1	0
Defense Finance and Accounting Service	4	0	2	2
Defense Investigative Service	1	0	0	1
Defense Logistics Agency	18	0	6	12
National Security Agency	6	6	0	0
DoD Science and Technology Labs	3	2	1	0
Totals	**88**	**27**	**33**	**28**

Table 6. *Size of Organization versus Likelihood of Success*

Size of Organization	No Success	Some Success	Significant Success	Total
Small	12	3	12	27
Medium	8	13	11	32
Large	14	2	13	29
Total	**34**	**18**	**36**	**88**

formance results. Any volunteer meeting these requirements is automatically predisposed to making changes in the way they do business. It is possible that the cases that would prove Roberts and Wargo (1994), Demchak (1995, 1996) or Wilson (1989) correct simply never volunteer to become labs; those that volunteer may be exceptional cases. Nevertheless, it does not appear that mission or organizational complexity necessarily dooms public sector organizations to miss the mark.

Ubiquitous Success Factors

According to NPR doctrine, managerial innovation depends on several factors that can be influenced by the reinventors themselves. Where these factors are absent or attenuated, reinvention usually fails.[5] This is held to be so regardless of the innovation's content or the organization's identity. These factors are:

- Commitment at the top of the organization
- A meaningful, clear vision, a set of goals, and a plan of action
- Organization-wide understanding of the vision, goals, and plan of action
- A sense of urgency
- An understanding of obstacles to change and persistence in overcoming them
- Performance measures and a willingness to learn from one's mistakes
- Recognition of successes and extraordinary efforts
- Institutionalization of continuous improvement

To understand the relative significance of these factors, we talked with representatives from more than seventy of the DoD's labs, in most cases, several representatives and the Reinvention Lab coordinators from each of the military departments and defense agencies. In some cases follow-up interviews were conducted. From these interviews, we developed the following conclusions and observations about the major factors, listed above, that we identified:

1. Committed Leadership

Most of the lab representatives we talked to believe that solid support from senior managers is the *sine qua non* of reinvention. Representatives of successful labs consistently praised the support of top management; failures, more often than not, blamed their bosses. Certainly, based on DoD's ten most successful reinvention efforts: travel reengineering; training support; Defense Logistics Agency's PrimeVendor program; recycling at the Defense Distributions Depot, Susquehanna (DDSP); supplies distribution in Korea; the Marine Corps recruit direct-deposit program; etc. (see below), we would have to conclude that this claim has merit. Unequivocal top management support was an element common to all of these efforts.

In some of these cases, however, grassroots reinventors exploited circumstances to win the support of top leaders. The rising cost of dairy products and office supplies enabled Colonel Redding Hobby of the 20th Area Support Group, Taegu, Korea, to convince his commanding general to let him change supply distribution, although the system that was replaced had been in effect for over forty-three years. PrimeVendor was driven by a General Accounting Office report recommending commercialization of food supply to the military. Environmental quality laws drove the recycling initiatives at DDSP. In other cases, top managers initiated change.

Regardless of the source, reinventors need continued support from top management to overcome resistance to change. Loss of top management support usually leaves the reinventors vulnerable. In several cases, it rendered their best efforts ineffectual. Consider, for example, the US Army Forces Command (FORSCOM), Fort McPherson, Georgia. FORSCOM was designated a Reinvention Laboratory in December 1994. The Strategic Systems Division, reporting directly to the FORSCOM chief of staff and participating in command planning at the highest levels, was subsequently created to manage FORSCOM's reinvention efforts. As long as reinventors from the Strategic Systems Division had the support of FORSCOM's senior leadership, their efforts prospered. They received the resources they needed, waiver requests were automatically granted, and everybody in FORSCOM wanted onto the reinvention bandwagon. Innovation flourished.

Then a new head of Strategic Systems came to FORSCOM. He had no commitment to reinvention. Subsequently Strategic Systems lost its favored place in the headquarters organization, reporting directly to FORSCOM's chief of staff. Instead, it was placed six steps down in the chain of command. Reinventors in FORSCOM lost access to the resources they needed; their waiver requests failed; and junior personnel replaced key decision makers from the core staff elements of FORSCOM on the reinvention team. The Strategic Systems representatives we spoke to expressed considerable frustration; a few pronounced the reinvention process at FORSCOM dead.

We would also note that Reinvention Labs in DoD departments and agencies with a reputation for managerial innovation—the DLA, the Air Force, and the DoD Science and Technology Laboratories—seem to be more likely to have made successful changes in the way they do business than those in DoD departments and agencies with a reputation for managerial conservatism (see Tables 1 and 2).

2. A Clear Vision and a Plan of Action

The second characteristic of successful reinvention teams appears to be an ability to envision a payoff and to figure out how to make it happen. The reinvention team at DDSP, for example, had a vision for conservation of packaging materials and pallets—100 percent recycling, nothing less would do. Reinventors at the Marine Corps Recruit Depot also had a vision. They started with a directive from DoD to use electronic funds transfer to pay active duty personnel. But they went far beyond that goal, envisioning a system in which Marine recruits were introduced to the world of credit cards and checking accounts and trained in personal financial management. As a consequence, not only did the Marine Corps achieve substantial savings through direct deposit, theft from Marine recruits decreased and their personal savings substantially increased.

3. Organization-Wide Understanding

The most successful reinvention lab representatives consistently stressed the importance of communication—up, down, and all around. David Whipple of the Naval Postgraduate School (NPS), for example, stressed the importance of communicating the NPS's vision of itself as the Navy's corporate university to the Navy brass and the Office of the Secretary of Defense (OSD), to its potential customers, and to every member of the organization. Moreover, he claimed that the NPS's vision and its plan of action had been successful in large part because they were not imposed from top down, but were crafted with the participation of all the members of the organization.

Another example, Admiral Leonard Vincent, head of the Defense Contract Management Command, personally briefed each of his commanding officers about the importance of the Process Orientated

Contract Administration Services program (PROCAS). Furthermore, he made a videotape that was shown to every employee of the Defense Contract Management Command, which communicated the vision, need, and strategic plan for implementing PROCAS.

4. A Sense of Urgency

Revolutions are not made leisurely. Large-scale organizational change must be pushed forward by a sense of urgency—by a need to act and act now. Otherwise, nothing may ever get done. As Senior Master Sergeant Dave Griffin of the Air Combat Command's Process Waste Elimination Action Workout program,[6] one of DoD's more successful Reinvention Labs explained, in order to accomplish results, his team tries to create an "atmosphere of crisis in order to prod people to seek solutions to problems that otherwise might not seem very important to them."

The significance of an "atmosphere of crisis" is also illustrated by the example of the Army Management Engineering College (AMEC). Originally a small (150-employee) unit located in Rock Island, Ill., AMEC did just what its name implies: taught the Army's industrial engineers how to do time and motion studies, develop workload standards, and, more recently, practice Total Quality Management. By 1989 the unit had established a reputation for expertise in the area of quality management, practicing TQM internally as well as preaching it externally to its customers.

When DoD training budgets fell after the end of the Cold War, the college found that it had to rely more on its customers (that is, other organizations within DoD and, increasingly, among other federal agencies) for funding. As is often the case, harsh conditions inspired an appreciation for the urgency of change among the members of this organization. The college threw out its traditional academic structure of deans and department heads. Instead, its faculty reorganized themselves into self-directed teams reporting to an executive board. They also assumed responsibility for marketing AMEC's various training and consulting services in addition to their regular teaching and research duties.

In 1993, with the National Performance Review just getting under way, AMEC's former head, Colonel Jack Prior, convinced his superiors in the Army Materiel Command, AMEC's parent organization, to designate the college one of the government's first Reinvention Labs.

When we spoke to AMEC's then-current head, Chuck Sommer, he described a vibrant, customer-focused organization offering state-of-the-art management training and consulting to a variety of clients throughout the federal government. Sommer reported that AMEC was almost completely self-supporting, with more than 70 percent of its operating expenses covered by revenues, and announced that it was moving toward privatization as an employee-owned company, becoming the second Employee Stock Ownership Plan carried out under the auspices of the NPR (the first was Office of Personnel Management Federal Investigation Service). As the adage says, what adversity does not kill, it strengthens.

At each stage of the process of organizational transformation, AMEC was propelled forward by the urgency of its situation.[7] The Army keeps threatening to shut down the college (a predicament shared by many of the Reinvention Labs, including all of the DoD Science and Technology laboratories).

5. Understanding the Obstacles to Change and Persistence in Overcoming Them

There is no substitute for persistence. Labs that demonstrated persistence and creativity usually succeeded in improving business processes. Many of the reinventors admitted that a lot of their ideas were half-baked at the outset. In contrast, those who understood the obstacles they faced, adopted realistic plans, and who persisted in their efforts to overcome road blocks were also much more likely to report measurable performance improvements.

Jerry Clemens of the Special Operations Logistics Division, Defense Distribution Depot, Susquehanna, referred to the process they used to identify and overcome barriers to success as the Plan/Do/Study/Act cycle. These barriers included DLA policies, DoD rules and regulations, presidential orders, and statutes. Where rules and regulations were identified to be the main obstacle to change, waivers were requested. Where statutes got in the way of achieving 100 percent recycling, Clemons's team looked for entirely different ways to accomplish what they were trying to do. And, finally, when it turned out that they were refurbishing many more pallets than they could use, the depot commander, at considerable risk to his career, decided to sell the refurbished pallets. Without this decision, $350,000 in revenues would have been lost.

Joe Harris, Chairman, Training Support, Army Forces Command (FORSCOM), noted that most of the obstacles faced by his reinvention team were a lot closer to home: fear on the part of base commanders that "their installation" would lose capacity and their unwillingness to accept near-term losses in return for long-term gains. This team's solution lay in paying careful attention to their customers' needs. They found that most base commanders wanted "support on demand, not owned support." Hence, the key to this team's success lay in a "careful assessment of what should be regionalized and what should be divested to local units, of tailoring service requirements to local needs, and of pay-back options."

As an example of how consistent pressure was needed to overcome cultural resistance to change, Harris cited his encounter with Army Personnel Command (PERSCOM) over the "uniform photo" that goes in every soldier's personnel file. PERSCOM representatives insisted that they had to have a 4x8-inch photograph. This is a nonstandard size and required specialized cameras and film and, more significantly, could not be easily digitized. When he asked why the Army had to have a 4x8 inch uniform photograph, he was told "that is what the regulation requires." A careful search uncovered no such regulation. Then, when PERSCOM representatives were apprised of that fact, they replied, "there is still a need for uniformity; that's the way it has always been done." Consequently, Harris went over their heads, taking the case for digital photographs to the Army chief of staff. In this instance, the reinventors won because they could point to a concrete example of a better alternative.

6. Performance Measures and a Willingness to Experiment

The Reinvention Laboratories that have unambiguously achieved significant operational improvements are also those that are most committed to measuring their accomplishments. Every one of the labs reporting significant changes in the way they do business also reports that they have established one or more metrics by which their performance can be measured.

The travel reengineering lab benchmarked DoD performance against best commercial practices. DDSP measured cost, cycle time, and customer service against "world-class" standards. PrimeVendor aimed for a 40 percent reduction in service charges, inventory levels, and warehouse space. The Air Combat Command's Action Workout teams build activity measures into every project, spending two to three weeks on preparation and data review before trying to change anything. They focus on cycle time and service quality—including rework, work hours, space utilization, overproduction, transportation and conveyance, inventory, unnecessary motion, unnecessary processing, and waiting time. Moreover, as Senior Master Sergeant Dave Griffin explained, the workout team consciously treats their efforts as experiments: "We don't know ahead of time that we will be successful, and we won't know if we are unless we have a good baseline to weigh our results against." He also noted that "the Action Workout's success depends on tolerance for failures," and concluded that "leaders must be willing to accept failure, if processes are to improve."

The Air Force's 45th Space Wing Reinvention Laboratory carries trial-and-error learning even further. The space command gives the lab an annual budget, which they are free to use as they please, as long as the net savings they find for others within the command exceed their own budget. According to Elbert E. Witt, "We don't pretend to find the answers to other people's problems; they come to us with their proposed solutions." These proposals must include a rudimentary cost/benefit analysis as well as an assessment of advantages and disadvantages of the proposed change. After evaluating the proposal on the basis of likely payback, the lab either accepts the proposal or rejects it. Reinvention costs are treated as investments and are kept distinct from operating costs, allowing for clearer, more objective evaluation.

We would note here that activity cost measures were especially important to many of the labs that could show unambiguous performance gains (see Thompson 1998). For example, activity costing enabled DDSP to analyze alternatives before they acted and to document savings after their actions were carried out. This exercise also made them aware of wasteful operating practices—such as using $30.00 per hour government employees to sort wood when local civilian labor would do the job for $7.50 per hour.

In fact, almost all of the labs have invested in performance measurement. One problem is that their metrics are based on local operating data. They cannot be verified by basic transaction records from the DoD's standard system of accounts. Consequently, owing to flaws in the federal government's bookkeeping and accounting systems, few of the reinventors' success stories can be substantiated by hard data. Without this data, it is difficult to know precisely what to make of the reinvention enterprise—aside from applauding the extraordinary efforts of the reinventors.

7. Recognition of Successes and Extraordinary Efforts

Reinvention Laboratories are supposed to empower people down the chain of command in the organization to use their knowledge of the system's workings to make things better and publicly to reward them for their efforts. The Hammer Award is one way the NPR celebrates success and rewards people for their contributions.

8. Continuous Improvement

The goal of the reinventors is to institutionalize continuous improvement. The DoD has always been characterized by islands of administrative innovation. One lab representative put it this way: "Mid-level managers in DoD are used to seeing new initiatives emerge on the scene almost every year; they're like new tunes on the Hit Parade—they reach great popularity, shine brightly for a time, then quickly fade, unnoticed by those too jaded to remember the lyrics or the melody."

Some of the more successful Reinvention Laboratories are already trying to figure out how to institutionalize what they have done; a few are thinking about institutionalizing continuous improvement. Most, however, are still struggling to implement basic changes or receive waivers.

The NPR is an attempt to prevent the current management reform initiatives in DoD from fading from the charts like a fallen top forty tune. Still, a lot more work will be required to convince DoD middle managers, let alone its rank and file, that the reinvention initiatives are more than merely the latest management fad to sweep through the organization. Many lab representatives want deeply to believe that this is indeed the case, but even they are often dubious.

Contingent Success Factors

Most of the problems faced by DoD's Reinvention Labs are ubiquitous. For innovation to take place, such problems must be overcome in all organizations, not just those found in the public sector. Indeed, we do not believe that public sector organizations are necessarily more change resistant than others.[8] Nevertheless, some of the barriers to managerial innovation faced by the labs seem to be, if not unique to government, especially difficult in the DoD.

The first is inadequate financial accounting and cost measurement systems. These make it hard for lab managers to show that performance improvements mean savings. In the short run, it might be acceptable to take the reinvestors at their word, especially where they have developed satisfactory benchmarks, and reward them accordingly—perhaps, as several of the lab representatives suggested, by allowing "labs that cause direct dollar savings . . . to retain savings as an incentive to keep innovating." In the long run, however, shortcomings in its accounting and control systems will likely defeat wholesale efforts to reform DoD's business practices.

It is very hard for us to reconcile DoD financial management priorities with its needs. In our opinion, the highest priorities of any system of accounting and control should be mission support. Instead, DoD efforts are focused on compliance with legislative intent and fiduciary control; these are by-products not the objective of well-designed accounting and control structures.

A second factor that militates against reinvention efforts in the DoD is management turnover—bosses change by design every one to three years. This inhibits initiative. Inexperienced managers tend to cling to what they know best—rules, regulations, standard operating procedures. It also leads to short time horizons.[9] Furthermore, management teams in DoD do not move from assignment to assignment together. Instead, DoD treats individual managers like interchangeable parts, to be moved around from one slot to the next, without consideration for organizational performance or team cohesion. There may be good and sufficient reason for this style of personnel management where combat units and direct combat support units are concerned, but for the two-thirds of DoD that provide support services, it makes no evident sense.[10]

To the extent that the DoD is serious about revolutionizing its business practices, a claim made by its senior officials with increased frequency in recent months, these two areas appear to be especially deserving of attention.

Notes

1. The original National Performance Review (NPR) report, *From Red Tape to Results* (Gore 1993) was issued in September 1993, and it was accompanied by thirty-three reports that amplify and clarify the NPR vision. Taken together these reports total more than 1,900 pages and take up six inches on the bookshelf. They focus on changing the culture of the federal bureaucracy (*Improving Customer Service, Creating Quality Leadership and Management, Transforming Organizational Structures,* and *Streamlining Management Control*), reinventing processes and systems (*Reinventing Human Services Management; Mission-Driven, Results-Oriented Budgeting; Improving Financial Management; Reinventing Federal Procurement, Rethinking Program Design;* and *Reengineering through Information Technology*), restructuring relationships between the federal government and the states, the private sector, and individual agencies. The NPR office has also published three yearly updates—most recently, *The Best Kept Secrets in Government* (Gore 1996) and *The Blair House Papers* (Clinton and Gore 1997)—recommitting the Clinton Administration to reinvention during its second term office.
2. The data collected for this report were gathered from telephone surveys conducted with managers of Reinvention Laboratories from the DoD. These are self-reported results, and, of course, there is a potential for a strong bias to report positive results due to organizational and/or political pressures to do so. However, respondents

seemed willing, even eager, to report failures or problems associated with their reinvention effort.

3. Others attribute governmental inertia to the political process itself, especially the checks and balances inherent to the American political process, etc. Clearly, however, these factors cannot explain the success of some labs and the failure of others—variables that do not vary cannot explain any variance. Moreover, these explanations assume a fact not in evidence, that governmental organizations are less innovative than others.
4. We are not entirely sympathetic to this line of argument, especially the version that stresses so-called "bottom line" measures: profitability, return on assets, economic value added, etc. Smart managers in the private sector pay more attention to non-financial performance measures (the kind that are available to public managers) than they do to financial ones. This is because they can affect the former directly, the latter only indirectly. Moreover, non-financial measures better predict future performance than do current measures of financial performance (Kaplan and Norton 1996; Anthony and Govindarajan 1998).
5. Of course, these success factors are similar to those found elsewhere. For example, John Kotter (1996) offers the following eight steps to overcoming obstacles to change: establishing a sense of urgency; putting together a powerful team to lead change; creating a vision; communicating the new vision, strategies, and expected behavior; removing obstacles to change and encouraging risk taking; recognizing and rewarding short-term successes; identifying people who can implement change; and ensuring that the changes become part of the institutional culture for long-term transformation and growth. (See also Rainey, 1997)
6. Action workouts focus on eliminating waste and improving work center productivity, concentrating on such things as over production, waiting time, excess motion, rework, and redundant processing. Fifty-two, ten-person Action Workout teams were in operation throughout the Air Force when this paper was written.
7. Unfortunately for AMEC, this sense of urgency was evidently not shared by others outside the college. Shortly after its designation as a Reinvention Lab, AMEC requested waivers on eleven different Army and DoD regulations. One of the most critical had to do with overhead charges: Army financial management rules prohibit organizations like AMEC from charging full costs to customers. The Army General Counsel advised that as long as the college remained on the Army's budget books, it was prohibited from paying its own way—recovering overhead costs through fees "would constitute an illegal augmentation of appropriated funds." The waiver request was not granted.

AMEC next turned to the Defense Business Operations Fund. This $100 billion revolving fund was designed to consolidate management and accounting for business-type activities throughout DoD—all the activities that have both customers and suppliers in DoD. A key component of the Business Operations Fund was its use of full costs to establish fees for services provided to DoD. Under the "unit-costing initiative" fees were supposed to reflect fully distributed average total costs rather than direct costs as was previously the case (Thompson and Jones 1994, 86–90). "We were one of the first volunteers for the Business Operations Fund," Sommer said. "Everybody else was nervous about the competitive pressures; we wanted them." Since the Army Material Command was a part of the Business Operations Fund, AMEC's application was promptly approved.

Then the Army Materiel Command decided to get out of the training business: "Not one of our core functions," AMEC officials were told. According to Sommer, this was not a matter of funding. "We could pay our own way," he claimed. "But we counted against Materiel Command's personnel ceiling." Consequently, the college moved in a different direction. An Army feasibility study concluded that AMEC could survive as a privatized, self-supporting, employee-owned enterprise. In the meantime, however, full time equivalent (FTE) caps were relaxed and the Army Materiel Command decided that the elements of the college associated with the Defense Acquisition University and the Army's School of Engineering and Logistics should remain in-house. This meant that the feasibility study had to be done all over again. With its completion, plans to take the college private were resumed.

Sommer later explained that "we were sure that we were finally on our way to privatization." But the Army balked, this time over the cost of privatization, estimated at $1 million over three years or about twelve thousand dollars per faculty member per year—including funding for Army oversight and conversion staff and a "trustee contract" similar to the one the Office of Personnel Management awarded to the Federal Investigation Service when it went private. Shortly after we talked to Sommer, the Army decided that AMEC would be assigned to the Training and Doctrine Command and funded from direct appropriations just as it was prior to the reinvention journey. As for Sommer, he has left the college.

8. Arguably this notion reflects the segregation that characterizes American management study. Those who study public administration are often unfamiliar with the frequency of failed change in business. Those who study business administration are equally unaware of the extent of highly successful change and innovation in the public realm (Rainey 1997). We would note one barrier to wholesale rein-

vention within DoD that we have not observed elsewhere to such a degree: an unwillingness of even committed reinventors to shed employees, although large-scale productivity improvement in DoD is impossible without the elimination of hundreds of thousands of jobs.

9. This propensity is explicit in the criteria used by the 45th space wing to decide which projects to tackle: projects must pay back an investment in three years or less, the longer the duration of benefits, the higher the hurdle rate used. This means that the investments supervised by the 45th space wing are explicitly biased toward short-term wins and against projects with far higher net present values. This problem could be mitigated if operating managers were held responsible for meeting appropriate financial targets, including responsibility for covering the cost of both the working and fixed capital that their entities use (see Anthony and Govindarajan 1998, chap. 7; Thompson, 1999).
10. The logic behind frequent management turnover is that it reinforces standardization across the military forces, which makes it easier for diverse units to work together and increases the robustness of individual units against damage—one merely has to replace the damaged parts and the unit is as good as new. However, several very successful military forces—the Israeli armed forces, for example, or the German army—practice a very different philosophy on the assumption that such units can be good as new only if they were not very good to start with. Moreover, the tradition of frequent command turnover in the American armed forces had its origins, not in an attempt to enhance mission capabilities, but in the desire of civilian authorities to crush the entrenched political power of the military bureaucracies and to break up alliances between the military bureaus and congressional subcommittees (Huntington 1961, 311–12).

Chapter 10

*Reforming State Social Services through Contracting: Linking Implementation and Organizational Culture**

Barbara S. Romzek and Jocelyn M. Johnston
The University of Kansas

Introduction

Privatization and contracting present public agencies and nonprofits with substantial challenges as they institute new program reforms (DeHoog 1984; Smith and Lipsky 1993) and attempt to meet governmental standards for implementation and accountability. Often such reforms involve complex procedures and confused beginnings (Peterson, Rabe, and Wong 1986). The process of implementing such reforms frequently reveals weaknesses in the underlying policy rationales and unintended consequences for new policy actors.

To understand the dynamics of a social welfare reform, the implementation of that reform, and the organizational culture of the agencies involved in the reform, we analyze the experiences of nonprofit agencies that have contracted to provide Medicaid case management services for the elderly in the state of Kansas. The reform, authorized by a waiver from the U.S. Health Care Financing Administration (HCFA), transfers several Medicaid functions from the traditional state Medicaid agency, the Department of Social and Rehabilitation Services (Social Services).[1] Administrative responsibility for Medicaid services for the elderly has been shifted to the state's Department of Aging (Aging), and case management is now provided under contract with the state's nonprofit Area Agencies on Aging (AAAs).

Under a HCFA waiver granted to Kansas, Social Services contracted for case management services with the AAAs effective Janu-

*We want to acknowledge the research assistance of Kara Lindaman and Denise Musser and the support of the Department of Public Administration for this project.

ary 1997 and transferred administrative responsibility for all Medicaid services for the elderly to Aging effective July 1997. The state legislation authorizing the privatization initiative specified that the AAAs would be the provider of choice for case management services. The waiver essentially established a system of managed care for the frail elderly through a single-point-of-entry case management design. Under the waiver, clients have access to one application process and one AAA case manager who determines the entire array of social services which they may need and for which they qualify.[2]

This case provides insight into the complexity of using contracting to effect social service reform. More specifically, the reform seeks to capture the flexibility and cost effectiveness of a capitated managed care model for Medicaid case management services for the elderly. We explore the policy rationales behind the reform and the interactions among components of the reform, including policy design, implementation processes, administrative cultures, and the working relationships between the nonprofits and state monitors. Our results indicate that the program has had mixed success in incorporating theoretically critical components of policy implementation. Furthermore, the reform has had substantial impacts on the nonprofit contractors responsible for Medicaid case management, particularly in the areas of administrative culture and relationships with state monitors.

Implementing Reform

The implementation literature offers theoretical perspectives and identifies several key elements that should be observable in a successful implementation process.[3] With these elements in mind, we conducted interviews with many key actors involved in the reform. These actors include the directors of the AAAs, frontline case managers working for the AAAs, and executive-level employees of Social Services and Aging. We assess the extent to which important implementation components have been incorporated by the participating organizations, and we explore the effects of the implementation on the cultures and accountability of the contracting nonprofits.

Theoretical Models of Implementation

Implementation models tend to be relatively complex, in part because of the contextual complications of implementation (Matland 1995; Goggin et al. 1990; O'Toole 1986). Nonetheless, several common variables emerge from the literature. In our case, the literature on intergovernmental implementation offers an especially useful theoretical framework because there are several hierarchical features in the relationships among the agencies. The AAAs are contractually accountable to Aging, which is in turn accountable to Social Services; Social Services is ultimately accountable to HCFA as a condition of its receipt of Medicaid funds. Thus, the "authority" which characterizes many intergovernmental arrangements is clearly manifested in this case.

Van Meter and Van Horn (1975) suggest that in an intergovernmental context, implementation is enhanced when goal consensus exists among the actors/agencies, when the amount of change required by the new policy is minimal, and when the implementors are favorably disposed to the new policy. Others have noted the importance of the capacity of the implementor (Derthick 1970; Williams 1980; Goggin et al. 1990) and flexibility for local implementors (Maynard-Moody, Musheno, and Palumbo 1990; Williams 1980). Perhaps most importantly, the theoretical validity of the policy design is considered critical to successful implementation (Pressman and Wildavsky 1984; Mazmanian and Sabatier 1983).

We find that most of the Van Meter and Van Horn conditions appear to have been met in this case. Our data indicate the presence of essential goal consensus, minimal to moderate change entailed in the reform, and a favorable implementor (AAA) disposition toward the new policy. We focus next on a detailed analysis of the theoretical role of the implementor in the reform process and on implementation dynamics that influence the capacity and performance of the implementor.

The Role of the Implementor

We focus here on two particular components of implementation theory: the implementor's capacity and disposition toward the policy. The incentive system incorporated into the policy is a major determinant of the implementor's disposition. Without adequate incentives, implementors are unlikely to be favorably disposed. In the intergovernmental context, and in this case, incentives include financial compensation for program administration and service delivery.

Financial incentives are not the only incentives available to policy makers. Technical assistance and monitoring advice facilitate implementor capacity and increase the palatability of the policy to implementors (Derthick 1970; Williams 1980; Peterson, Rabe, and Wong 1986; Van Meter and Van Horn 1975.) Thus, technical assistance serves multiple purposes: it fosters capacity, goal consensus, and a positive implementor disposition, each of which is fundamental for successful implementation.

This idea is addressed indirectly by Van Meter and Van Horn (1975), who draw upon Etzioni's (1975) work on compliance systems to understand the forces at work in obtaining policy compliance. Etzioni identifies a variety of compliance systems available to organizations based on coercive, normative, and/or remunerative power. Van Meter and Van Horn contend that when policymakers are attempting to obtain compliance in an interorganizational or intergovernmental context, normative and remunerative powers are most commonly used. In the context of this policy reform, remunerative powers include allocating funds and rendering technical assistance. Normative power is exercised through socialization into shared values and the cultivation of professional alliances.

Despite the wide range of sanction options available, the federal government rarely threatens to withdraw or withhold funds or to use other coercive powers (Wright 1988; Derthick 1970). Instead, the national level negotiates with state and local officials. Bargaining among levels of government typically leads to an acceptable level of cooperation and compliance over time (Matland 1995; Sabatier 1991; Ingram 1977; Derthick 1970; Wright 1988; Peterson, Rabe, and Wong 1986; Van Meter and Van Horn 1975; Williams 1980). As a program matures it gives rise to an important element of the policy context: the professionalized bureaucrat. (Derthick 1970; Peterson, Rabe, and Wong 1986). The professionalized bureaucrats link the intergovernmental levels through a set of shared values; they identify with the program, its clientele, and their bureaucratic counterparts at other governmental levels. Gradually, the shared values and relationships among these bureaucrats/policy professionals become the vital "cement" that holds the multiple levels of government together (Peterson, Rabe, and Wong 1986). Professionalized bureaucrats would be favorably disposed to the initiative, exhibit adequate implementation capacity, and play an important part in eliciting necessary support among state and local politicians.

Policy Rationale

Most implementation theorists stress that successful implementation requires a policy which is theoretically valid. We turn now to the policy rationale that supports the actual transfer decision in our case.[4] Bearing in mind the theoretical focus on policy validity as a requirement for successful implementation, it is important to examine how the original components of the policy rationale have been affected during the implementation process. Our interview data allow us to assess the viability of these components. Table 1 summarizes our conclusions.

Table 1. *Comparing the Policy Rationale and Implementation Dynamics*

	Policy Rationale	Implementation Dynamics
Cost Neutrality	Reformed Medicaid service delivery strategy should cost no more than that in the pre-reform SRS system. Somewhat ensured through capitated nature of the reform.	AAAs uniformly viewed contractual compensation for case management as inadequate. One AAA barely avoided bankruptcy six months into the reform.
Flexibility/Streamlined Bureaucracy	Flexibility would enhance the "local" advantages of the AAAs. A leaner administrative structure would further enhance program efficiency. Objectives include minimized bureaucratic constraints and reductions in the size of state Medicaid workforce.	State laid off all direct care workers but retained many caseworker/front line staff and program managers in new monitoring and administrative positions. Flexibility is evident. However, the AAAs seek greater uniformity, standardization, and written procedures; in other words, they seek features of a more bureaucratic structure.
More Professionalized Case Managers	AAAs intended to upgrade requirements for case managers responsible for Medicaid elderly.	AAAs hire case managers with higher-level credentials than SRS caseworkers. But AAA case managers are monitored by former SRS caseworkers/frontline staff who are perceived as less qualified. Monitors lack legitimacy from perspective of AAA case managers and directors.
Advocacy Expertise with Elderly	AAAs and Aging have long history of advocacy with elderly and with elderly-oriented service provision.	Aging advocacy experience with elderly is clear. However, administrative capacity for complex intergovernmental program is questionable at this point, as is capacity for contractual oversight. AAAs appear to be "driving" Aging policy despite their contractual status.
Better Service to Clients	AAA case managers can provide better service to clients due to single-point-of-entry design, higher professionalism, more intensive case management plans, and expertise with elderly.	Potential for higher levels of client service exists but has been compromised, thus far, by administrative overload that imposes burdens and time constraints that interfere with client service.
Single Point of Entry	Foundation of the policy. Allows clients to obtain information about all available state/federal services from one caseworker, with whom client can establish rapport.	Several of the AAAs have adopted a more fragmented approach to case management, dedicating selected staff to Medicaid only. Fragmented structure thwarts single-point-of-entry design and intent.

1. *Cost neutrality.* As the plans for privatization through contracting with AAAs were finalized, it became apparent that the cost savings rationale might be unrealistic. In recognition of this, the reform rationale shifted from cost savings to cost neutrality. This is consistent with other reforms in Medicaid which incorporate capitation/managed care designs.[5]

Reality. When Aging and the AAA officials lobbied the legislature to transfer administrative responsibility for the program, they emphasized their capacity to deliver case management services more efficiently. During the early months of the reform, AAA directors began expressing skepticism that they could provide quality services for $30 per hour; by October 1997 this skepticism had intensified. One AAA nearly filed bankruptcy in fall 1997. After intervention from Aging, the AAA redesigned its delivery system, case management supervision was discontinued, staff case managers were laid off, and a few were rehired under contract. Although client services survived this crisis, there has been a clear toll on staff and management. The experience of this AAA, the consistency of the financial concerns expressed by the other AAA directors, and the subsequent increase of the reimbursement rate to $40 per hour provides evidence that the cost savings component of this policy rationale may be ill founded.

2. *Flexibility/streamlined bureaucracy.* One of the important arguments in favor of transferring case management for the Medicaid elderly to the AAAs stemmed from the view that AAAs offer a more "local" perspective on the needs of the elderly. In addition, compared to Social Services, the AAA administrative structure was lean. Thus, in keeping with the current government reform paradigms, including devolution, the policy was built partly on the notion of a decentralized, flexible system.

Reality. State Social Services employment dedicated to Medicaid services for the elderly has been substantially reduced. Some Social Services caseworkers and related personnel were retained to monitor the reformed program, and a few others were hired into case management positions by the AAAs. Despite the expansion of Aging staff, there has been a net reduction in state employment. This is due in part to the termination of all state-provided, direct-care services; most former state direct-care providers have been employed by private-for-profit and private-nonprofit organizations (i.e., home health agencies, etc.)

More interestingly, the flexibility emphasized as a policy rationale and by implementation theory (Maynard-Moody, Musheno, and Palumbo 1990; Williams 1980) has proven to be a mixed blessing. Because the Medicaid waiver was new to all agencies, they each faced difficult challenges and unknown policy terrain. Many of the policy details were unclear; others were evolving as the agencies responded to emerging issues during the implementation process. These uncertainties made it especially difficult for AAAs as they sought advice and technical assistance from state agencies on the finer points of the policy. One AAA director noted that although all parties to the new system strove to minimize rules and regulations, "it's gone too far." The AAA directors and case managers were frustrated by the lack of structure. In the absence of adequate technical assistance from Social Services and Aging, the AAA directors wanted more "written policies and procedures, uniformity" across the state, and standardization of policy. As a result, at the one-year point in the implementation process, the AAAs sought the reassurances of "bureaucratic" structure. The AAAs wanted better technical assistance but found it to be of uneven quality from Social Services and Aging. The unevenness was due in part to the difficulty of finding and retaining appropriate "point persons" who could provide consistent advice over time. The respected "point person" at Social Services—as well as several other experienced Medicaid program staff who might have facilitated a smooth transfer of the technical assistance function over to Aging—rejected offers of employment at Aging.

3. *A (more) professional group of case managers.* Under the reform, case management services were to be delivered by AAA case managers who were experienced with the elderly and were well versed with other federal and state programs for the elderly. In the view of Aging and the AAAs, the AAA case managers would offer superior service, in part because of the fact that AAAs required higher levels of education/experience compared with Social Services case managers.

Reality. This component of the policy rationale seems to have been met. The AAAs have filled many of their case management positions with trained social workers and nurses. However, some of the other jobs have been filled by personnel with backgrounds similar to those of the pre-reform Social Services caseworkers: bachelor's degrees with some experience. We note one important complication. The state Medicaid monitors are perceived by many AAA directors and case managers as less qualified than those over whom they have monitoring authority. Our data indicate that this is not uniformly true and that some monitors have qualifications comparable to the AAA case managers. Yet in many cases, better-qualified AAA case managers are being overseen by state monitors with less "expertise" in case management for the elderly. In part, this complication is due to the nature of the monitoring function in the reform. The monitors are directed to focus on technical features of service delivery, with an emphasis on the requirements of the state's information systems and federal rules and regulations. Nonetheless, the perceptions are clear: AAA case managers—and their directors—believe that they are accountable to less-qualified persons. In many instances, the complication is exacerbated by the fact that these monitors were displaced from their original Social Services jobs due to the reform, and lingering resentment continues to affect the interpersonal relationships of the case managers and monitors.

4. *Advocacy expertise with the elderly.* Aging and the AAAs have a long tradition of advocacy for elders; consequently, they have a legitimate claim on expertise with this population. Their pre-existing mission—service to seniors with an emphasis on fostering independence and enriching lives—is consistent with the basic objective of the Medicaid waiver (i.e., providing in-home support for income eligible elderly and minimizing the need for institutionalization in nursing homes).

Reality. Aging's tradition of advocacy and service to seniors continues unquestioned. From the perspective of service delivery and comfort levels for elderly clients, this component of the policy rationale seems valid. However, a large question concerns the capacity of Aging to administer a major segment of the Medicaid program. The question of AAA capacity is less clear and is certainly affected by the adequacy of resources. However, most AAA actors indicate that clients have experienced minimal disruption during the transfer, and this has been confirmed by a patient satisfaction survey.[6]

While there is little doubt that advocacy is important to successful service for the elderly, traditional Medicaid administration includes features that may conflict with advocacy (i.e., gatekeeping, regulation, cost control). Perhaps more importantly, the management of a large intergovernmental program, coupled with the contractual relationship with the AAAs for case management services, requires field oversight, a strong accountability system, and some distance from the contractor on the part of Aging. Earlier in the implementation process, interview respondents indicated that they eagerly awaited the transfer of administrative responsibility from Social Services to Aging. When asked to comment on whether the transfer had met their expectations, most AAA directors indicated some frustration with Aging's performance to date, frequently citing communications problems. This frustration is certainly due in part to the enormous growth of Aging in response to its new responsibilities.

In terms of accountability and distance from the AAAs, our data also suggest that the AAAs are currently driving the implementation process. The AAA directors and staff report that they are "training" Aging. Social Services officials remain concerned about the influence of the AAAs on Aging management and the capacity of Aging to lead in the Medicaid policy arena.

5. *Better service to clients.* The original agreement between Social Services and Aging included provisions that would maximize case management intensity. This concept was carried out in the form of a caseload limit for AAA case managers. The transfer agreement stipulated that Medicaid caseloads were to be limited to forty, a number far lower than comparable caseloads under the pre-existing Social Services system.

Reality. Our data suggest that those delivering case management services to the elderly experienced administrative overload during the transition year. The need for case managers to spend large amounts of time adhering to Medicaid requirements affected the time available for actual case management. Case managers are strongly committed to their clients and to the provision of high-quality case management, but they are somewhat frustrated by the paperwork and documentation requirements of the new program. The AAA's general interest in greater clarity and structure (mentioned above) concerned the criteria under which the quality of their case management would be reviewed. They sought to establish boundaries for professional discretion, not to restrict it.

6. *Single point of entry.* The major underlying premise of the transfer is that the AAAs can offer clients a single-point-of-entry approach to needed services; under this approach the elderly client faces only one application process and deals with one case manager for all required services. AAA case managers can consequently assess the client's needs and tailor a service package from virtually all federal- and state-level publicly funded services for this clientele.

Reality. When asked why they thought that they provided case management services more effectively than Social Services, nearly all AAA directors mention the single-point-of-entry design as crucial to their case management success.[7] Prior to the new system, AAA staff would have to refer appropriate seniors to Medicaid staff, and vice versa. However, our interviews reveal an interesting paradox. Despite the fundamental role of the single-point-of-entry design in the new policy, the administratively demanding nature of Medicaid has led to a system in which some AAA staff are dedicated to Medicaid only. Several AAAs have adopted a staffing pattern in which certain case managers are assigned to non-Medicaid case management and others are assigned to specialize in Medicaid case management. Thus, it appears that at least in some AAAs, a relatively fragmented approach has been adopted.[8] In these instances, case managers who assess a client's needs and who decide that the client requires services from a different program then transfer the case to a different AAA case manager.

In essence, these variations in AAA case management structures suggest that the single-point-of-entry design, the cornerstone of the new service delivery strategy, has been partially rejected by some AAAs. Several AAA directors have decided that the original Social Services approach—specialized staff assigned to specific programs—may outweigh the benefits of a more integrated case management approach.

In order to enhance our understanding of the impact of the policy rationale on the implementation process, we turn now to an exploration of the characteristics of the parties to the reform and to the interaction between organizational culture and the implementation experiences of the key agencies involved.

Implementation/Organizational Culture Linkages

There is a reciprocal relationship between cultures and the implementation processes (Meyers, Glaser, and MacDonald 1998; Meyers and Dillon 1999; Keiser 1997; Keiser and Meier 1996). Agencies' institutional interests and cultural mindsets bear on implementation decisions (Rourke 1984). Both bureaucratic politics and the demands of the implementation process reflect the prevailing values and institutional interests of participants. The cultures of the agencies involved in the implementation affect the parties' perceptions of viable strategies and their reactions to change initiatives (Garvey 1993; Ott 1989; Schein 1992). Likewise, implementation decisions have the potential to have dramatic influence on the cultures and missions of those agencies involved in the reform (Trice and Beyer 1993).

Organizational Culture

The Medicaid reform waiver has substantially altered the external and internal environments of each of the key agencies involved in this reform; it presents them with new levels of complexity as they seek to respond to a reconsideration of the role of government in the area of social services, to a shrinking conception of the appropriate scope of government, and to an expansion in the definition of legitimate service delivery systems. For example, Social Services lost line responsibility for a large component of one of its major programs, Medicaid. While it retains ultimate fiscal responsibility for the state's role in Medicaid, Social Services no longer provides services directly and must work through Aging, AAAs, and private direct service providers. Aging took on a new administrative role and ballooned in size and budget responsibility. It administers a program that originates with a federal agency (Health Care Finance Administration), is overseen by a peer state agency (Social Services), and delivered by nonprofit and for-profit contractors. The AAAs took on a new program and a substantially more needy clientele which expanded the size and complexity of their operations. They provide case management services under contract without any control over the private direct-care service providers. They have little influence over the federal program design and have strained relations with the state agency charged with fiscal and legal authority for the program (Social Services). And they must work with a monitoring agency (Aging) that is still building the administrative infrastructure to support its new responsibilities.

While our primary interest is in the interaction of the implementation experience and the culture and values of AAAs and their staff, the culture of the two key state agencies in this policy reform, Social Services and Aging, substantially influences the implementation experience of the AAAs. We briefly profile the pre-reform cultures of the relevant agencies as background for the subsequent discussion.

Kansas Department of Social and Rehabilitation Services (Social Services)

Prior to the reform, Social Services was a large, cumbersome, umbrella state welfare agency; its culture emphasized a rules-and-regulations approach to program management and a client entitlement approach to service delivery. Social Services caseworkers frequently worked in segmented programs and had high caseloads (sometimes up to 150 cases) which made it difficult to establish personal relationships with clients. Several caseworkers could be working on a single case, with one focusing on medical needs, another on housekeeping needs, and so on.

Kansas Department of Aging (Aging)

Prior to the reform, the Kansas Department of Aging was a small agency of eighty people, with a budget of approximately $20 million that was mostly federal funding passed through to nursing homes; its culture emphasized advocacy and an ombudsman role. As part of the transition, Aging has doubled its staff to 166 employees and has a proposed fiscal year 1999 budget of $324 million. Aging has undergone a substantial reconfiguration from a pass-through and advocacy agency to a regulatory agency. Under the Medicaid reform, Aging is responsible for the management and oversight of the contract with the AAAs within the bounds of the Medicaid program waiver authority.

Area Agencies on Aging (AAAs)

The AAAs were initially set up in response to the Older Americans Act of 1965 with a role of advocating and facilitating elderly access to services (i.e., congregate meals, Meals on Wheels, transportation, and assisting the elderly in gaining access to Medicaid services from Social Services). AAAs also provide state-funded services for the elderly under a program called SeniorCare, which is designed to serve the near-poor elderly. Services offered include meal centers, home health services, etc. AAAs derive most of their funding from federal, state, and county governments; as such, they are typical of nonprofits that have emerged in response to the availability of government funds (Smith and Lipsky 1993). AAAs are led by an appointed director and governed by boards consisting of representatives and elderly advocates from each county within the AAA geographic region. There are eleven AAAs in Kansas, and they provide coverage for all 103 counties in the state. A few of the AAAs are county agencies, receiving a stipulated portion of property tax revenues in addition to state and federal funds. However, most are certified nonprofit agencies.

Interagency Relations

Interagency relations are best characterized as interdependent. The cooperative agreement between Social Services and Aging seeks to avoid duplication and minimize the monitoring duties under the new arrangement. These relationships involve reciprocity but not between equals. Social Services is in a stronger position than Aging, but Social Services needs Aging and the AAAs because the economic, political, and social realities dictate that there is no going back to the old Social Services model. Social Services retains control and final authority through its role as designated fiscal officer for the Kansas Medicaid program under the federal Medicaid waiver. Any changes Aging would like to make in the administration of the program must be submitted to Social Services and *if they do not object,* the change can go forward.

Not surprisingly the reform has generated tensions, animosities, and hurt feelings between Social Services and the AAAs. AAAs lobbied vigorously for the opportunity to provide targeted case management services for Medicaid elderly; they felt they could be more effective and efficient than Social Services. With the privatization reform the long-time Social Services staff felt that all the time they invested in the Medicaid program was unappreciated and that "their" program was being "taken away" from them. Social Services staff felt that supporters of the reform were saying they "had not done a good job" with the Medicaid program. Some of this resentment was directed at the AAAs; they had lobbied for the program with the explicit message that the AAAs could and would do a better job. AAA directors report that this resentment has not diminished much over time. One commented that Social Services staff members "still hate us."

The Culture of AAAs

One of our primary interests is to understand how the AAAs have been affected by their assumption of the case management responsibilities for the frail elderly in the state of Kansas. As a result, the AAAs face substantial administrative and service delivery challenges as they cope with changes in the type of clientele, the volume of cases, and the urgency of care for those clients. In response, the AAAs have hired more people, changed the mix of skills on staff, experimented with using contract employees, opened satellite sites, and increased their reliance on technology. The AAAs face new challenges of program implementation with the case management program—challenges that are likely to affect their internal integration and that may threaten the agencies' survival (Schein 1992; Ott 1989). We explore those dynamics in the discussion that follows.

Artifacts

The most visible components of organizational culture are the artifacts, or constructed physical and social environments; they are the visible and tangible results of behaviors, including office layouts, dress codes, technology, norms, rites, and rituals. The cultural artifacts typical of these AAAs are those familiar to most community-based nonprofit agencies. Their facilities tend to be low tech, human service storefront operations, typically located close to other social services to maximize opportunities for client access. The self-identification of AAA members is as advocates for the elderly which provide services that supplement government programs.

Staff Growth

All the AAAs hired additional case managers and more clerical or administrative support staff to cope with the increased paperwork and bookkeeping obligations of the contract. AAAs used a variety of approaches to staffing for case management, but most either hired case managers as AAA employees or contracted with individuals for case management services.

The AAAs were especially emphatic about the importance of using a different mix of staff credentials than those used by Social Services: specifically, they sought higher professional credentials than typically found among state case managers. AAA case managers tend to be social workers and nurses, often with B.S., M.S.W., or R.N. credentials. One AAA director expressed this sentiment: "When you're dealing with questions of health and mental capacity of clients, the decisions regarding plans of care are important. I think it's unacceptable to use nonprofessional people as [Social Services] did. Nonprofessionals aren't going to understand the complexity and be able to make judgments in the best interests of clients."

The change in the size of staff created the need to integrate newcomers into the work group through more supervision and socialization of new case managers into the norms of the agency. For some AAAs, especially those in the more metropolitan areas, the expansion was easier to absorb into the existing facilities and administrative infrastructure because the proportions of new case managers were not large enough to influence the group dynamic. In smaller units, a few new caseworkers could have noticeable impacts. There were undercurrents of misunderstanding and jealousy on the part of some AAA employees regarding contract employees who had different terms and conditions attached to their employment. For example, some AAA regular employees resented the flexibility of the contract employees who worked out of their homes.

Satellite Sites and Technology

Increased caseloads required AAAs to rent more space and sometimes move operations because of the need to expand their operations. Some AAAs with especially large geographic areas of service set up satellite offices and set up caseworkers in geographically dispersed in-home offices. This presented new management challenges due to reduced face-to-face interaction among staff and long-distance supervision. In areas of the state where population dispersion makes substantial travel demands on case managers, or where case managers are contractors, case managers find themselves with minimal opportunity for interaction with other case managers. Such conditions require more attention to administrative procedures, cultivation of shared service norms, and coordination by the AAAs.

All AAAs resorted to increased reliance on technology, including computers, electronic phone-answering devices, and faxes to cope with the increased scope of billing, bookkeeping, and client contact. Needless to say, while such devices are necessary they are often especially difficult for elderly clients to adjust to.[9] Prior to the reform, computers tended to be used for advocacy and communication purposes, such as newsletters, mailing lists, etc. The Medicaid program led the AAAs to a preoccupation with computerization, in part because AAA plans of care are submitted to the Department of Aging via the computerized Medicaid Management Information System (MMIS). Many of the AAAs had to upgrade substantially their fiscal management skills to keep up with administrative demands.

Cash Flow Problems

Prior to the reform, case management services in Social Services were often cross-subsidized, allowing disproportionately high staff costs in one program to be partially subsidized by other program funds. AAAs do not have access to these funding alternatives; they have less operational flexibility and are more vulnerable to cash flow problems. Contractors frequently face problems related to the failure of governments to live up to their payment obligations (Milward 1996). In the first year, reimbursements to the AAAs often were several months late; substantial amounts of time and energy were expended on billing protocol at the expense of service provision; and frequent modification of government rules created financial crises for the contractors. One aspect of the problem was the inadequate reimbursement rate set by the state for the case management program.

This review of the experience of AAAs reveals agencies under the stress of transition. The increased administrative complexity led to a reliance on administrative and technological aids that have somewhat diminished the agencies' human touch. The increased number of clients and volume of communication needed to handle the program resulted in substantial impacts on the physical and social environments of AAAs. For example, the need for electronic equipment, computers, and space have all put some distance between AAA staff and the elderly. The increased caseload has also created administrative pressures regarding coordination and cash flow. The situation has been stressful for all concerned. Case managers report difficulty keeping up on details of other programs for the elderly, somewhat diminishing their ability to serve as a single point of entry for the elderly.

Values

Organizational values reflect the group's shared sense of what ought to be and how one ought to behave. Those shared values and beliefs drive behavior; other values are sometimes only espoused, either as rationalizations or aspirations for the future (Schein 1992). Thomas

Jeavons (1994, 189–92) identifies the core value for nonprofits as: morally responsible service with more instrumental values of integrity, openness, accountability, service, and charity. The values of integrity, openness, accountability, and service are common in the public sector as well. When agencies find themselves under stress, the values of the enterprise are put to the test. Important instrumental values are re-examined, fundamental values reaffirmed, and merely espoused values are revealed as ideals rather than values in use. Such has been the case for AAAs under this Medicaid reform.

The values of the organizations involved in the reform are important factors to be considered in the implementation process. The parties to this reform are in general agreement about most of the values listed above. The accountability and openness values are of particular importance in our analysis. Other values that emerge from the unique missions of the agencies examined in our study include: dignity and independence for the elderly, client advocacy, cost consciousness, and staff professionalism. While the three key agencies in this reform reveal little conflict over three of these values, there is less agreement about the professionalism value.

Professionalism, with its emphasis on specialized knowledge and service to clients, is a basic value of the AAAs. The trend toward professionalism in nonprofits has been widespread since the end of the Reagan presidency (Hall 1994) with human service programs being seen as requiring more than amateur approaches and volunteers (Salamon 1995). The AAA commitment to professionalism is reflected in AAA hiring patterns as they sought to staff up for their new case management responsibilities with individuals with higher levels of professional credentials. This response by the AAAs is consistent with Smith and Lipsky's (1993) observation that when nonprofits take on clients who are needier than previously served clients, agencies tend to broaden the qualifications of their staff as a way to cope.

The interaction between the cultures of the organizations and the implementation process indicates that the Medicaid reform has exerted significant effects, particularly on the pre-existing culture of the AAAs. While the amount of policy change involved for the AAAs can be viewed as moderate, the administrative disruption has taken a toll on the AAAs, with particularly high costs accruing to the AAA directors and case managers. The AAAs had to adjust to a large increase in their caseloads, significant changes in the neediness of their clientele, notable increases in staff size, and new coordination challenges. In other words, the capacity of the AAAs as implementors of this Medicaid waiver has been severely tested. The AAA response to the challenge—the increased use of professionals—has helped to some extent by expanding the substantive credentials of the frontline case managers. But this strategy has created conflicts by exacerbating tensions between state monitors and case managers in the contract monitoring phase of the relationship.

The Missing Link: Weak Professional Bonds

This investigation reveals a fundamental weakness in the implementation process due to a lack of cohesion between frontline program workers (AAA case managers) and the monitors from the "higher" state level—what some have called the "cement" (Peterson, Rabe, and Wong 1986) which can serve to reinforce intergovernmental management relationships (Wright 1990; Gage and Mandell 1988). What is needed is the development of a consensus among social service professionals about accepted practices or service protocols relevant to the case management responsibilities. Policy guidelines and shared ethical norms provide cognitive maps for professionals as they navigate the case management terrain and exercise discretion regarding plans of care for the frail elderly. The positive interpersonal interactions which might lead to more effective service delivery from the AAA case managers and which might enhance their service capacity have been few and far between. Instead, these relationships have been characterized by mutual distrust, and occasionally, by outright hostility and resentment. This situation is due in part to the state's decision to avoid layoffs for many state workers by using former state caseworkers to monitor new AAA caseworkers.

As is true in most public sector and nonprofit organizations, multiple accountability relationships are the norm (Romzek and Dubnick 1987; Kearns 1996; Radin and Romzek 1996; Johnston and Romzek 1997). Smith and Lipsky (1993, 12) note that professional commitments of dedicated human service workers often protect against some of the more severe problems of accountability that can occur under contracting. The external review of client plans of care by state Medicaid monitors is a serious point of friction between monitors and AAAs over the scope and criteria used in external reviews. Aging's perspective on its Medicaid monitors is that they should focus on processes/forms for accuracy and policy compliance. In this capacity the role of the state monitors is to make sure that the plans of care are in compliance with federal rules and regulations.

The AAAs' perspective on these reviews is that the state has not provided sufficient clarity on the standards by which their case management will be reviewed and that state monitors are ill equipped to review the case managers' work. The shared values regarding service to elderly clients are apparently insufficient to overcome the fact that monitors do not have legitimacy in the eyes of the AAA staff. As a consequence, AAAs have expressed a strong need for a Medicaid policy and procedures manual to help them know in advance the criteria under which their plans of care will be reviewed. While they report that the paperwork demands get in the way of providing good service to clients, they nonetheless welcome greater clarification from the state as to the relevant rules, regulations, and service criteria as a way to minimize tension over external reviews.

Friction is generated by the level of scrutiny and the amount of time it takes for case managers to respond to the audits. The accountability criteria require case managers to keep what they consider "excruciatingly careful records," such as accounting for their time for the work week in fifteen minute blocks.[10] AAAs are not used to as many audits and reviews as they encounter under the Medicaid program. The case management contract stipulates that ten percent of the cases be audited by the state each month. Case managers are quick to point out the inefficiency of such a sampling strategy and wonder why Aging monitors cannot pull a smaller random sample. AAA staff view the character and nature of this scrutiny as intrusive, redundant, and distracting from their central mission of ensuring that the frail elderly receive the care they need to stay in their homes. Case managers spend substantial amounts of time preparing files for review and responding to reviewers' inquiries and comments, and they resent the fact that the review results are so slow. Typically it takes three or four weeks for the results of a review to be reported to the case manager. (In some instances, results have not been reported for up to four months.)

While tension between monitors and the monitored is not unusual, some of the friction is due to status differences and holdover sensibilities of former state caseworkers who now work as Medicaid monitors. The state monitors typically do not have professional credentials as high as those of the AAA case managers. Aging's position is that it does not take the same level of professional skills to be a state monitor as it does to be a case manager because Medicaid monitors do not have significant client contact except in the instance of home audits. From the perspective of AAA staff, their work is subject to oversight from state monitors with inferior education levels and qualifications. AAA staff have little respect for state monitoring staff. Several commented on how poorly prepared they were for their new duties. One noted, "We couldn't believe how little they know about their jobs. We had to train them." This reaction is consistent with problems noted by Smith and Lipsky (1993, 109) when judgments are questioned and reviewed by auditors who lack the training of those whose practices they challenge.

A second source of tension relates to sensibilities regarding monitoring the performance of individuals doing one's old job. In some instances state monitors are overseeing case management protocols for clients that the monitors worked with as Social Services caseworkers before the reform. Thus, the first-line "principals" (the state monitors) to whom the AAA "agents"are accountable are overseeing case managers who, in effect, occupy the positions from which they were displaced. Some of these reviewers have negative feelings about having "lost" the Medicaid program to the AAAs. Some former Social Services case managers bring to their monitor jobs the old Social Services rule-and-regulation and entitlement approach to social services. Others bring negative attitudes with them when they shift over to Aging. Respondents widely report problems with "difficult" reviewers. Upon probing for further information, several respondents qualified their answers, saying they had not had a personal experience with difficult monitors. This is similar to the phenomenon often reported in public opinion surveys of government employees; while the general perception is negative, individuals report that their own personal experiences with government employees are positive (Goodsell 1994).

In summary, the positive features of technical assistance, monitoring, and informal consulting—features which theoretically have the potential to facilitate good intergovernmental and interorganizational working relations and successful implementation—have failed thus far to materialize. Ironically, this element of the implementation process may be due entirely to the desire of Social Services to avoid the personal hardships of staff layoffs. By creating "principals" out of displaced staff, Social Services may have unwittingly crippled a critical component of the implementation process.

Conclusion

This paper reports on the implementation experience of key actors involved in a significant privatization initiative in social welfare reform: an effort to develop a single-point-of-entry to Medicaid services for the frail elderly under contract with regional nonprofits throughout the state of Kansas. We offer insights into the implementation experiences of the nonprofit contractors who actively sought and received responsibility to provide Medicaid case management services. As a work in progress, this reform represents an effort to tap into the flexibility and expertise of nonprofit agencies for implementation of a managed care model of Medicaid services.

The nature of the policy reform is evolving in response to implementation challenges that have emerged. Some of the underlying rationales behind the privatization initiative have been realized. The reform has afforded greater administrative flexibility, program decentralization, and increased professionalization of the Medicaid case management services. Other policy rationales behind the reform have been modified or found to be of questionable validity. The cost neutrality rationale appears to be out of reach for this reform. There are indications that some of the AAAs find the single-point-of-entry organizing principle to be problematic. Some AAAs have found it easier to segregate Medicaid case management services from other services they provide. The intriguing twist on this segmentation strategy (which is contrary to the single-point-of-entry model) is that those AAAs which have followed the segregated model have had the fewest cash flow and reimbursement problems. There are signs that while flexibility in administrative arrangements are preferred, case managers are uncomfortable with the lack of definition in program guidelines regarding case management per se. In contrast, case managers and AAA directors are nearly unanimous in their calls for a policy and procedures manual and clarification of the fine points of case management.

The weakest link in the implementation process appears to be the lack of collegial working relationships between the contract monitors and the contracting agency directors and case managers. Admittedly, oversight and monitoring relationships are often less than cordial, but in this kind of reform into uncharted territory, a more cooperative, technical assistance relationship could facilitate the intent of the reform. The "cement" which often facilitates intergovernmental and interorganizational relationships—and which enhances the capacity of implementer agents—has proven to be elusive thus far in the implementation process.

The experiences of the AAAs in the state of Kansas thus far highlight the challenges facing nonprofits as they seek a greater role in service provision for the elderly. Their administrative capacity has expanded and they now play a larger role in the politics of human service policies in the state. They face the challenge of coping with these changes. The AAAs have undergone a period of substantial stress created by the administrative challenges associated with growth in staff and caseload, logistical complications due to geographic dispersion, and the greater neediness of their new clientele. As they cope with the demands under the contract, the AAAs find that their obligations under the contract have stretched their administrative capacity to the limit and have altered their priorities and values. And, in the case of one AAA, which was pushed to the verge of bankruptcy by cash flow and reimbursement issues, the experience has forced a reconsideration of its basic role and survival as a human service provider. AAAs find cash flow problems and paperwork/documentation requirements to be burdensome.

The result has been a steep learning curve for AAAs as they seek to meet their obligations under the contract and administer a program that is undergoing substantial reform. This experience has afforded some reality shock to AAAs, a result that is consistent with Salamon's observation that the marketization of human service delivery has important consequences for nonprofits (1995). Salamon notes that the advocacy orientation of nonprofits, as policy innovators and social critics, is endangered by the penetration of market-type relationships into the social service arena. The lesson in this experience for AAAs is: Be careful what you ask for. You just might get it.

Appendix

Methodology and Data

To identify and document the organizational cultures and implementation dynamics involved in this reform, we interviewed three key groups of officials. The initial round of interviews was conducted just as the reform took effect (January–March 1997), a second set of interviews was conducted ten months into the reform (October 1997), a third set was conducted 22 months into the reform (October 1998). The interview groups consisted of:

1. Key state administrators within Social Services and Aging and the current chair of the legislative committee responsible for overseeing the program transition from Social Services to Aging.
2. Ten of the eleven AAA directors, as well as statewide AAA administrators responsible for transition issues.
3. Several frontline AAA case managers.

Using semi-structured personal interviews, we asked members of each group to respond to a standard list of questions. The questions were designed to identify key issues in the implementation process and to assess all actors' understanding of and capacity for managing the new system, including its contractual features. Forty-five interviews were conducted. To supplement the interview data, we obtained and reviewed a number of relevant administrative and legislative documents concerning the transfer. Our objective was to use both types of data in order to understand better the impetus for the actual privatization decision, the policy rationale of the reform, the implementation dynamics and experiences, and the cultures of the organizations.

Notes

1. We use shortened state agency names as a mechanism to minimize the frequent repetition of lengthy official agency names.
2. The reform has several policy goals. They include shrinking the size of the state Medicaid bureaucracy and reducing state payroll expenses associated with the program (Johnston, Davis, and Fox 1998). The expectation was that many Medicaid caseworkers would find employment with private service providers and with the AAAs. The reform was also based on an expectation that a reassessment of nursing facility residents would reveal a number of elderly who were functioning at high enough levels to be able to leave the nursing facility for supported living in the community. Reducing the number of nursing facility residents is one of the long-term goals of the reform, as is delaying the entry into nursing home facilities of the elderly still living independently in the community. Another important goal for the reform transition was to minimize disruption to Medicaid and AAA clients.
3. For example, see Van Meter and Van Horn (1975); Van Horn (1979); Mazmanian and Sabatier (1981, 1983); Pressman and Wildavsky (1984); O'Toole (1986); Matland (1995); Goggin et al. (1990); Gage and Mandell (1990); and Wright (1990).
4. The design of the Medicaid waiver is a legitimate point of analysis, but the decision to transfer administrative and service delivery authority is our primary research interest.
5. Although Social Services officials may have been somewhat skeptical about cost neutrality, the capitated/managed care features of the transfer provide strong constraints on cost increases, thereby enhancing the probability of cost neutrality.
6. The satisfaction survey, conducted by Social Services, focused on client awareness of the transfer and Social Services/Aging/AAA communication with clients regarding the transfer. Over 90 percent of the clients indicated satisfaction with these particular segments of the transfer.
7. It is important to note that not all interview respondents felt that AAA case management was more effective than Social Services. Several respondents also indicated that a major factor in AAA effectiveness was the relatively small caseload. Prior to the reform, Social Services caseworkers sometimes managed over 100 cases. The original agreement between Aging and Social Services stipulated that AAA case managers could manage a maximum of forty cases. That

limit was recently lifted. In the view of some respondents, removal of the forty case limit threatens the ability of the AAAs to provide more effective case management relative to the pre-reform Social Services system.

8. One director, who manages an AAA which receives significant county funding, mentioned striving to reach a more integrated approach to case management. Thus, this director seeks to avoid fragmentation and to adhere as strictly as possible to the single-point-of-entry design.
9. During our own phone calls to some AAAs, we encountered voice mail menus that were frustrating. Occasionally we would even get full voice mailboxes which prevented us from leaving messages. Needless to say, such technology lacks the human touch that most people expect from human service programs, especially for an agency dealing with seniors, many of whom are not comfortable with this technology.
10. References to "billable hours" abound in our interview data. One adjustment required of the AAAs was documentation of time spent in Medicaid case management. Originally, the AAA case managers were keeping track of time in increments of minutes. More recently, they have been authorized to bill in quarter-hour increments, which has provided them some relief from time-consuming record keeping.

Chapter 11

Quasi Markets and Strategic Change in Public Organizations

James R. Thompson The University of Illinois–Chicago

Since the inception of the National Performance Review (NPR) in 1993, its sponsors have offered up a variety of "success stories" as evidence of the efficacy of their reforms. Annual reports issued for the years 1994–97 include multiple examples of units that have applied reinvention principles to restructure service delivery methods with beneficial results. In general, the units cited are relatively small in size. The Federal Emergency Management Agency, with 2,500 employees, is one of the few exemplars of agency-wide reform. Many of the success stories involve individual offices with a few hundred or fewer employees. There is no evidence to date of transformation of any of the large "production" (Wilson 1989) agencies such as the Internal Revenue Service (IRS) or the Social Security Administration. Yet the achievement of NPR's ambitious goal of improving trust in government will require changes in agencies with broad citizen contact.

The techniques endorsed by NPR to improve organizational performance, total quality management and business process reengineering, have not fulfilled their promise. At the IRS, where a major emphasis was placed on quality management during the late 1980s, success has been spotty, limited to a few offices and units where management was willing to invest the time and resources needed to make it work (Theodore 1997; McAuley 1997). Business process reengineering has been an even greater disappointment. The Tax Systems Modernization effort at the IRS which was to incorporate restructed business processes met with an ignominious end when Congress terminated funding; an effort to reengineer the disability claims process at the Social Security Administration has fallen far behind schedule and faces an uncertain future (Davis 1998; U.S. General Accounting Office 1996, 1997).

This chapter examines an alternative intervention, the Performance-Based Organization (PBO), that has been used with some success overseas to induce change in large public agencies. As head of the NPR, Vice President Gore has proposed that several, mostly smaller federal agencies be designated PBOs. To date, however, Congress has acquiesced in the creation of only one, the Student Finance Agency in the Department of Education.

The essence of the PBO model, which has been most fully developed in Great Britain and New Zealand, is to provide service delivery units a degree of autonomy from policy makers in order to induce greater attention to issues of service quality and operating efficiency. The PBO represents both an institutional innovation and an organizational intervention. The intent of its designers was that the PBO serve to catalyze fundamental change within the service delivery units. It is this dimension of the phenomenon that is of primary interest here.

This chapter argues that, for the purpose of understanding the organizational consequences of a change from conventional government agency status to a PBO, it is useful to conceptualize the PBO as a form of "quasi market." The term quasi market has been utilized to describe a variety of mechanisms intended to "mimic the effects of markets . . . within publicly owned settings" (Bennett and Ferlie 1996). Various elements of the PBO that derive from its market-like character, such as substitution of a contractual arrangement for a hierarchical relationship between department head and service delivery unit head, serve as a basis for explaining the impact of this innovation at the organization level.

As an introduction to a discussion of the PBO as an organizational intervention, the evolution of the concept in the context of Prime Minister Thatcher's public service reforms in Great Britain is tracked. The model was formally introduced as part of Thatcher's "Next Steps" program in 1988. Although the PBO model is in place in New Zealand as well, this discussion will focus primarily on Great Britain because the experience there offers particularly useful insights into the organizational implications of this type of reform.

The PBO model is but one element of a global public service reform movement the themes of which have been grouped under the heading of the "New Public Management." Ideas related to the New Public Management, including the use of private sector management techniques, the introduction of market mechanisms into the bureaucracy, and a "disaggregation" of "formerly monolithic units" (Hood 1991) have been particularly influential in the Anglophone countries.

Subsequent to a review of the Thatcher public service reforms, the theoretical basis for the PBO is reviewed and critiqued. Sponsors of this innovation borrowed ideas and concepts from the institutional economics literature including public choice, transaction cost, and principal-agent theories. The conclusion here, discussed below, is that an alternative way of understanding the reform better accounts for the outcomes observed. That alternative is based on the conception of organizations as complex, multidimensional social systems. Intervening in such systems for the purpose of inducing change requires the disruption of multiple subsystems, which the market-like features of the PBO permit.

The Thatcher Public Service Reforms

The Next Steps program is the latest in a series of reforms to the public sector initiated by Prime Minister Thatcher after taking office in 1979. The first of those reforms came to be known as the "Rayner Scrutinies" after Lord Rayner, whom Thatcher recruited from the private sector to find ways to introduce efficiencies and enhance the performance of the public service. Whereas the Rayner Scrutinies were targeted to specific programs and departments, the Financial Management Initiative (FMI), launched in 1983, was a government-wide effort to specify performance measures and to allow greater discretion on operational matters to lower-level mangers. FMI was succeeded by Next Steps in 1988.

Each of the three programs was somewhat ad-hoc in approach; Zifcak (1994, 16) observes that Prime Minister Thatcher "did not enter office with a clear and coherent programme of management reform." She did, however, set some clear political parameters for the reform program; "to reduce civil service numbers and remould civil service management in the image of the private sector" (Zifcak, 16). The broad principles on which the reform program was based included (1) providing rewards for the display of managerial skills as well as for policy skills among top civil servants and (2) decentralizing authority from departmental headquarters to operational managers (Metcalfe and Richards 1987). A brief history of each of the two reform efforts that preceded Next Steps follows.

The Rayner Scrutinies

Upon taking office in 1979, Prime Minister Thatcher appointed Derek Rayner as her special adviser on efficiency and head of the newly created Efficiency Unit within her office. Rayner deliberately sought to avoid the development of a "grand scheme" for reform. Instead, he sought to "set in train numerous small-scale initiatives designed to produce discernible benefits in a relatively short time" and thereby "demonstrate that there were serious shortcomings in the management of the civil service" (Metcalfe and Richards 1987, 7). Rayner's objective, according to Metcalfe and Richards, was "lasting reforms of structures, systems, personnel policies and deeply ingrained attitudes and beliefs" (Metcalfe and Richards, 7). Key tenets of Rayner's approach were that "reform had to be an internal process" and that "commitment to change within departments at both official and ministerial levels was vitally necessary if there was to be a transformation in the whole managerial culture of Whitehall" (Metcalfe and Richards, 8).

While some successes were achieved, in general the Rayner Scrutiny program failed to achieve its key objectives, most prominently to change the culture of Whitehall and to catalyze broader change from the small-scale initiatives (Zifcak 1994; Fry et al. 1988).

The Financial Management Initiative (FMI)

The Rayner Scrutinies were followed in 1983 by the FMI, which incorporated the following managerialist elements:

- The establishment of clearly defined objectives and of measures to track the progress of those objectives;
- The decentralization to line managers of responsibilities for both resources and operations.

In contrast to the Rayner Scrutinies, which targeted individual programs, FMI was government-wide in scope.

By 1988, Thatcher and her advisers, most prominently Robin Ibbs, Rayner's successor, concluded that FMI was not accomplishing the objectives they had set out; management responsibilities had not devolved from the central staff units and departmental headquarters to line units, and no broad change in basic beliefs and attitudes had occurred (Zifcak 1994; Painter 1995). Identified as a major obstacle to the reform program was the reluctance by Treasury and department-level management to relinquish control over the operating units (Zifcak 1994; Greer 1994):

> The principal obstacle which lay in the path of the FMI had been the resistance of the Treasury to a relaxation of central controls. This resistance had been mirrored in departments where central finance and establishment offices were at best cautious and at worst actively resistant to the transfer of managerial authority to operational managers. (Zifcak 1994, 81).

Other problems with FMI that arose included: (1) there was a recognition that for civil servants at the department level, promotions were based more on policy expertise than on managerial acuity (Zifcak

1994): (2) FMI became focused almost exclusively on budgetary matters to the exclusion of personnel and other management concerns (Gray and Jenkins 1991); and (3) cultural issues arose as evidenced where authority was delegated but managers were reluctant to act (Zifcak 1994). The Next Steps initiative "took direct aim at these points of resistance" via a number of primarily structural innovations (Zifcak 1994, 81).

The Next Steps Initiative

The critical change made under Next Steps was the creation of semi-autonomous units, called "executive agencies," within departments. Agencies have primary responsibility for the delivery of service while departmental headquarters are to focus on policy development. Chief executives of the agencies are selected via a competitive process open not only to career civil servants but to those from outside the public sector. The chief executives are given three-year renewable contracts and are eligible for bonuses contingent upon meeting the targets set forth in the framework document. Contracts, in the form of "framework documents," are intended to serve as a primary accountability mechanism for the chief executives. The framework documents specify both a set of measures by which the performance of agency heads is to be measured and flexibilities with regard to personnel, budgetary, and financial matters which they are to be granted.

The purpose of making explicit the granting of flexibilities to chief executives was in part to deter undue interference by both the Treasury and departmental representatives in operational issues. According to Hunt (1995, 79), the intent was that the minister not issue further directions to the chief executive beyond the framework document except "if major changes in direction are necessary or circumstances arise which were unforeseen." Agencies, in turn, are required by the Treasury to make efficiency gains of at least 1.5% annually on "running" or administrative costs. Treasury has also mandated a market-testing initiative whereby agencies are required to identify services that can be contracted out and to compare the cost of contracting out with that of providing the service in-house.

The actual flexibilities granted vary substantially among agencies depending on factors such as whether and to what extent the agency generates revenue in support of its operations. In cases where self-generated revenue covers most or all of the running costs, agencies were moved from gross to net accounting systems allowing more discretion in how funds were spent. In 1994 agencies were granted substantial responsibility on pay and classification matters although Treasury retains control over pay settlements and total payroll. Agencies have also gained authority in the areas of recruitment and training (Talbot 1997a).

Since its inception in 1988, the Next Steps reforms have been widely implemented. One hundred-thirty executive agencies have been created. These agencies include 75 percent of the total membership of the Civil Service (Talbot 1997b). While no overall evaluation of Next Steps has been undertaken, the program has been praised as "the single most successful civil service reform program of recent decades" by a Parliamentary committee and, perhaps more tellingly, has been supported by the Labor Party (Roberts 1995). Reports have identified improved operational efficiency and enhanced quality of service at individual agencies such as the Vehicle Inspectorate and the Employment Service (Oliver and Drewry 1996; Fogden 1993). Two independent observers concluded that,

> Generally the changes, which are seen by the agencies as combining freedom with accountability, have operated to improve not only performance and concern about the individual customer but also profitability, and they have resulted in much more flexible and specialist corporate structures and working relationships with devolved responsibility (Oliver and Drewry 1996, 111).

Theoretical Foundations of the Next Steps Initiative

The theories in which Next Steps and the PBO model are purportedly grounded are examined below for the purpose of ascertaining the intended effect of this intervention at the organizational level. Whereas the New Zealand reform program had an explicit theoretical grounding in public choice theory and institutional economics (Boston et al. 1996), the British program did not. Nevertheless, key tenets of these theories, as well as of managerialism, are clearly apparent in the British model.

Public Choice Theory

Key assumptions adopted from public choice theory that have been incorporated in the Next Steps program include:

1. The necessity of separating the policy and service provision functions of government. The public choice rationale for this separation is that self-interested behaviors on the part of bureaucrats will lead to bias in the policy advice provided to decision makers. However, no provision has been made for an

independent source of policy advice in Great Britain as has been done in New Zealand.

2. The necessity of providing explicit incentives to ensure that priority is given to the objectives of improved efficiency and enhanced service quality. Public choice theory highlights the potential for discrepancies between the objectives of the government and those of subordinate officials. Attention is directed to systems of incentives that lead to greater congruence between the two. The key incentives offered chief executives for the accomplishment of the objectives set forth in the framework documents include a pay bonus and an enhanced prospect of reappointment.
3. The need to avoid producer capture and bureaucratic empire building by making service delivery functions "contestable" via competitive tendering. Moving to a contract-based relationship between department and agency can, in some cases, serve as a prelude to privatization or market testing (Greer 1994).

Principal-Agent Theory

Principal-agent theory also provides justification for the agency structure. Eisenhardt (1989, 58) cites two problems with which principal-agent theory is concerned, where "(a) the desires or goals of the principal and agent conflict and (b) it is difficult or expensive for the principal to verify what the agent is actually doing." In principal-agent theory, attention is devoted to how the principal can induce the agent to act in ways consistent with the principal's objectives given the agent's propensity to act in self-interested ways. An important constraining factor is the costliness to the principal of information about the agent's behavior. The two generic solutions offered to the problem goal alignment are (1) for the principal to devise mechanisms to monitor the behavior of the agent or (2) to enter into a contract whereby outputs are specified. The traditional approach in bureaucratic settings has been for the principal to monitor the agent's behavior via hierarchical and other control mechanisms including budgetary, personnel, and regulatory systems.

Principal-agent theory highlights the availability of alternative mechanisms for inducing cooperation such as the monitoring of outputs. According to Eisenhardt (1989, 59), "The argument is that such contracts co-align the preferences of agents with those of the principal because the rewards for both depend on the same actions, and therefore the conflicts of self-interest between principal and agent are reduced." The framework documents that serve as a contract between the chief executive and the minister ostensibly represent a shift from behavioral monitoring to output monitoring.

Transaction Cost Economics

Transaction cost issues relate to PBO's primarily with regard to privatization and market testing. Transaction cost theory specifies conditions under which in-house service provision may be less costly than contracting out. For some agencies that deliver services for which there are multiple private-sector providers, such as Her Majesty's Stationery Office, which prints official documents for the government, agency status proved to be an intermediate step to privatization. For many other agencies, however, no such competition exists. In such cases transaction cost economics suggests that services can be provided more efficiently in-house (Deakin and Walsh 1996).

Managerialism

Also important in the formulation of Next Steps is a vein of thinking that has been identified as managerialism. Pollitt (1993, 2) identifies the following elements of managerialism:

- The main route to social progress now lies through the achievement of continuing increases in economically defined productivity;
- Such productivity increases will mainly come from the application of ever more sophisticated technologies;
- Management is a separate and distinct organizational function and one that plays the crucial role in planning, implementing, and measuring the necessary improvements in productivity;
- To perform this crucial role managers must be granted reasonable "room to maneuver" (i.e., the right to manage).

Also associated with managerialism is Alfred Chandler's 1962 work identifying and comparing the unified or functional and divisional forms of organization. Chandler argues the necessity of decentralizing authority via the "divisional form" in part on the basis that, in a turbulent environment, top management would otherwise experience an information overload (Vancil 1978). Various of Chandler's successors have endorsed the divisional form on the basis that it generates co-alignment between the goals of the divisional manager and headquarters.

Greer (1994, 46) comments that, "the basic premise of Next Steps is to devolve power from the centre and to leave agency managers free to run the day to day operations of their agencies." Decentralization of the management function has been promoted based in part on the premise that management decisions should be made by "experts" with collateral authority over agency operations and in part on the basis that senior civil servants give priority to policy rather than management "not only because it demands immediate attention but because that is the area in which they are on familiar ground and where their skills lie, and where ministerial attention is focused" (*Improving Management in Government* as quoted by Fry et al. 1988, 432).

Critiques of the Institutional Economics Explanation

A variety of criticisms have been leveled against institutional economics as an approach to understanding the behavior of individuals in organizations. One line of criticism is that the rational, self-interested behavior assumed by public choice theorists does not acknowledge the extent to which behavior is "embedded" in social relations (Granovetter 1985). Thus opportunism may be constrained by factors such as empathy, community, and morality (Jencks 1990).

A second argument is that the institutional economists do not adequately account for the extent to which power differentials can affect the interaction between parties independent of what utilitarian considerations would dictate (Eccles and White 1986). Finally, questions have been raised about how to apply the principles of institutional economics to public organizations where efficiency considerations are likely to be secondary (Moe 1991a). In addition to these more generic concerns, a number of problems arise when institutional economic principles are applied to the Next Steps framework.

Principal-Agent Theory

Consistent with principal-agent theory, the framework document can be regarded as a contract between government and agency with the government as principal and the agency as agent. In the simple configuration illustrated in Figure 1, the framework document serves to co-align the objectives of principal and agent by specifying the principal's objectives and offering the agent incentives for achieving

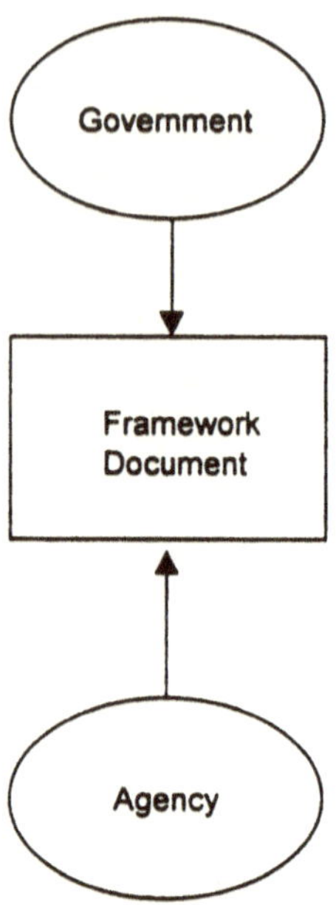

Figure 1. Negotiating the "Framework Document" Under Next Steps—The Theory

those objectives. However, this depiction oversimplifies the actual relationship between government and agency.

Figure 2 better illustrates the apparent reality of that relationship. The framework document is actually negotiated among four different groups; the agency, the Office of the Minister for the Civil Service (which has overall responsibility for the Next Steps program and is part of the Cabinet Office), the department, and the Treasury (Greer 1994). This four-way arrangement is illustrated in Figure 2. The problem that arises in the context of principal-agent theory is that the government has assigned somewhat conflicting objectives to its different agents; Treasury given a mandate to hold down expenditures, the minister and departmental management addressing policy concerns, and the chief executives charged with implementing operational efficiencies and service enhancements. The conflict is most apparent with regard to Treasury's general reluctance to make the broad grants of discretionary authority to the agencies that Next Steps doctrine implies is necessary if fundamental change is to occur at the agency level (Greer 1994).

A second issue relating to the viability of principal-agent theory in accounting for the effect of Next Steps at the agency level is whether the incentives provided chief executives are of sufficient

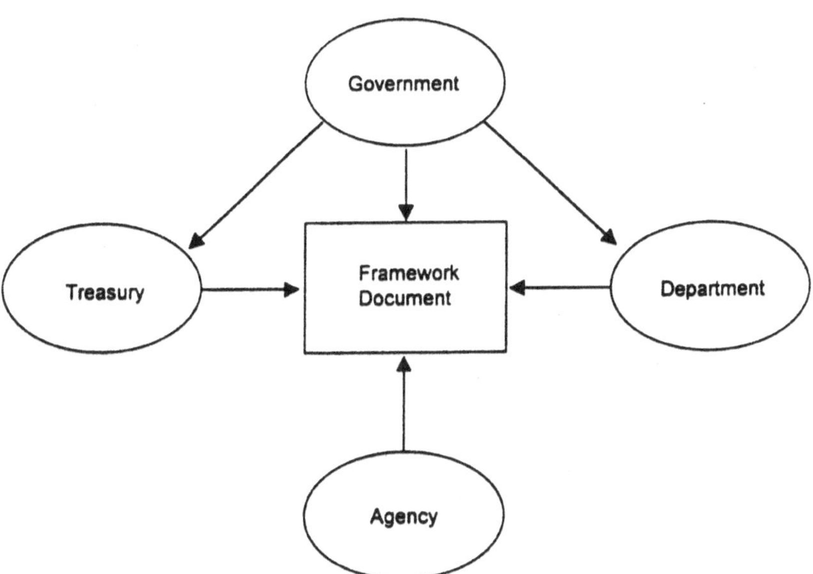

Figure 2. Negotiating the "Framework Document" Under Next Steps—The Reality

magnitude to actually affect behaviors. For example, chief executives recruited from within the civil service who wish to retain their civil service status are eligible for a bonus equivalent to only 5 percent of their salary (if they are willing to relinquish their status they are eligible for a 20 percent bonus). A similar problem pertains to bonuses paid subsidiary management within agencies where "the sum paid to individuals is marginal compared to their overall salary" (Carter and Greer 1993, 414). An incentive structure has also been established to reward agencies for holding down expenditures by allowing them to retain a portion of any underrun. Again, however, the amount is so small in many cases that the incentive effect is likely to be negligible (Greer 1994).

Transaction Cost Economics

Transaction cost economics investigates the relative efficiency of performing a function in-house via hierarchical mechanisms versus contracting out. Theorists suggest that in-house production is more efficient where (1) information asymmetry exists between buyer and seller and (2) where there are a small number of providers. In the case of the Next Steps agencies, it is apparent that (1) information asymmetry is high—agencies have a great deal more information about the production process than do departments—and (2) there are generally very few, in many cases only one, providers. Considerations from the view of transaction cost economics would therefore dictate against use of the PBO framework for most agencies (Deakin and Walsh 1996).

Markets versus Hierarchies as a Continuum

Transaction cost economics presents markets and hierarchies as dichotomous choices. A counterargument is that markets and hierarchies represent the two ends of a continuum, with most transactions having both market and hierarchical features (Hennart 1993; Bradach and Eccles 1991). While the Next Steps program is overtly contractual, multiple hierarchical elements are apparent. First, chief executives are appointed for three-year terms, with reappointment subject to approval by the minister making apparent that the parties are not on equal footings. Second, both departments and Treasury exercise influence over agency operations beyond what is specified in the framework document via requirements for annual business plans. Third, ministers and staff units at the department level exert extensive influence on the day-to-day operations of the agencies despite theoretical prescriptions to the contrary (Hogwood 1993).

The PBO as a Global Intervention

The arguments presented above challenge the conventional interpretation for how the introduction of the PBO model affects the behaviors of both agency and ministry personnel. The institutional economics explanation relies on assumptions which are not honored in the context of Next Steps. An alternative explanation relies on an understanding of the PBO as a "global intervention" within the complex organizational system that public agencies represent. The construct of "market" with which the intervention is associated is utilized to gain insight into the organizational impact of this intervention.

The "Market" Construct

The concept of markets incorporates a number of diverse elements. Markets are contrasted with central planning as economic institutions that allocate resources; they are contrasted with "authority systems" (Lindblom 1977) as "political-economic alternatives"; and they are contrasted with hierarchies and networks as a means of coordinating human activity (Thompson et al. 1991). Markets also represent an ideology (Barber 1977). The focus here is on the market as an alternative to authority systems as approach to organizing. However, the other dimensions of this construct are also relevant to the effect of the quasi market as an organizational intervention.

Markets have a number of important social implications when contrasted with authority systems:

1. Markets imply a degree of a decentralization with decisions made by independent consumers. In a market system "no authority needs to set priorities or come to any other judgment about what is most important to produce. People—consumers, suppliers, businessmen—simply decide whether to buy more or less of any given commodity or service" (Lindblom 1977, 72). No "consumer" mechanism is incorporated into Next Steps, yet the principle of decentralization, whereby the framework document sets terms of exchange that specify the scope of authority of the chief executive, is reflected in the design.
2. Markets provide a degree of transparency to transactions via the price mechanism. Whereas in a hierarchical system transactions are subject to conflicting sets of incentives (Lindblom 1977), the price system allows the transaction to occur according to a single measure of value. In a bureaucracy line managers may be subject to conflicting directives from different actors: political overseers may seek improved performance while staff units place emphasis on procedural compliance. Performance measures serve as a proxy for price by specifying the terms of exchange and clarifying priorities.
3. The price mechanism serves as a metering device that "facilitates the payment of rewards in accord with productivity" (Alchian and Demsetz 1972, 778). The performance measures specified under Next Steps serve a similar purpose by metering the performance of the chief executive. They further facilitate metering by the chief executive of his/her subordinates.
4. A related aspect is that markets are impersonal and "automatic"; "they carry with them their own system of rewards and penalties, incentives and sanctions, which are imposed automatically" (Beetham 1991, 137). There is no competition for most of the service delivery functions under Next Steps but there is an implicit element of automaticity incorporated into the framework documents whereby if performance objectives are met, rewards in the form of bonuses and potential reappointment will be forthcoming.
5. The concept of "markets" also represents an ideology incorporating a specific set of values, among them efficiency, equity,

and freedom (Barber 1977). As such, the program was highly compatible with the outlook of the prime minister and the Conservative Party that she represented.

6. The concept of markets also has important political implications. To the extent that there is a true competitive market, consumers gain the power to select among various alternatives. This is turned on its head to some extent under Next Steps where the purchaser, in this case the department, loses authority to some degree. The program does retain the principle of disaggregated decision making however.

The PBO as a Quasi Market

Next Steps incorporates some market features while excluding others. The key market-like element is the substitution of a contractual for a hierarchical relationship between agency head and minister. As noted above, the contract triggers various market-like features. Hennart, using institutional economics as a context, distinguishes between markets and firms as "economic institutions" and the "price system" and hierarchy as "methods of organizing" (1993, 531). While "markets are institutions that predominantly use the price system of organizing" (531), both markets and firms can use a mix of the price system and hierarchy. The critical distinction between the price system and hierarchy is that "the price system rewards agents on the basis of their outputs [whereas] hierarchy rewards on the basis of behavior (inputs)" (531), and further that "while prices indirectly guide behavior by rewarding output, hierarchy directly controls individuals by specifying behavior and rewarding compliance" (534).

Accepting Hennart's (1993) distinction between economic institutions and methods of organizing as well as between the price system and hierarchy, it is apparent that the framework document used as a contractual vehicle in Next Steps is intended to mimic a price system by rewarding on the basis of outputs and that it is intended, to some extent, to substitute output measurement for hierarchical control. A second market-like element in the Next Steps arrangement is the specification of performance measures which can serve to make provision of a service contestable by either internal or external vendors.

The Quasi Market as a Global Intervention

The hypothesis offered here is that the effect of Next Steps is a consequence of the multifaceted nature of the quasi-market intervention it represents. This effect can be understood by investigating the implications of the quasi market for different organizational elements or "subsystems." Different theorists have identified alternative sets of organizational "subsystems." This analysis relies primarily on Tichy's (1983) list (political, cultural, and technical) modified to incorporate elements from that of Burrell and Morgan (1979). As a PBO, the Next Steps initiative represents a "global" intervention, impacting each of the major subsystems.

Intervening in the Structural Subsystem

The quasi-market intervention represented by Next Steps was explicitly a structural intervention targeted at reporting relationships and at the reward system. Reporting relationships were changed by substitution of the "contractual" arrangement between agency head and minister for one that had previously been exclusively hierarchical. Creation of the chief executive position and the accompanying redefinition of the agency head's role represented a major structural innovation. The most prominent changes in the reward system included subjecting the chief executive to reappointment every three years.

Intervening in the Political Subsystem

Whereas the institutional economics perspective places emphasis on incentives as a mechanism for influencing behavior, a political perspective places an emphasis on shifts in power among the actors. One effect of Next Steps has been to enhance the power of the chief executive vis-à-vis both the Treasury and departments. This is a consequence of several features of the structural changes that have been introduced. For example, the existence of the framework document can enhance the power of the chief executive when confronted with interference by either Treasury or the department in operational matters. Greer (1994, 26) observes that the existence of a contract specifying limits on this interference may serve to deter interference and provide the chief executive with a degree of autonomy:

> . . . if, for example, the Treasury were not playing the Next Steps game and delegating agencies with additional 'freedoms', then this failure to play by the Next Steps rules would be blatantly obvious through the published agency framework documents and business plans which outline the boundaries in which agencies must operate.

As noted above, although interference in agency matters continues to occur, the net effect of the contractual arrangement is to establish greater equality between the parties (Zifcak 1994).

Intervening in the Managerial Subsystem

Managerialism highlights the legitimacy of management as a profession and the manager's "right to manage" (Charlesworth, Clarke, and Cochrane, 1996). In the context of Next Steps, the granting of additional authority to chief executives was regarded as necessary in light of the policy focus of managers at the department level. Designers of the program presumed that top officials do not have and are not rewarded for management skills. Identifying an individual with such skills, specifying managerial responsibilities, and providing that official with a greater degree of autonomy enhance the pursuit of managerial values.

The managerial subsystem addresses the role of the manager in organizational affairs. The Next Steps formulation envisions a more entrepreneurial role for the agency head than had been the case under the traditional arrangement. This role is highlighted by the additional status accorded the chief executive as a consequence of (1) selection according to a competitive and open process, (2) receiving a three-year appointment with some guarantee of tenure during that period, (3) the additional flexibilities granted in the framework document, (4) the semi-autonomous status granted the agencies, and (5) the explicit sanction of the government of the objectives to be achieved. The program deliberately places substantial responsibility on the chief executive for effecting change in agency operations.

Intervening in the Cultural Subsystem

The cultural explanation of quasi markets is closely affiliated with the institutional explanation. Smircich (1983) offers alternative understandings of the concept of organizational culture. One refers to culture as "networks of subjective meanings or shared frames of reference that organization members share to varying degrees and which, to an external observer, appear to function in a rule-like or grammar-like manner" (348). The cultural perspective places emphasis on the socially constructed nature of reality. Markets can be understood as socially constructed and as containing an important symbolic dimension (Hoggett 1996).

Zifcak (1994) quotes a Second Permanent Secretary to the effect that the agency concept itself is largely socially constructed:

> What is an administrative agency—it is nothing, it's an administrative unit but people feel its part of the family. . . . The very act of having a ring fence means that within it people can be given greater freedoms and responsibility than otherwise its an act of faith (86)

The market as an institution embodies certain rules, norms, and expectations that, according to some observers, have had a profound effect on the behavior of agency employees. That effect takes the form not only of having performance goals specified and greater discretion offered to managers, but also the threat of the external market via competitive tendering. Hoggett (1996, 15) argues,

> . . . there can be no doubting the powerful effect that markets are having on the behaviour of the vast majority of public sector employees . . . the attempt to shift public sector organizations' culture by persuasion, example, training, etc. appears to have failed. However, the introduction of markets and competition to vast areas of the public sector since 1987 does appear to be bringing about a major change in the way in which workers and managers behave. . . .

Hoggett describes the Next Steps programs and the accompanying changes as creating a new set of "meta-level rules," which he identifies as an "extremely effective form of 'hands-off' control" (25).

This shift constitutes what Brown (1978) describes as a change in the organizational "paradigm." An organizational paradigm, according to Brown, consists of "those sets of assumptions, usually implicit, about what sorts of things make up the world, how they act, how they hang together, and how they may be known" (373). In fundamentally disrupting traditional assumptions about the public service such as low priority given management considerations, lifetime tenure, preeminence of the Treasury, and exposure to competition, the Next Steps program appears to meet his criteria for a paradigm shift.

The institutional elements of Next Steps work both internally and externally. The quasi-market approach may obtain its own legitimacy based on the general legitimacy accorded "the market" in the broader society. This feature is particularly important from the perspective of the political overseers. Legitimacy of the intervention derives both from the market aspects and from emulation of private-sector practices (managerialism).

Conclusion

The problems facing those who seek to change the operations of large governmental bureaucracies in accordance with reinvention principles are formidable. In addition to the matter of devising new organizational models that allow improved efficiency and enhanced service, the would-be change agent has to confront issues of culture and of power. The cultural problem is essentially one of changing the unstated "rules" which govern the behavior of members. The power problem is that of decentralizing authority over operational matters to line managers.

The British experience provides some evidence that introducing market-like features into the bureaucracy can serve as a solution to these problems. The Next Steps intervention, itself primarily a structural intervention, has, according to a number of observers, changed both the written and unwritten rules of behavior in these organizations and facilitated a shift in power to agency heads who, via the framework documents, are provided with a mandate to improve performance. Those changes, at least in some instances, appear to have set the stage for operational improvements.

There are a number of implications of this analysis for the American reform experience. First, it raises questions about the efficacy of programs such as the Government Performance and Results Act in leveraging change. Simply introducing performance measures as an isolated intervention is unlikely to transform the behaviors of organizational members. GPRA in many ways parallels the Financial Management Initiative in its structure, with the performance measures introduced as a means of gauging programmatic impact. If, however, the intent of the program is to change officials' behavior, it would appear that a broader intervention along the lines of Next Steps is required.

Recent experience provides no reason for optimism that Congress will approve wide-scale implementation of PBOs in the U.S. None of the seven pilot PBOs submitted by the Clinton administration has been approved in Congress. One implication of the quasi market as an organizational intervention, however, is that it is subject to being implemented at subsidiary organization levels. Thus, a large agency with an extensive field structure could create an internal quasi market by emulating the features of the Next Steps program: creating a contractual arrangement with field unit heads; granting additional operational authority to these heads in conjunction with the use of performance measures as a means of accountability; allowing open competition for the unit head slots; and providing for the use of incentives in the form of job retention and additional pay to mimic the PBO concept. Some structural changes would be required to effect such a program, but most would be within the scope of authority of the agency head. It appears that if bureaucratic reform is to become a reality, interventions with a broad effect such as this will be essential. The British experience with the quasi-market concept to date appears to hold some promise in that regard.

Part IV

Models and Frameworks: New Approaches to Public Management

Chapter 12

Organizational Configurations: Four Approaches to Public Sector Management

Nancy C. Roberts Naval Postgraduate School

Public sector management presents major conceptual challenges to managers. There are competing models of governance (Peters 1993), of public management (Stevens 1997), of values (Quinn and Rohrbaugh 1981; 1983), and of disciplinary perspectives which serve as the foundation for the field (Lynn 1996). Public managers have a number of choices in response to such conceptual complexity. They can limit their frame of reference or paradigm and assume there is "one best way" to be a public manager, learn the best way, and apply it to whatever context or situation they confront. This alternative presupposes that there is one best way of public sector management and that it is understood well enough for application to public organizations. Alternatively, they can develop a contingency approach to management and match organizational characteristics such as strategy, structure, tasks, or processes to fit particular situations. This option assumes that research has progressed to the point where the contingencies are well defined and understood and are applicable to the manager's particular context. Or, third, the public managers can take a holistic stance and assume that only a certain number of organizational configurations are possible. This alternative posits that configurations cluster organizational characteristics systematically. Thus organizational environments, strategies, structures, processes, and cultures cohere into expected patterns. Public managers would first identify and then manage to these patterns to be successful.

This chapter takes a configurational approach. The goal is to assist public managers in conceptually developing a logic of action that acknowledges the complexity of public management and yet makes this complexity more manageable by putting into bold relief the major configurations that are used in practice. Four configurations are identified: the Directive Configuration, the Responsive Configuration,[1] the Adaptive Configuration, and the Generative Configuration. The first section describes the four configurations and uses examples to ground each one in organizational reality. Research support for the configurational approach is presented in the section following. The chapter concludes with a brief summary of the implications in taking this configurational approach for public sector management.

Organizational Configurations

An organizational configuration is defined as a "constellation of conceptually distinct characteristics that commonly occur together" (Meyer, Tsui, and Linings 1993, 1175). Also referred to as "gestalts" or "archetypes," configurations represent a clustering of organizational attributes (e.g., environment, strategy, structure, culture, beliefs, processes) that fall into coherent patterns. Rather than treating an organization as composed of constituent parts that may be adjusted or fine-tuned independently of one another, a configurational approach takes a "holistic stance" and assumes that the parts of an organization "take their meaning from the whole and cannot be understood in isolation" (Meyer, Tsui, and Linings 1993, 1176). Thus organizational elements are expected to cohere and be related in stable and understandable ways. Rather than relying on bivariate analysis, organizational inquiry can be based on the patterning of organizational elements (Miller and Friesen 1984, 15). From this perspective, organizations are considered to be constellations of interconnected parts; to gain an understanding of them one needs to examine their overall gestalt rather than their individual properties or elements.

Configurations are derived in two ways. Some are theoretically identified as ideal types based on a priori distinctions. For example, Weber (1947) distinguished among charismatic, traditional, and bureaucratic types of organization; and Burns and Stalker (1961) compared and contrasted organic and mechanistic forms of organizing. Other configurations have been developed inductively through the empirical classification of data. Miller and Friesen (1984) used statistical manipulation of organizational information in large samples to identify the clustering of variables and their relationships. For those reliant on empirical classification, configurational research begins with large data sets. For those reliant on a priori distinctions, configurational research begins with theory-based dimensions deductively derived to identify and distinguish among the configurations. This chapter takes the deductive approach which has been found to explain performance better than inductively defined configurations (Ketchen, Thomas, and Snow 1993).

Dimensions of Efficiency and Effectiveness

Reliant on a priori distinctions, this exercise begins by identifying two basic dimensions of organization performance—efficiency and effectiveness—on which there has been extensive research (Ostroff and Schmitt 1993). Efficiency refers to the "capacity to produce results with the minimum expenditure of time, money, or materials" (*Websters* 1971, 725). Efficiency thus focuses on the input-output ratio (Pennings and Goodman 1977). To be efficient is to do things well, to attend to the internal organization by refining, routinizing, formalizing, elaborating on existing knowledge, and making short-run improvements. Effectiveness, on the other hand, is defined as "productive of results" (*Websters* 1971, 724). The focus is on doing the right thing and it is determined by an absolute level of either input acquisition or outcome attainment (Pennings and Goodman 1977). It comes from an understanding and interpretation of the external environment as it signals what ongoing adaptations in goals, outputs, and outcomes are required.[2]

Both efficiency and effectiveness play an important part in organizational performance, yet in the competition for resources each can interfere with the other, thereby resulting in a tension between the two. Efficiency depends on "focus, precision, repetition, analysis, sanity, discipline, and control" (March 1995, 5). Effectiveness, on the other hand, through the process of adaptation to the external environment, relies on "serendipity, experimentation, novelty, free association, madness, loose discipline, and relaxed control" (March 1995, 5). While effectiveness thrives on exploration and experimentation, efficiency attempts to drive them out (March 1995, 5). Consequently, public managers need to make choices between the levels of efficiency and effectiveness they intend to pursue. Figure 1 illustrates four possible combinations, identified as configurations or ideal types, that can be theoretically derived when public sector managers seek different levels of efficiency (horizontal dimension) and different levels of effectiveness (vertical dimension).

Directive Configuration

The Directive Configuration resolves the tension between efficiency and effectiveness by configuring an organization for optimal efficiency with less attention devoted to effectiveness. In this configuration, public managers pursue efficiency by running their organizations like well-oiled machines (Miles, Snow, and Meyer 1978; Mintzberg 1996a). They avoid issues of adaptation to the external environment that require reexamination of current operations. In-

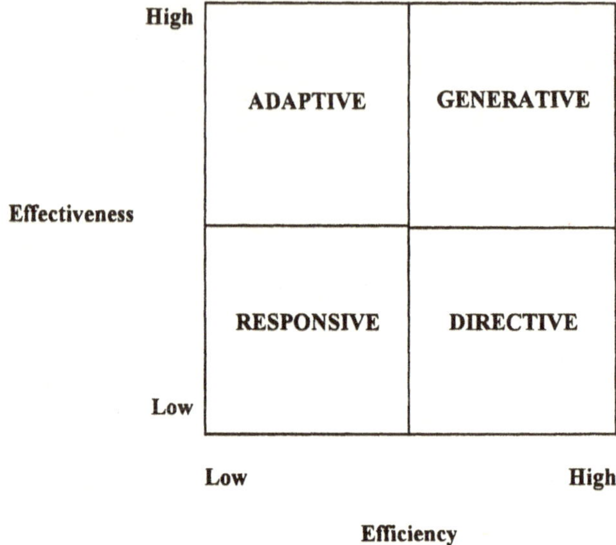

Figure 1. Organizational Configurations

stead, they focus on maintaining internal order, thus attempting as much as possible to cut the organization off from any disruptive external influences. Serving as the locus of decision making, managers insist on a common direction to set goals and objectives in order to keep members accountable. They require formalized jobs and standardized work to maintain orderly, reliable, and coordinated activity. They oversee uniform policies that cover rights and duties, promotions based on competence and merit, and impersonal role relations to ensure the smooth flow of work. Using both budgetary and operational controls to monitor actions, they oversee organizational changes geared to improving operations. Since change can disrupt orderly routines, they minimize it unless it is deemed essential. When forced to make major change, they take on the role of strategic planner and driver of the organizational system by issuing top-down directives to modify standard operating procedures. (See Table 1 for an elaboration of the Directive and other configurations.)

A navy aircraft carrier during peace time operations is an organization that approximates this ideal type. Its environment is stable, with a well-defined threat structure (e.g., the Soviet Union during the Cold War). Every effort is made to protect the carrier from the vagaries of the environment, both natural and man-made, in order to minimize the risk to this multibillion-dollar investment. National security policy is implemented by the Department of Defense and the Armed

Table 1. *Summary of Four Configurations*

	Responsive	Directive	Adaptive	Generative
Purpose	react to politics/ play politics	order; minimize uncertainty	innovate	learn
Organizational Type	neutral organization; political organization	machine bureaucracy	adhocracy	network; virtual organization
External Environment	competing coalitions, stakeholder conflicts, regulated environment	stable; simple	hypercomputative; complex	turbulent, complex; hard to separate internal/external parts
Direction Setting and Planning	muddling through; piecemeal, disjointed planning; partisan mutual adjustment	top-down, comprehensive hierarchy of goals and strategies; sequential planning process	vision and values drive from top; strategies emerge from throughout organization based on experimentation and groping along; strategic choice activates politics	strategic issues identified by top; strategies emerge from stakeholder collaborations
Basis of Decision Making	responsive to political authority; political decision making; garbage can process	rational, technical analysis	rational analysis in technical core; politics at mid-level and at strategic apex	dialogue and deliberation of strategic issues; co-learning

Table 1. *Summary of Four Configurations* (Continued)

	Responsive	Directive	Adaptive	Generative
Change Initiated by	shifting political alliances	strategic apex sets new course	finding new opportunities through explorations & experiments	stakeholder collaboration
Organizational Structure	none characteristic unless political coalition establishes temporary authority	mechanistic; centralized, functional;	organic, decentralized, project management	cellular forms of organizing; multifunctional, self-organizing teams, partnerships, alliances, joint ventures
Organizational Tasks/Jobs	ill defined; fluid; determined by associations	standardized; specialized; formalized	expert based; nonstandardized to support the project/program	cross training; jobs expanded & enlarged to empower self-managed teams
Organizational Coordination	through interplay of politics and coalitions	through hierarchy, specialized work, SOPs, and routines	through liaisons, coordinating committees, task forces, & mutual adjustments	through info.-sharing and mutual adjustments among network members
Implementation	unaligned design elements; lack of coherence among organizational parts	top-down alignment of design elements with org.'s direction	alignment with vision through experiments	alignment between strategic issue and action plan

Table 1. *Summary of Four Configurations* (Continued)

	Responsive	Directive	Adaptive	Generative
Controls and Evaluation	based on inputs and pleasing political authority	based on rules; standardized inputs required per unit of output	based on feedback linked to vision and outcomes and customer satisfaction	based on norms for learning; feedback linked to issue, outcomes, and stakeholder satisfaction
Organizational Norms	appearance of responsiveness to political authority	order and stability	teamwork; creativity; invention; flexibility	active listening; collaboration; appreciation of differences
Role of General Manager	crisis manager or power broker	planner; controller	visionary; champion of innovation	steward; teacher; designer
Role of Organizational Member	firefighter or political actor	"soldier"	entrepreneur; innovator	co-learner
Central Skills	manages crisis; bargains and negotiates; forms coalitions; conducts power analysis; builds a power base	conducts rational analysis and cost-benefit analysis	inspires others to action; builds enthusiasm and commitment; articulates vision; manages conflict	focuses on key issues and questions; structures and facilities dialogue; evokes trust in process; leads large-group collaborations
Metaphor	fire fighting; gamesmanship	machine	mountain climbing	DNA; holograms

Services through a strict chain of command that reaches from the president to the shipboard commander. Plans, Programming, Budgeting, and Systems (PPBS)—a top-down sequential planning process introduced by Secretary of Defense Robert McNamara in the 1960s to link comprehensively department policy and functional and operational plans with budgets and systems—sets the broad parameters for carrier activity. The onboard structure is functional, with centralized decision making and coordination based on hierarchy and standardized operating procedures. Inputs acquired (dollars and personnel) and surrogate output measures (readiness) serve as the mechanisms of control and evaluation. Effectiveness is not an issue (it is assumed to be consonant with U.S. national security policy), so the carrier concentrates its efforts on efficiency by rehearsing and improving its many activities (e.g., carrier plane landings and takeoffs). And, as is typical of all machine bureaucracies, tasks are standardized, specialized, and formalized. Discretion and flexibility are minimal in deference to the norms of order, stability, and respect for higher authority.

Responsive Configuration

The Responsive Configuration relieves the tension between efficiency and effectiveness by minimizing attention to both dimensions. What this means in practice is that public managers do not push their organizations toward effectiveness or efficiency, nor do they make much effort to reconcile the competing demands between the two. Considering issues of effectiveness at one moment and efficiency the next, they oversee organizations that produce inconsistent, disjointed patterns of activity in response to competing demands in the political environment. Without an underlying logic to inform actions, they fail to provide coherent, integrated policies to guide the organization as a whole, either for the purpose of efficiency or for the purpose of effectiveness. Consequently, organizational members emulate the managers' "muddling through" with their own patchwork of poorly coordinated decisions (Lindblom 1959; 1979). Some compare the decision process that results from these interactions to a "garbage can" where problems, solutions, decision makers, and choice opportunities are thrown together as independent streams linked by their simultaneity in time, not by any logic or order (Cohen, March, and Olsen 1972).

In their attempts to be responsive to the external political forces swirling about them, public managers are forced to make a choice. They can assume the role of crisis manager, an option which requires them to douse political fires whenever they erupt and accommodate demands of contentious stakeholders. Or, alternatively, they can become power brokers in their own right, joining the political fray, building a base of power, and developing strategies and tactics to protect their self- and organizational interests. Whether they choose the role of crisis manager or broker of power, however, emergent organizational policies are the result of partisan mutual adjustments made in response to competing demands in the political context (Lindblom 1959; 1979).

Robert Reich (1990, 3–4) played out the role of crisis manager during a two-month period at the Federal Trade Commission. He participated in deliberations on the regulations that would require cigarette manufacturers to label packages and advertisements with a warning if their brand contained tar and nicotine above a certain level. On a day-by-day, moment-by-moment basis he attempted to respond to one stakeholder after another, ranging from those on the Hill in the House Commerce Committee, to various representatives from the press, to lobbyists from the American Tobacco Institute, Common Cause, the American Cancer Society, and Ralph Nader's Health Group, along with different groups within the Commission such as staff members from the Division of Marketing and Advertising, the general counsel, and the FTC chairman himself. Eventually, he comments, the " . . . 'brushfires' were doused. Accommodations were made, and compromises reached" (4). When considering whether it was a good rule, he admitted that he did not know and was only relieved that it was no longer his responsibility.

Rather than subject himself to the competing demands of his many stakeholders and the vagaries of the political process, Robert Moses took on the role of power broker. Beginning as a parks commissioner in New York City, he amassed resources to the point that he is considered by some to be one of the most powerful public officials in the United States during the twentieth century (Caro 1974; Pfeffer 1992). Moses started by accumulating positions that initially appeared to be of little importance. Over time he expanded his reach by gaining more detailed knowledge of how the New York building process worked (e.g., contracting, insurance, performance bonds, legal and banking services). In so doing he built a very large resource base from which to operate, trading knowledge, information, and contracts for power. Ultimately, an "army" of union members, construction firms, legal firms, and bankers constituted his supporters. Over his 44-year career, he managed to build 12 bridges, 35 highways, 751 playgrounds, 13 golf courses, 18 swimming pools, and more than 2 million acres of parks in New York, displacing over 500,000 people in the process and influencing generations of city planners and urban development specialists both nationally and internationally (Pfeffer 1992).

Adaptive Configuration

The Adaptive Configuration seeks to optimize organizational effectiveness, downplaying interests in efficiency. Public managers achieve organizational effectiveness by adapting to the external environment and meeting customer needs. They take on the role of champions of innovation to unleash entrepreneurial and innovative behavior throughout their organizations (Miles, Snow, and Meier 1978; Mintzberg 1996b). They decentralize decision making so it rests on the shoulders of organizational members who are closest to customers, substituting customers for bosses as the basis of authority. They rely on members' up-to-date knowledge to signal what adaptations and innovations in products and services are required to attract and keep customer support. To ensure a continual stream of new ideas and keep the creative juices flowing, they reward risk taking and innovative ideas and design decentralized organizations that focus on collaborative projects and cross-disciplinary teams. Reliant on a general vision of the future rather than insistent on specific goals and objectives, they encourage "groping along" in the search for new ideas rather than planning (Behn 1988). Flexibility, creativity, exploration and experimentation are far more important to them than rigid adherence to internal order and control.

Research and development organizations are typical of those in the Adaptive Configuration. NASA during the 1960s, under the leadership of James Webb, is a good example. When Webb took over as NASA administrator, his stated purpose was to develop an agency that "could be as innovative in the management of all its activities as it was in its scientific and technical work" (Webb 1969, 141). Innovative management was essential because the organization faced many uncertainties and unknowns. Given a very general mandate by President Kennedy to land a man on the moon within the decade, NASA's goals were "neither fixed nor . . . precisely determined" (Levine 1982, xix). The agency had to settle a host of issues: what type of hardware should be developed; how the organization should be designed and run; whether to do all of the design and development work internally or to contract it out; and whether to put the emphasis on man or machines in space. Addressing these issues required exploration and learning from experience. No one had the formula for what had to be accomplished. "There were important areas of unpredictability, areas where none of the experiences of man could tell us what would be needed or how it could be provided. Yet we had to go ahead despite these uncertainties. The only way we could learn was to do" (Webb 1969, 147).

Unable to prepare for substantive and administrative conditions that could not be foreseen, Webb reasoned that it made sense to build an agile organization where innovation would be more important than stability: "You have to have a system that permits, encourages, and even forces flexibility and adaptive innovation on the part of those people—including the executives—who are responsible for its various elements" (Webb 1969, 143). Thus NASA went through various organizational changes to ensure flexibility and to induce a state of "organic flux" (Webb 1969, 142). The efforts produced a loosely coupled, decentralized system reliant on program offices and field centers for project management (Levine 1982). The intention of senior management was to give the centers what they needed to get the job done. Individual managers also were given the authority to act independently when the situation warranted it: "The nature of tasks and demands change too rapidly for a static setup to be effective" (Webb 1969, 160). Although managers were expected to be knowledgeable in sound management doctrine and practice, they also were required "to do a job without exact definition of what it (was) or how it should be done" (Webb 1969, 136). "In the area of uncertainty, the executive would have to find his own way. Nobody could tell him precisely what to do; there was no precedent to which he could look; there was a blank area in his job description" (Webb 1969, 147). Consequently, NASA searched for those who could "work effectively when lines of command crisscross[ed] and [moved] in several directions rather than straight up and down," those who could "adjust to several bosses at the same time," "work effectively in an unstable environment and live uncertainty and a high degree of personal insecurity" (Webb 1969, 136). Since nothing could be "taken for granted," "fully anticipated," "prepared for in advance," or "programmed with complete surety," there had "to be a readiness and an ability on the part of the individual to cope with the unexpected and unknown from within and without. Maneuverability of the whole and the varied parts [was] essential for success" (Webb 1969, 169). As Webb admitted, "we accepted a large degree of organizational instability to achieve the necessary degree of maneuverability" (Webb 1969, 135).

Generative Configuration

The Generative Configuration demands optimal efficiency and effectiveness. No longer content to make trade-offs between efficiency and effectiveness, as in the Directive and Adaptive Configurations, public managers strive for the optimum on both. They search for ways to reconcile competing expectations emanating from the two dimensions: short-run and long-run perspectives; global and local considerations; individual and collective needs; social and economic concerns; security and freedom; change and stability; diversity and commonality of purpose. Managers who not only cope with the tension between the two dimensions but move well beyond it have been called masters of paradox (Handy 1994; Quinn and Cameron 1988).

Central to the resolution of paradox is the public manager's reliance on stakeholder collaborations. In fact it is through collaborations that the manager is able to achieve both organizational efficiency and effectiveness. Efficiency derives from networked stakeholders working together in the pursuit of common means; effectiveness derives from networked stakeholders working together in the pursuit of common ends. An example from public management is illustrative. When confronted with a budgetary crisis, a district superintendent called for a collaboration among district stakeholders to cut the budget (Roberts 1985). Stakeholder deliberations over a period of four months resulted in a set of recommendations which were unanimously approved by the Board of Education in a matter of minutes. The process was responsive since all stakeholders were invited and did attend. Greater efficiency occurred because the stakeholders, meeting face to face in open fora to share information, voice their opinions, and make recommendations on what should be cut from the budget, avoided costly delays and legal battles typical of the budget-cutting process. Effectiveness was achieved because customers (students and parents) agreed that the Board of Education's recommended changes would enable the district to maintain a quality education while adapting to the recession that had gripped the state.

Stakeholder collaborations take many forms, including multifunctional teams, partnerships, joint ventures, and alliances (Kanter 1989). As temporary arrangements of stakeholders who can be both internal and external to the organization, collaborations require participants to come together quickly to exploit some opportunity or solve some problem that each acting independently could not address. The point is to leverage intellect (Quinn 1992; Quinn, Anderson, and Finkelstein 1996) and promote people's generative learning—learning that develops their capacity to create new solutions to old problems rather than settle for adaptive learning that only prepares them for coping (Senge 1990). The intent of generative learning is to open up new ways of looking at the world and to encourage a deeper understanding of a system and its underlying dynamics. Generative learning becomes possible through dialogue—an open, deliberative, problem-solving process—that requires stakeholders to listen carefully to one another, respect one another's differences, and pool their information, resources, and skills in order to deal with complex social issues for which there are no right answers (Roberts 1997; Roberts and Menker 1998). When convening public deliberations, public managers assume the roles of steward, teacher, and designer. Their function is to manage the creative tension between a vision and current reality, invite participation in the resolution of that tension, and ensure a process in which generative learning can take place (Senge 1990; Roberts and Bradley 1991; Roberts 1997).

Finding public organizations that exemplify all the characteristics of the Generative Configuration proves to be more difficult than it was for the first three configurations. Experimentation is underway on various aspects of the Generative Configuration, but no one organization exists, as far as this researcher is aware, that exemplifies the Generative Configuration in its entirety. Instead, we find evidence of organizations moving in fits and starts toward what is often referred to as the "new management paradigm" (Levine and Luck 1994) or the "postmodern organization" (Fox and Miller 1995). There are: stakeholder dialogues and deliberations to craft public policy and organizational direction (Reich 1990; Roberts and Bradley 1991; Roberts and King 1996; 1997); learning strategies to review organizational procedures and chart new courses of action (Garvin 1993; Senge et al. 1994); measures of outputs and outcomes to track and improve organizational performance (Kamensky 1996); dedications to customer service and the offering of only those products and services that add value (Halal 1994); improved organizational processes through reengineering, outsourcing, and quality improvements to ensure greater efficiencies (Hammer and Champy 1993; Hammer and Stanton 1995; Osborne and Gaebler 1992); and experimentations with the new networked organizational forms and their boundaryless character (Ashkenas et al. 1995; Snow, Miles, and Coleman 1992). While lacking an exemplar, there is sufficient evidence to warrant discussion of the Generative Configuration and its contours.

Research Supporting Configurations

The configurational approach to management has provoked interest on the part of practitioners and scholars, and support continues to grow as researchers test the various configurations in different organizations and environments (Meyer, Tsui, and Linings 1993). While the Generative Configuration is evolving and has not been examined in its entirety as a separate configuration, it captures an important element—the network structure—that has been missing from traditional criteria and that is recommended for identifying new configurations in the future (Ketchen, Thomas, and Snow 1993).

Evidence for the Directive and the Adaptive Configurations is particularly strong (Doty, Glick, and Huber 1993), especially when the two are represented in the model formulated by Miles and others (1978). Researchers have found, for example, a continuum on which high performing organizations tend to position themselves. At one end of the continuum is the Directive Configurations (The Defender in the Miles, Snow, and Meyer 1978 model) and at the other end is the Adaptive Configuration (The Prospector in the Miles, Snow, and Meyer 1978 model). This continuum is represented in Figure 2 as a diagonal running between the Directive Configuration and the Adaptive Configuration.

High-performing organizations tend to position themselves as ideal types at either end of the continuum. Other organizations have been found at varying points along the continuum, in effect creating hybrids which pursue different degrees of efficiency and effectiveness. Miles, Snow, and Meyer (1978) refer to the hybrid at the center point on the continuum as the Analyzer. It has a dual focus: it seeks the flexibility inherent in the Adaptive Configuration and the control and order characteristic of the Directive Configuration. Incorporating features to accommodate both stability and change, hybrids often

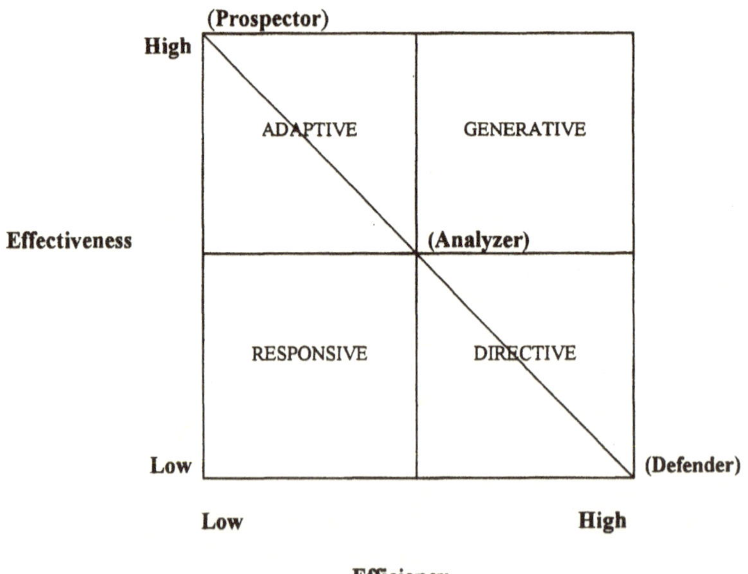

Figure 2. Miles, Snow, and Meyer Continuum and the Four Configurations

adopt a matrix structure (Miles, Snow, and Meyer 1978, 75). A matrix permits subunits to have disparate processes in order to accommodate both stable and dynamic areas of operation. For example, a matrix organization can locate and exploit new products and markets, keeping flexibility in certain portions of its operations while simultaneously maintaining a firm base of traditional products and customers in the stable portions of its domain.

Alternative organizational arrangements and hybrids also have been described by Mintzberg. Professional Bureaucracies (Mintzberg 1996c) combine the efficiency of machine bureaus with the adaptations and innovations that professionals bring from their fields. The Diversified Configuration (Mintzberg 1996d) enables a corporate entity to set up a set of semi-autonomous units that are coupled together by a central administrative structures. Some of the subunits can pursue effectiveness through innovation and change; others can mine traditional products and services to achieve greater efficiencies. Thus the overall corporate entity can benefit because it combines subunits striving for either effectiveness or efficiency.

There are some disadvantages to hybrids located on the diagonal between the Adaptive and Directive Configurations, however. Researchers have demonstrated that the greater the similarity between the Analyzer and one of the ideal types at either end of the continuum, the greater the increase in performance. This finding suggests that ideal types are better performers than hybrids, although a hybrid can still be a good performer (Doty, Glick, and Huber 1993). Hybrids on the diagonal also downplay stakeholder participation in critical decisions, at least in comparison to the Generative Configuration. In the current environment, when the public and its stakeholders expect greater involvement in the decisions that affect their interests (McLagan and Nel 1995; Thomas 1995; White 1988), this may be a risky strategy. For example, stakeholder collaboration is now required through the Government Performance Results Act (Kamensky 1996), which mandates collaboration among a range of stakeholders from Congress to customers.

Research evidence to support the Responsive Configuration comes from a variety of sources. In the business literature, organizations falling into this configuration are often treated as reactors—poor performers that fall into a deficit or "residual" category because they are considered neither effective nor efficient (Miles, Snow, and Meyer 1978; Doty, Glick, and Huber 1993). Alternatively, in a highly regulated environment organizations falling into this configuration are viewed as good performers (Miles, Snow, and Meyer 1978; Snow and Hrebiniak 1980; Doty, Glick, and Huber 1993). This treatment takes the latter perspective. Consonant with a line of public administration and public management theory and research that emphasizes the responsiveness of public organizations and public managers (Kearney and Sinha 1988; Rourke 1992; Stivers 1994), the Responsive Configuration is viewed as an ideal type in a political economy which requires organizations to be accountable to the public by anticipating and responding to its concerns. Responsiveness, not efficiency or effectiveness, becomes the primary driver under these circumstances. Whether public managers view their roles as crisis managers who strive to accommodate competing political interests or whether they see themselves as power brokers who promote their preferred interests, responsiveness becomes their raison d'etre.

Implications and Conclusion

Four deductively derived configurations of public management have been identified. The first three—the Directive, the Adaptive, and the Responsive—have a tradition in public management and are supported by research as noted above. The fourth, the Generative Configuration, follows the recommendations for future configurational research by updating the first three configurations and incorporating interorganizational linkages and a new organizational form—the networked organization—as its major feature (Ketchen, Thomas, and Snow 1993). Both the Responsive and the Generative Configurations capture characteristics particularly relevant in the public arena. Each acknowledges the importance of stakeholders to the organization's performance: the Responsive Configuration assumes a competitive model of stakeholder relations where stakeholders bargain, negotiate, and compete with one other to achieve their ends; the Generative Configuration assumes a collaborative model of stakeholder relations where stakeholders participate in public dialogues and deliberations in the search for a common end.

The four configurations simplify the management jungle of competing theories and models for public managers and, at the same time, raise into bold relief public management's fundamental questions: How efficient are we and how efficient must we become, given the imperative to reduce costs and conserve resources? How effective are we and what adaptations, if any, are needed to meet customer needs in a changing environment? How responsive are we to stakeholder issues and how responsive must we be, given competing political interests? And ultimately, how can we be efficient, effective, and responsive when optimizing all three aspects of public management can push us into paradoxical dilemmas that are difficult to resolve?

The new configuration—the Generative Configuration—offers public managers a way to resolve their paradoxes and move beyond simple trade-offs between efficiency, effectiveness, and responsiveness, but the path it offers is not an easy one for public managers to take. Stakeholder collaborations in the Generative Configuration can produce greater organizational efficiency, effectiveness, and responsiveness (Roberts 1985), but they do not always do so (Gray 1989; Kaboolian 1995). Public dialogues and deliberations can increase the divide between contentious stakeholders as well as diminish it. Conflicts, a natural part of the give and take in a democratic society, do not always get resolved through collaborative means. And there is much to learn in establishing and leading stakeholder collaborations in order to make them successful (Bunker and Alban 1997).

Despite these uncertainties about the Generative Configuration, there is progress in linking the configurations to organizational performance. Two of the ideal types (Directive and Adaptive) have been demonstrated to be high performers, and the third (Responsive) a good performer in a regulated environment. Thus we find there are multiple paths to high organizational performance supporting the equifinality assumption that an organization can reach a same final state from differing initial conditions and by a variety of paths (Katz and Kahn 1978; Van de Ven and Drazin 1985).

And finally, in taking a configurational approach to public management, managers would do well to remember that the component parts of each ideal configuration, summarized in Table 1, "fit" together. Fit—"the consistency across multiple dimension of organizational design and context"—reveals the extent to which organizational components are mutually reinforcing and compatible (Doty, Glick, and Huber 1993, 1201). When the components fit and are patterned after a configuration's ideal, the organization is expected to be a high performer; deviations from ideal types perform less well. Therefore, when undertaking change projects, public managers would be advised to consider how well the anticipated changes fit with their organization's current configuration. Wholesale adoption of techniques because they are promoted as "good business practice" from the private sector, without consideration of configurational fit, risks misaligning the organization and its component parts. Before the launching of organizational change, it would be prudent to ask: What configuration best describes my current organization? Which configuration would be ideal for my organization? Do the changes I champion move me closer to the ideal? Introducing change without addressing these questions runs the risk of reducing rather than improving organizational performance.

Notes

1. In earlier representations of the four configurations, the Responsive Configuration was titled the Reactive or the Reactive/Political Configuration (Roberts 1995). The name has been changed to avoid any negative bias implied by the terms "reactive" and "political" and to underscore the positive aspects of the configuration.
2. I am indebted to Bradley and Pribram (1996) for their distinction between efficiency (internal operations) and effectiveness (external adaptation).

Chapter 13

Dissecting the Black Box: Toward a Model and Measures of Government Management Performance

Patricia W. Ingraham and Amy E. Kneedler
Syracuse University

Introduction

This chapter presents a model that can serve as a theoretical framework for evaluation of government management, a sphere of assessment that has mystified scholars, public managers, and government reformers alike. The model is the centerpiece of the Government Performance Project, an initiative of the Alan K. Campbell Public Affairs Institute at Syracuse University funded by the Pew Charitable Trusts. The Government Performance Project seeks to address three important questions for government and its constituents: First, how well do governments perform? Second, how does public management relate to performance? Third, can public management and government performance be improved? The ultimate goal of the project is to create and apply measures of the ability of public entities to effectively translate resources into desired outcomes.

To pursue research into the performance of government entities, it is necessary to address directly the key intervening variable in the classic performance equation that relates resources to results. This key variable is government management, an element traditionally dismissed as a somewhat mysterious "black box." The black box characterization has developed because, while most would agree that government management in utilizing resources also influences policy results, few have attempted rigorous analysis of what government management involves and how it operates. That is, we really do not know very much about what is inside the box. In this chapter, we begin to dissect the black box by proposing a model of government performance and discussing approaches to measuring management effectiveness.

The proposed model specifies the key relationships between overall policy performance (the ultimate results of government action) and government management performance (the degree to which a public entity's administration is effective). The model further demonstrates how government management is underpinned by particular component systems, or management subsystems, that may be analyzed. We propose that there exist four key distinct but interrelated management subsystems: financial management, human resources management, information technology management, and capital management. We further believe that these subsystems can be integrated in an overall ability to lead and manage public organizations for results and, therefore, to link management quality to the overall performance of governments.

Here, we first set the stage for our model through a brief review of the literature to illustrate the gaps left by studies that attempt to understand government behavior in policy implementation without accounting for the character and impact of public management. We then present a new model of government performance and identify targets for research. Finally, we address some possible approaches to empirical measurement of management effectiveness.[1]

The Tradition of Approaches

The merit of public management research turns on the question of whether the effectiveness of public management can be related to overall policy performance. Above, we referred to the classical policy-performance equation that relates resources to results, where resources are inputs into the black box of public management, wherein processes transform the inputs and produce results as the outputs of policy. In this model, represented in Figure 1, public management is an assumed mechanism—an administrative apparatus that traditionally has not been well specified. Historically, it is this model that is implicit throughout much of the academic concern with government performance, from the classical public administration orthodoxy, which viewed the administrative apparatus as neutral and straightforward, onward. Under the guise of scientific management, the business of public management was reduced to the optimally efficient translation of men and materiel into outputs and thus lacked substantive impact on performance (Goodnow 1900).

At least since the mid-1940s, though, American public administration has rejected the idea that administration is a neutral actor in the public policy process, as captured by Norton Long's declaration

Figure 1. The Classical Policy-Performance Equation

that "the lifeblood of administration is power" (Long 1949, 257). Policy analysts in the 1960s and 1970s recognized the fallacy of the neutral administration construct but still considered public management as relatively unimportant in the performance equation. Standards of rationality and economic efficiency dominated this field, and thus, the relative amounts of inputs and outputs, measured in terms of cost and utility, were the focus of attention. To the extent that management received any attention, it was through limited and simplistic inclusion of size- and structure-related variables such as size of budget, number of personnel, or degree of centralization or decentralization (Peters and Heisler 1983). The views of more contemporary thinkers have served to dispel this attitude, as exemplified by Donald Kettl's recent assertion that "public management matters, and it matters because the quality of public management shapes the performance of public programs" (Kettl and Milward 1996, 1). The question this assertion begs is How?

The standing of public management as an operational element in performance suffered blows from another quarter with the emergence of early policy implementation literature, which saw the administrative apparatus as a source of multiple veto points and thus an obstacle to the success of government policies (O'Toole and Montjoy 1984). Pressman and Wildavsky (1984) and many others have argued that in the movement from policy adoption to policy output, public management, operating in a local context dominated by powerful political factors, has the ability to shape, distort, and sometimes redefine policy goals in ways that are important, often negative, and essentially unpredictable. Earlier implementation analyses thus recognized that something about management matters, but there is little in their case-analytic findings that specifies what that is.

The emerging "third-generation" implementation literature addresses some of these issues. It suggests that lack of "connectedness"—common purpose, communication, and integration—across units of government and public organizations poses significant problems for implementation (O'Toole 1996; Provan and Milward 1995). Policy design research has also revealed that clarity of purpose and of objectives is centrally important (Schneider and Ingram 1997; Meier and McFarlane 1995; Hogwood and Peters 1985). Integration, clarity, and communication therefore surface as central variables in several bodies of policy research.

Thus, even though scholars have generally analyzed the black box in simplistic or unidimensional terms, there is ample support in recent literature for the idea that management is a key and complex component in the policy-performance equation. There are two primary sets of literature that are now actively engaged in exploring important related questions. These two areas, the development and applications of principal-agent theory and the studies of interorganizational networks, will be considered briefly as important context for our model.

Agency Theory and Management Performance

Principal-agent theories include several variations on a formal model of bureaucracy attributed to Niskanen (1971) that attempt to predict bureaucratic behavior under specific sets of assumptions, the most common of which involve the characterization of individuals as rational actors seeking to maximize their utility within dyadic exchange relationships. In their simplest form, these models cast the legislature as a unitary principal who seeks to ensure that its agent, the public bureaucracy, acts to fulfill the principal's intent. This relationship is fundamentally problematic because the principal lacks information about the agent's abilities, preferences, and behavior.

Three aspects of these models are salient in the policy-performance equation. The first is their concern with the "moral hazard" problem, driven by the inability of the principal to observe the agent's action (Bendor 1990), which threatens the legislature's ability to ensure that bureau performance is aligned with policy goals and which undergirds the issue of managerial control. A second important factor is that the principal cannot fully specify and direct the actions of the agent but instead provides broad guidance, leaving the agent to design programmatic details—exactly the quandary identified by early analyses of implementation. Third, these models implicitly depend on the question of what determines organizational effectiveness and thus are shaped by the nature of the mechanisms by which policy is implemented and objectives are pursued. Hence, agency theory is pertinent to understanding public management and performance because of its central concern with controlling and directing bureaucracies to accomplish desired outcomes.

Agency theory has met with sharp criticism largely because the predictive power of the models is very sensitive to changes in the character of the assumptions involved. Worsham, Ringquist, and Eisner (1997) argue that agency theory is excessively simplified and reminiscent of early implementation research. They suggest alternatives that could make the theory more realistic, such as consideration of multiple principals and agents contending with many, often vague and sometimes conflicting, policy dimensions within a complex web of relationships. Many critics also assert that the role of institutions, thus far neglected by principal-agent models, must become a focus of analysis. Along these lines, Terry Moe claims that the most serious difficulty of the postulated principal-agent relationships is that they portray government bureaucracies "as black boxes that mysteriously mediate between interests and outcomes. The implicit claim is that institutions do not matter much" (1987, 475). Moe (1991a, 1991b) asserts that institutional arrangements and organizational factors are, in fact, of prime importance. In short, the agency models' descriptive and explanatory power is diminished because the rich complexity within and across public agencies is ignored when bureaucracy is treated as a rational, homogenous monolith.

We add a criticism of our own to the chorus of calls for agency models more reflective of reality. A significant limitation to the way public institutions are represented in most formal models is that the impact of government management on policy performance is ignored, if not implicitly denied. We speculate not only that organizational arrangements and factors are significant but that the nature of public management contributes powerfully to the effectiveness with which public agents are able to translate principals' intents into outcomes. A variation on the principal-agent relationship that accounts for management—that is, one that acknowledges and incorporates specification of the intervening variable in the policy/performance equation—would yield a more accurate and productive portrayal of bureaucratic behavior and influence.

Interorganizational Networks and Integration

The dominant focus of the literature on networks traditionally has been from two perspectives: resource dependence and transaction cost economics, which focus on the organizational-level outcomes that derive from network involvement but which give little attention to the performance of the network as a whole system (Provan and Milward 1995). Moreover, much of the research has focused on the structural aspects of networks rather than on the managerial problems that arise under interorganizational circumstances and constraints (Mandell 1990). Also, study of interorganizational networks often rests on variations of principal-agent theory to explain organizational behavior, and thus meaningful predictions of network behavior can be limited by the assumptions of rational models (O'Toole 1996).

Emerging now in the interorganizational network literature is a recognition that a focus on organizations as the units of analysis is insufficient because the performance we seek to understand requires a sense of the cooperative strategy of the entire network and of the development and achievement of common objectives based on this larger whole (Provan and Milward 1995; Mandell 1990; Porter 1990). This new focus represents expansion in the conceptual foundations of this scholarship from an atomistic perspective on the components of organizational effectiveness to a broader view of the dimensions of network performance.

Implicitly, the notion of integration, both as a means of arranging and coordinating service provision and as a deeper concept that describes the nature of operational, managerial, political, and even social linkages within and among organizations, is becoming central. Provan and Milward, in their preliminary theory of network effectiveness, cite integration as a key factor and assert that "the basic building block of any network study is the linkages among the organizations that make up the network" (1995, 10). Reduced fragmentation, greater coordination, and minimized duplication are among the advantages they hypothesize result from integration in the context of service provision through a linked network. We suspect that these benefits may accrue from integration generally, including integration of management systems across an organization or a government. This holistic view that networks comprise a number of actors working as a cohesive whole to achieve an overall purpose also introduces the need for strategic leadership and management to develop, communicate, and effect a comprehensive vision for the larger system. Again, the relevance of this view of strategic leadership and management to coordinating administrative systems across agencies and within governments is clear.

The state of interorganizational scholarship hints at an emerging empirical relationship between the study of policy implementation by public agencies, the refinement of formal models of bureaucracy, and the development of theories of integrated service network behavior and effectiveness. At this stage, however, the progress and convergence of these fields are hampered by limited treatment of the role and nature of management in the overall performance of these public systems. No doubt the importance of public management has not simply been overlooked. Rather, the absence of a framework for understanding and measuring management effectiveness has probably caused these factors to be omitted. One potential contribution of the model we propose here is to inform other fields of research in which management is likely to be a critical ingredient.

The Performance Model

In this section, we propose a model that describes the key relationships inherent in government management. We present the model in three stages. First, we identify the assumptions on which the model is based. Next, we locate government management in the policy system. Finally, we focus in more detail on three dimensions of government management that affect government's ability to be effective: the management subsystems, the degree of integration, and a system of managing for results. In particular, we note the significance of factors such as leadership, information, resources, and organizational learning for management.

Assumptions

Our model is based on a foundation of assumptions that are widely accepted, but relatively untested and somewhat controversial. The base assumption is that management matters in the overall performance of government—that is, effective management is positively related to effective performance. A multitude of prescriptions for performance enhancement in both the private and public sectors depend on this assumption, and public administration and public management have attempted to base disciplines on it. In the literature of these fields, though, there has been little development of formal, empirical linkages between government's management capability and the performance of public entities. This presumed association can be ignored no longer. Discussions about the nature of effectiveness and reform efforts aimed at improved performance are integral to contemporary debates about the continuing role of government in society—and thus rigorous analysis of and prescriptions to improve government performance must also consider the thorny issue of how to assess government management.

A second assumption is that effective management is fundamentally concerned with the extent to which the various functions of management are performed within and contribute to a holistic management system, a concept we follow network theorists in characterizing as the degree of integration. We mentioned in the introduction to this chapter that management is composed of distinct component systems that have typically been considered as separate functions, a legacy that has flowed from early twentieth-century conceptions of public administration. We argue that good management depends not only on the good performance of each of these systems independently, but particularly on the extent to which these management subsystems are marshaled around consistent objectives, are mutually enabling, and are well coordinated. In short, management systems in combination, not isolation, create the heretofore unmeasured concept of effective management.

Finally, we assume that sound leadership has a positive influence on effective management and thus on overall government performance. We argue that leadership contributes to each management subsystem but is most significant in its alignment of these systems within a coherent and cohesive administrative framework. Here the notion of vision commonly identified in the leadership literature emerges to frame mission, consequent goals and objectives, and organizational and societal values together within a broader purpose. The linkage between leadership and performance manifests itself in the extent to which leadership operates through formal, systemic performance-based activities.

In addition to these assumptions, it is important to note that this model specifically emphasizes performance, a concept assigned various definitions and connotations in the literature. Two distinct types of performance are implicit in this model. The first is policy performance, which is how the outputs of public institutions are felt by society as outcomes and which is the ultimate dependent variable in the model. Here performance refers to the degree to which obligations and requirements are fulfilled as promised or expected. Normatively good performance thus connotes successful achievement of stated objectives. The second is management performance, which refers to administrative effectiveness or how well public entities accomplish their administrative functions.

The Big Picture: Government Management in the Policy System

The "big picture" of the relationship between government management performance and overall policy performance is portrayed in Figure 2. From this perspective, it can be seen that our model elaborates on the classical conceptualization in which resources and policy are transformed by public administrative institutions into outcomes. In the model presented here, government management is the intervening variable in the policy-performance equation. As such, it drives policy performance and is influenced by several factors, including politics, policy direction, available resources, and environmental factors. Management, in turn, fundamentally comprises management subsystems—financial management, human resources management, information technology management, and capital management.

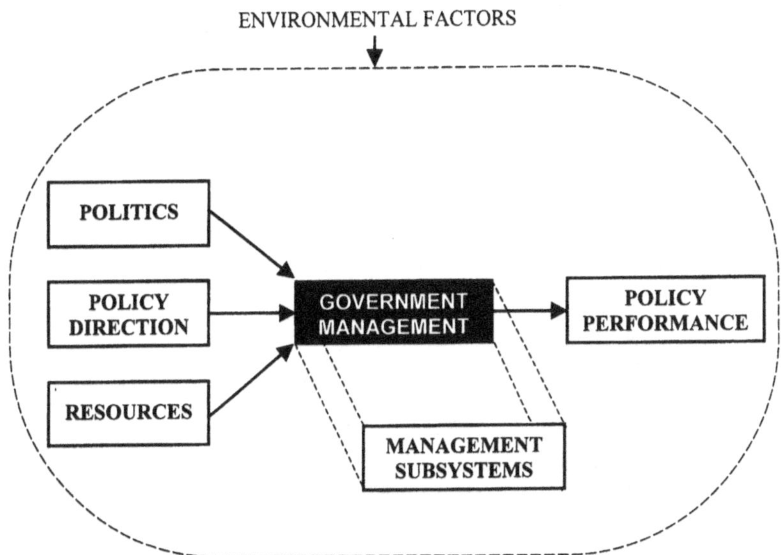

Figure 2. The New Performance Model—Government Management in the Policy System

We note explicitly that a variety of environmental factors affect all components in the government performance system. Most recent implementation and urban finance literature recognizes the dramatic impact that local conditions can have on the character of programs, their outcomes, and thus policy performance. While these factors are considered exogenous to this model, as Figure 2 shows, they embody a broad array of influences, including properties of the larger context within which the government operates and properties of the government's jurisdiction, such as socioeconomic conditions, demographic characteristics, and the physical environment. It is easy to see that environmental factors might affect public management subsystems. Human resources management, for example, is likely to be affected by demographic characteristics such as the size and qualifications of the available labor pool. Capital management would likely be affected by the physical environment and factor markets.

A Closer Look: The Dimensions of Management

We have identified three fundamental dimensions to management capacity. The first is the set of management subsystems, presumed common to almost all government settings, that embody the intrinsic administrative activities of governments. The second is the set of

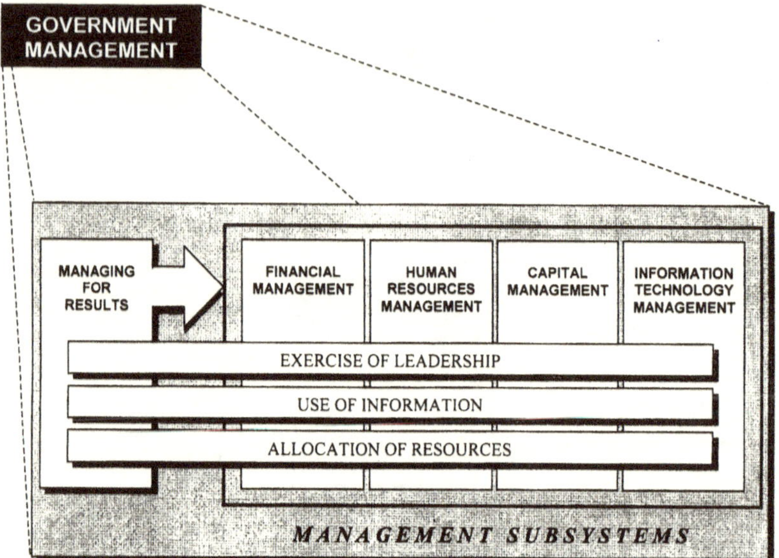

Figure 3. The New Performance Model—The Dimensions of Management

integrating factors that facilitate the orchestration of these management subsystems in a coherent totality. The third is the existence of a formal managing-for-results system that lends a substantial framework to organizational learning processes. An ideal type of the relationship among these dimensions is shown in Figure 3. Each dimension is discussed in turn below.

Dimension No. 1: The Management Subsystems

There is widespread agreement—as evidenced by the tables of contents of mainstream public administration texts—that there are several core administrative functions that all governments perform. This perspective undoubtedly emerged from the work of Weber (1946) and Taylor (1911) and most prominently from Gulick's classic POSDCORB typology (1937) but also reflects more contemporary thought. For example, Rosenbloom (1989), in his discussion of the practice of public administration, devotes significant attention to the core functions of budgeting and human resources management. Cohen and Eimicke (1995) additionally include gathering, organizing, and using information as a key managerial tool in the public sector. We conclude that for most governments and for most policy areas, four broad core systems are likely to be present. The characteristics of the subsystems that underpin government management are summarized below.

Financial management. Government financial management systems distribute and manage money for public purposes through processes such as procurement, accounting, cash management, and reporting. Financial management includes both budget allocation and budget execution systems. A financial management system that supports performance must determine the appropriate level of resources, allocate those resources according to strategic priorities, and spend money effectively and accountably. Key components of the effectiveness of the financial management subsystem include the ability to engage in accurate revenue and expenditure forecasting, a long-term focus, the practice of planning for contingencies, awareness of the linkage between cost and performance, and appropriate flexibility (Meyers 1996).

Human resources management. Government activities are typically highly personnel intensive. Thus, personnel systems, concerned with recruiting, retaining, motivating, training, and terminating public employees, are a key element of public institutions. Key components of the effectiveness of the human resources management subsystem include: the use of coherent rules and procedures, efforts at workforce planning, timely hiring, sufficient professional development programs, and meaningful reward structures and disciplinary actions. Because increased flexibility in the human resources management process has been a consistent focus of administrative reform, it is also important to consider where in the system and for whom such flexibility occurs.

Capital management. Capital management involves planning for, maintaining, and disposing of long-lived resources. This area is particularly salient for state and local governments where capital spending and stock management demands are typically more frequent than in federal agencies, although many federal agencies have large capital responsibilities. Key components of the effectiveness of the capital management subsystem include: active engagement in long-range planning and prioritization of projects, adequate budgetary resources for infrastructure maintenance and repair, and attention to the relationship between capital and operating budgets.

Information technology management. The quality and availability of information are crucial to the ability of managers and policymakers to make decisions and carry out the key functions of resource acquisition and policy implementation. Managing information technology includes the development, maintenance, and use of technological systems to collect, analyze, and communicate data. Especially in public institutions responsible for executing complicated programs and interfacing with large, diverse constituencies, information technology performs both primary and integrative functions. It not only responds to information demands particular to specific programs but also supports the information needs of the other management subsystems. Key components of the effectiveness of the information technology management subsystem include: the timeliness, accuracy, reliability, usefulness, and cost-effectiveness of data and the ability of all personnel to use the information systems.

Dimension No. 2: Integration

Within the context of government management, the relationships among the management subsystems just described and their contribution to management effectiveness are influenced by the degree of integration: the extent to which the management subsystems are orchestrated as part of a unified, cohesive whole with shared values, common goals, aligned objectives, and mutually supporting tasks. We suggest that integration is primarily accomplished through three key activities: the exercise of leadership, the use of information, and the strategic allocation of resources.

Exercise of leadership. In the realm of government management, leadership is driven by the ability of senior executive, appointed, and career officials to make decisions; to provide guidance and direction; to develop the institution's mission, vision, and values and communicate them to all its members; and to coordinate the behavior of all organizational components and subsystems to behave in a manner consistent with the institutional and broader public values to achieve the stated mission and ultimately to realize the policymakers' intent. The extent to which coherence across management systems and the capacity to move constructively toward public goals and objectives is achieved depends on leadership at both the political and executive levels, which presents a "duality of leadership" problem in most public organizations: elected and appointed officials formally lead the government but those in the career civil service also have an executive leadership function (Ingraham 1995). This issue is directly relevant to the analysis of the dimensions of management proposed here because political leadership provides one critical set of directions, resources, and supports for system creation and maintenance. Political leadership generally does not, however, interact specifically or consistently with the management systems we propose to analyze. Leadership of those systems is the responsibility of a different set of leaders: those located within the organizations. Successful interaction between these two sets of leaders both creates an overall vision for the governments and the management systems that support them and drives coherent, well-supported movement toward achieving this vision.

Use of information. The freedom, consistency, and speed with which managers cause information to flow throughout a government, the attention that managers give data, and the willingness of managers to share knowledge converge to facilitate or thwart the overall integration of the management subsystems. While the information technology management subsystem, a mechanism concerned with the collection and availability of timely and accurate data, supports the transmission and use of information, it is the interaction of government managers with information that can enable the management subsystems to operate in concert.

Allocation of resources. The decisions managers make about how resources will be generated and distributed across a government and the activities that facilitate this decision-making process influence the extent to which the management subsystems are configured to be mutually supporting. The classic example of such activity is the budget process, whereby managers negotiate over how money will be allocated; this process fundamentally communicates the collective perception of the government's goals and priorities. Another example is the location of capable human capital throughout the government. While such processes as recruiting and hiring personnel are the purview of the human resources management system, the placement of people at key points of intersection among the management subsystems affects the degree of cohesion in the system as a whole.

Dimension No. 3: Managing for Results

The dimension of managing for results concerns the extent to which a formalized system of performance management that facilitates a trend of improving effectiveness is present. Managing for results is the dominant mechanism by which leaders identify, collect, and use the information necessary to evaluate the institution's performance in pursuit of identified objectives, to make decisions, and to direct institutional actions. It is composed of a set of tools by which organizational learning processes are formalized. It is thus an important managerial function for leaders who seek to improve the ability of the management subsystems to support overall institutional behavior and ultimately to contribute to successful policy outcomes.

Governments that are managed for results focus continually on discovering the most effective ways of achieving their objectives. Such a results orientation rests on two vital components. The first is the ability to identify clear objectives. The second is a means to assess progress toward those objectives according to accepted criteria or standards, a mechanism often referred to as performance measurement. In addition to these components, a government's ability to manage effectively is driven by the characteristics and degree of integration of the management subsystems in that fully integrated governments are characterized by management subsystems that collectively influence management effectiveness via the presence of an interactive relationship between the management subsystems and the managing-for-results system, as shown in Figure 3. The vehicle for this interaction is the same set of forces that serve to integrate the management subsystems. In other words, the exercise of leadership, the use of information, and the allocation of resources all serve to bind performance assessment to administrative functions.

Toward a Methodology

Much of the above discussion has a commonsense we-have-always-known-that quality. In one sense, that is true. Several of the linkages outlined above have been assumed to exist, or have been tested in isolation from other parts of the performance model we propose here. Government management thus has been analyzed in simplistic or unidimensional terms, usually via size- and structure-related variables.[2] In addition, two crucial dilemmas confront analysis of government management. The first is that measuring effectiveness is arduous because goals are vague, multiple, or conflicting; are interpreted and prioritized differently by different actors; and differentially affect a variety of constituents. Even when goals are clearly identifiable, outcomes are commonly affected by environmental factors.

The study of interorganizational networks discussed above raises a second methodological issue that researchers of government management are likely to confront. The crux of the challenge arises from a fundamental assumption made by network theorists, analogous to our assumption that management matters to performance, that the structure and level of integration of the interorganizational system influence service outcomes. This assumption implies that effectiveness must be assessed at the network level, rather than at the level of subordinate organizations, to measure/assess overall outcomes. Similarly, governments, not their subordinate agencies, are the appropriate units of analysis in studies of management performance. Unfortunately, as Provan and Milward point out, effectiveness of complex systems is difficult to measure and there exists little "empirical evidence to support the presumed relationship between integration and network effectiveness or to indicate what network characteristics are associated with effective outcomes" (1995, 4).

Provan and Milward (1995) employed what they termed a "multimeasure, multiperspective" approach to address these challenges in their study of community mental health systems. They collected and aggregated both qualitative and quantitative data at several levels of analysis and attempt to explain network outcomes from the perspectives of several separate sets of actors in the system. Despite some important limitations, their discussion does suggest that comprehensive, multifaceted study is more revelatory in the examination of complex, integrated systems than more unitary approaches are likely to be. We, like Provan and Milward, propose to employ a multimeasure, multiperspective approach in the context of the Government Performance Project that will allow us access to both the nature of each separate management subsystem and its contribution to overall management capacity and the nature and consequences of integrative linkages among these subsystems.

Two very different options were initially available to the project and its designers. One option was to begin with prescribed principles of performance, or guidelines for attaining a prescribed performance behavior or level. There are examples of such an approach: the Osborne and Gaebler (1992) principles for reinventing government is one. The simplicity and rigidity of such an approach, however, risks subjecting governments and government agencies to a one-size-fits-all set of standards and principles. While there are certainly some uniform management principles, what constitutes good management probably differs profoundly depending on the setting.

The option we have chosen for the Government Performance Project is more derivative. It is based on a general consensus among academics and practitioners that several different management systems need to be examined if important performance levers are to be identified. Thus the project is proceeding in two stages. Our initial effort focuses on identifying and measuring the dimensions of management performance. In short, the research first addresses the middle of the policy-performance equation in an effort to specify the administrative black box. Later work proposes to test the relationship between managerial and policy performance.

Certainly, there are significant methodological and measurement concerns associated with this research. In this chapter, we have attempted to develop a theory of government management and to specify correctly the key relationships in this model. We have not tackled the admittedly complex details of how to pursue valid empirical analysis, but we would like to mention three areas to which empirical study of government management must attend. One obvious conundrum is the choice of valid criteria by which to assess the dimensions of management. Since the goal is to understand management holistically, not each individual management process in isolation, inquiry must focus on how each management subsystem enables or constrains the government's overall ability to accomplish its mission, goals, and objectives. Criteria must be oriented toward discerning the efficacy of the management subsystems, the aspects of integration, and managing for results.

Another important question is how to differentiate the activities of high-performing government from average behavior. Certainly one of the aims of public management research is to reveal what governments that are well managed do differently from those that are not. We propose that the characteristics of the management subsystems discussed above can yield measures that will help capture these differences. One innovative statistical technique for making distinctions according to level of performance using quantitative data is substantively weighted least squares (SWLS), as proposed by Meier and Keiser (1996) and developed further by Meier, Gill, and Waller (2000). SWLS is an analytical tool based on iterative use of weighted least squares regression that allows high-performing cases to be distinguished from average performers. Because of its potential to indicate not only which cases are high performers, but also along what dimensions and how dramatically they vary from the average performers, the SWLS technique may be a valuable tool for analysis of the quantitative data gathered in this project. It is also a good example of the kind of analysis we seek to accomplish—analysis that tells both us and the participants in the study what is unique about successful results-based management.[3]

A remaining—and fundamental—problem is that our initial focus proceeds in the absence of the policy-performance equation's traditional dependent variable, outputs/outcomes. Instead, we initially treat management itself as the dependent variable, despite lacking quantitative measures. We argue, however, that the dimensions of management may be examined via comparative analysis across governments and time, which would address directly one of the most consistent methodological problems of public management research: the inability to draw generalizations and to develop theory from case studies.

Conclusion

Ultimately, we seek to understand the relationship between management performance and policy performance. As governments move toward greater emphasis on results, they and the publics they serve inevitably focus on what contributes to good performance and what does not. Indeed, most modern reform efforts seek to improve public performance. At the same time, there is widespread recognition that many factors with a direct or indirect impact on performance are beyond the control of public organizations and their leaders. Elections matter; economic, social, and physical conditions matter; media definition of issues matters; the scope, scale, and perception of policy problems matter. These critical influences, however, cannot or should not be controlled by public organizations. On the other hand, the systems within and across governments for managing resources and translating them into public services are substantially influenced by public organizations. If we are to identify malleable components of the public performance equation, therefore, the quality of management and the subsystems that underpin it must be front and center. As Goggin et al. have said, "A sophisticated understanding of organizational capacity and its subtle influences on policy implementation would require descriptions of virtually the whole gamut of administration, from financial management to motivation, from information systems to affirmative action plans and their impact on the workplace" (1990, 120).

This model responds to the call for rigorous analysis of government management systems. It facilitates assessment of the contribution of public management to policy outcomes by providing a theoretical framework for cross-system, cross-government, inter government, and cross-time comparisons. Moreover, it supports both quantitative and qualitative analysis to permit conclusions that are richly descriptive and broadly revelatory. Substantively, this model can lend realistic detail to formal models of bureaucracy by disclosing the complexity and strength of the influence of management on organizational control and effectiveness. It can demonstrate the contribution of management dimensions to the ability of government to fulfill its policy promises through implementation. It can bolster the study of interorganizational networks by explaining how the concept of integration operates to orient multiple institutions toward common objectives. It can also further the field of public management itself by specifying the dimensionality of performance-based activity in government settings.

This work tackles head-on one of the most troublesome and enduring dilemmas of public management research—the issue of the character, role, and impact of government management. We seek finally to shed bright light on the answers to two very difficult questions: What goes on inside the black box? and How does it matter? The challenges inherent in exploring this challenging frontier of public management are unquestionably formidable, but the potential to expand significantly the common body of public management knowledge is sufficient reward to warrant this expedition.

Notes

1. The authors are very grateful to Jeffrey Brudney, Kenneth Meier, H. Brinton Milward, Laurence O'Toole, Mark Robbins, Saundra Schneider, Jeffrey Straussman, and particularly our colleague Philip Joyce for their helpful and incisive comments on earlier drafts of this chapter.
2. We do not mean to discount the influence that structure may have on the performance of public organizations. Moreover, in network settings, structure within and among organizations—or lack thereof—may have a significant role. As Laurence O'Toole has pointed out to us, structure is likely to affect the degree to which managers can have impacts on performance, particularly in network settings. He also acknowledged the difficulty of isolating the independent effects of structure from management, an important consideration in our quest to specify the impact of management capacity.
3. Kenneth Meier suggests that the development and application of SWLS proceeds, in part, from the notion that there are important intervening components missing from the classical public performance model. SWLS is a technique that may help to specify leadership and management behavior in the updated conception of management and policy performance that we propose here.

Chapter 14

Concluding Perspectives

Jeffrey L. Brudney, Laurence J. O'Toole, Jr., and Hal G. Rainey
The University of Georgia

At the close of this book, titled *Advancing Public Management*, it is appropriate that we consider in what sense the contents of the book may suggest in fact such an "advancing" of public management. This perspective emerges in the three distinct senses of the phrase.

First, the contributions in this book document clearly a number of lines along which scholars have made advances in research. As a result of the work represented here, we now know considerably more about public management. Sometimes, to be sure, that knowledge is far from complete and may even border on the frustrating. Indeed, one of the points emerging from several of the chapters is that it is crucial to frame the key questions about public management clearly and appropriately, whether those queries pertain to the relationship between agency culture and management, or how to identify the exemplar cases from which those interested in public management should learn lessons for "best practices", or how and to what effect public management can be reformed or reinvented.

The introductory essay of this volume charted some of the paths of advancement, as did the section clusters organizing the contents of the book. We comment briefly on these below. Others are identifiable from the chapters, even if not explicitly communicated through the overt structure of the volume. We mention a few of these in this essay. The general point is that the authors in this book, as well as many others at the conference, have made important advances in framing systematic and significant questions about public management and in beginning to find answers to them.

Second, scholarly understanding of public management is also advancing into the future. This volume not only documents recent progress in research, it also presages some likely and promising courses for the coming years. This concluding chapter also includes a consideration of this issue and mentions trajectories for future research that promise to be worthwhile in the years ahead.

Third, the kinds of research represented in this book carry implications for how to improve the practice of public management. Advancing public management in practice, then, is another sense in which the contributions in this volume should be assessed. Here, this chapter and the book speak less directly. A review of the chapters, however, indicates that most of the scholars included here would agree on the one central assertion that advancements in scholarship and research carry key implications for the practicing public manager.

This point might seem obvious, but the issue is tricky. As Bozeman (1993) has pointed out, there can be dangers in a research approach to the field that adheres too closely to today's immediate practical needs, the set of burning issues and challenges that fill the calendars and occupy the short-term agendas of most managers. But as the contributions to this volume attest, accepting this point by no means entails an antiseptic, ivory tower approach to scholarship. Many of the researchers whose work is included here have public managerial experience, and all frame their work in terms of what they regard as today's—and tomorrow's—pressing challenges for public management, in practice as well as in theory.

These "advances" must occur at least roughly in tandem for the joint enterprise to be worthwhile. And many of the themes expressed and emphasized in individual chapters—whether on the importance of managers' considering how to frame issues for broader political decision, or on what sense practitioners might make of the welter of efforts to reinvent government, or on what kinds of models might be needed for achieving different managerial objectives—echo this general theme. The best scholarship on public management is not constrained and controlled by the immediate needs on the front lines of management in government but should offer insights and findings that carry implications for altering and improving practice over the longer haul. This characteristic applies to the work in this book.

The volume suggests, therefore, several *kinds* of advancements. As indicated above, rather than attempting a comprehensive integration of the contributions of this book, we leave it to the separate chapters to offer on their own a considerable variety of conclusions and implications. And even the crosscutting themes are manifold. We select a few of these, nonetheless, for brief exposition.

It is useful to begin with the explicit frames of reference sketched by the volume's overall organization: the impact of public management, developments in methodology, the theme of reform, and novel frameworks.

The first section of this volume asks a crucial question: in government, does management matter? In so doing, the contributions here also raise the key related question: what are the scope and bounds of public management? While adopting a properly cautious stance—for, after all, public management is not the *whole* of governance, and a number of sources of influence over performance are not in managers' hands—the authors of these chapters portray with clarity a broad array of possibilities for managerial impact. While managers do not mold the clay of agency culture in some simple and dominant fashion, as Khademian shows, and while issues of complexity and measurement make it most difficult to show conclusively the extent of managerial influence, as O'Toole argues, management has considerable potential for shaping what government actually delivers. Hammond and Knott even suggest the significant range of discretion for political executives in policymaking itself that derives, perhaps ironically, from the apparent surplus of "principals" (i.e., influential actors and authorities) in a U.S.-style separation-of-powers regime. Most generally of all, Lynn indicates the multiple directions in which managerial influence can be exercised. Similarly, the volume shows, as Lynn also suggests, that both short-run and long-run channels of influence are important to consider.

The coverage of the nature and extent of public managerial impact suggests as well a variety of important lines of research activity to be pursued into the future: from studies of culture and management, to further refinements and new approaches to modeling the ways management matters, to considering the interactive impact of management and context. The contributions also imply a set of heuristics for practicing managers. Note the leveraging opportunities available to managers operating in networked settings, for instance, and consider the kinds of interactive effects skillful management can have by working via the multiple managerial subsystems sketched by Ingraham and Kneedler.

It has long been commonplace to observe that we need new kinds of tools, measures, research designs, and approaches to inquiry if we are to unpack the many complexities of public management. Some in the past have claimed that public administration, in particular, and also public management have sorely needed to embrace methodological developments generated in other fields of social science. The articles in this book—certainly including but not merely limited to those in Part II—provide clear evidence of methodological vigor. Scholarship on public management not only *reflects* the advancements in other disciplines but is itself *contributing* to the effort to move social science forward to explore key questions for the future.

This assertion does not amount to a naive claim of a relentless, neatly converging, ever-accumulating mountain of evidence. In fact the readings mirror a number of the unsettled methodological and epistemological questions of the social sciences more generally: qualitative versus quantitative inquiry, behavioral versus interpretive research, inductive versus formal and deductive strategies. But the contributions are not mired in sterile and sectarian disputes. Rather, for all their differences they suggest a common perspective at a broader level: to get busy with the important questions facing researchers (Rainey 1993); to use methods appropriate to the questions at issue and the data available; to treat seriously the requirements for replicability and clarity of exposition; and to craft designs and tools to understand public management with the ultimate aim of contributing to its improvement in the future. Empirical research in the service of substantively and practically significant questions is the common ground.

In this regard, and given this basis for exploration, the contributors offer applications of diverse techniques and designs, some quite innovative. The agenda of Meier, Gill, and Waller is no less than a union of rigor and managerial utility and the development of a markedly new set of techniques to help do the job. Further, the contribution of Maynard-Moody and Leland shows how outmoded some of the old methodological quarrels have become. For the research of these scholars is both interpretive in its epistemology—the investigation, after all, treats the stories of front-line public servants seriously—and also scientific in its design and execution. The work, in fact, was supported by the National Science Foundation, a relative rarity for even the most methodologically sophisticated public management scholarship.

Once again, many of the articles beyond the section on methodological frontiers reflect similar features. Ingraham and Kneedler's chapter, for example, describes a large research program that illustrates this point. They present an interesting model of public management capacity in their chapter in this book. The model guides their development of multiple methods to measure and score the relative management capacities of different agencies and government jurisdictions that they report elsewhere. (For some of the earliest results, see the February 1999 issues of *Governing* and of *Government Executive.*) The point is not to suggest that this set of essays necessarily constitutes the last, best word on methodology for public management scholarship. The evidence is strong, however, that while important questions and differences remain, a number of new and strikingly provocative approaches are under development. The subject of public management, happily, has attracted the right kind of attention and served as focus for a variety of fascinating efforts. The chapters just mentioned as well as others in this book demonstrate this point clearly.

And what of reform and all that? Should one conclude, as is so often observed on other subjects, *plus ça change, plus c'est la même chose*? The contributions of this book suggest, in effect, no. Reform and reinvention, along with related initiatives, have been consequential for public management as well as for the performance of governments. And some varieties of innovation are both inevitable and welcome. But calling for reform, as shown by Green, Jones, and Thompson along with Romzek and Johnston, is a far cry from getting it done. The success of such efforts is highly contingent on a set of variables that deserve attention from public managers as well as policymakers. Furthermore, as other analysts suggest, those interested in reform would do well to broaden their perspectives: outward, to the experiences in other nations as Thompson emphasizes; and conceptually, to sort and clarify the huge set of related but differentiable kinds of reform approaches and intents, as McGregor argues.

Once again, innovation into the future is a concern transcending many other contributions of this collection. Meier, Gill, and Waller advance the major premise that when properly used, analysis can and should be a tool for improving public management. And Roberts frames her dissection of several approaches to management in terms of the kinds of challenges—and, often, needs for change—bearing down on the managers of today and tomorrow.

All these comments and crosscutting themes in turn suggest the value of new models and frameworks for the analysis and understanding of public management. The two readings in part IV of the book are suggestive on this topic, not definitive. And, just as obviously, the readings explicitly placed under this heading are accompanied by a number of other chapters that touch upon the same theme, from the formal models of Hammond and Knott to the consideration of quasi markets as a potentially important model for institutional arrangements of interest to public managers—a topic addressed by Thompson.

The ideas about models and frameworks sketched in this volume should serve as bases for further model building and testing in the years ahead. The potential for some may be great. Ingraham and Kneedler's model of management capacity, for instance, is certainly not immune to challenge. But this perspective is explicit, linked to streams of research stretching back for decades, important for future practice and theory building, and integrated into an ambitious and careful data-collection process that can pay dividends for a considerable period. It is just such efforts that can contribute broadly to the understanding of public management and the development of further model-building efforts. The results are likely to be payoffs that we can now only dimly imagine.

Additional themes, besides those explicitly identified by the structure of this volume, are also readily identifiable in the preceding pages. One already mentioned in this concluding essay is the appropriate mix of relevance and rigor throughout the volume. A feature that distinguishes this collection is its attention to advancing careful research on the subject of public management and its contribution to advancing the performance of public managers as they operate on the front lines of governance.

Another obvious topic of significance emphasized in several of the chapters is the importance of "networks" in contemporary public management. Two chapters (those by O'Toole and by Kingsley and Melkers) address the subject directly; others (particularly the chapter by Romzek and Johnston, and also to some extent the chapter by Thompson) do not frame the analysis in precisely these terms but nonetheless acknowledge and treat seriously the multiactor character of much of today's public management. Since a volume published following an earlier National Public Management Research Conference included a section and several articles focused explicitly on this topic (Kettl and Milward 1996), it should be clear that this theme has captured the attention of many scholars and serves as a productive organizing point for some of the most significant research underway in the field. We can expect further work along these lines to pay large returns.

Another striking feature of this set of contributions, taken as a whole, is the heterogeneity of actors and levels involved in the central issues and tasks of public management. From the front lines (see, most obviously, the chapter by Maynard-Moody and Leland) to the top political executives (as modeled by Hammond and Knott), a variety of actors—including, in some instances, many not formally part of the apparatus of government—are involved in significant ways with the challenges of public management. The research published in this book focuses analytical attention at the several levels of management itself: of organization, of cross-organizational arrays, and of governance. When considered in conjunction with the first-mentioned theme above—does public management matter?—one is struck by the expansive, almost daunting, terrain on which the subject must be considered. Public management issues and research questions appear from the bottom to the top of government and from the managerial issues within line public agencies, to the challenges of managing public programs in complicated multi-actor settings, to the politico-managerial agendas of governance. This heterogeneity, in turn, is both energizing and potentially stultifying: there remains much to learn, and in many venues. The research agenda, accordingly, must be complex and must remain open to assessment via diverse theoretical and methodological approaches.

This point is not a mere echo of Lynn's reminder, in his introduction to part I, of Mark Moore's (1995) point that the public management function entails efforts in multiple directions: upward, downward, and outward. Rather, public management—the coordination of people and other resources to achieve legitimate public objectives—involves actors in many locales, not just the apex of public agencies; and it likely entails a multiplicity of approaches. Finding patterns, robust generalizations, and reliable guidelines for informed action in the face of this heterogeneity, these together constitute the set of challenges facing public management scholars in advancing our understanding.

If this imposing agenda seems sobering, at least there is this: the effort is in the service of a worthy, even ennobling, objective. Consider that the evidence offered in this volume, data drawn from studies designed in a variety of ways and aimed at managerial efforts by an array of different actors functioning at diverse levels, offers a consistent conclusion on one supremely important topic: the general quality of public-managerial performance. The voluminous literature on public bureaucracy, developed in earlier decades as well as recently, is filled with often negative and sometimes contradictory images of managerial performance. Two pictures in particular stand out: that of the stodgy, inefficient apparatus on the one hand, and the aggressive and unaccountable machine on the other. The careful research contained in this volume, however, sketches a quite different portrait.

Public management faces challenges, to be sure, but it is quite possible to find systematic ways to identify optimal performers (as Meier, Gill, and Waller have suggested); or to discern evidence that even those on the front lines are occupied with a form of self-management in the cause of defensible principle (as Maynard-Moody and Leland inform us); or to document collaborative partnering initiatives in which managers play an important role (as Kingsley and Melkers show); or to see remarkable and suggestive signs of managerial initiative—in the best senses of that term—in the reinvention laboratories of a huge federal agency (an unmistakable point of Green, Jones, and Thompson).

The public management evidence in this book, evidence that can be useful in outlining the kinds of advancements necessary in the future, shows a range of performance, but also degrees of principled action, innovation, competence, and effectiveness that belie the stereotypes so frequently proffered. In the upcoming challenge to advance public management, in both practice and scholarship, this theme—perhaps above all—can sustain the effort.

Biographies of Authors

Jeffrey L. Brudney is Professor of Political Science and Director of the Doctor of Public Administration program at the University of Georgia. He is the author of *Fostering Volunteer Programs in the Public Sector: Planning, Initiating, and Managing Voluntary Activities* (Jossey-Bass, 1990), for which he received the John Grenzebach Award for Outstanding Research in Philanthropy for Education. Dr. Brudney has published a large number of journal articles and book chapters in the areas of public administration and the voluntary, nonprofit sector and is the coauthor (with Kenneth J. Meier) of *Applied Statistics for Public Administration* (fourth edition, Harcourt Brace, 1997). In 1994, Dr. Brudney was selected as a Fulbright Fellow to Canada, where he served on the faculty of York University (Toronto) in the Voluntary Sector Management Program, the leading center in that country for study and practice in the nonprofit sector.

Jeff Gill is Assistant Professor of Political Science at California Polytechnic State University. His research focuses on statistical theory and political methodology generally applied to topics in American politics. Publications include "The Insignificance of Null Hypothesis Significance Testing," "Tightwads and Spendthrifts: Measuring Fiscal Behavior in the Changing House of Representatives," "One Year and Four Elections: A Study of the 1998 Capps Campaign for California's 22nd District," and "Formal Models of Legislative/Administrative Interaction." He is the author of *Generalized Linear Models: A Unified Approach* (Sage, 1999), and with Kenneth J. Meier, *Substantively Weighted Analytical Techniques (SWAT)* (Westview Press, 2000).

Mark T. Green is Assistant Professor of Political Science at the University of Colorado at Denver. His research focuses on public management and public policy. He has published articles and books on public sector reform, budgeting, public finance, and gambling policy.

Thomas H. Hammond is Professor of Political Science at Michigan State University. His research generally involves the development of formal models of organizational structures and political institutions. He is currently writing a book (with Jack Knott and Gary Miller) that presents a multi-institutional model of the policymaking process in the U.S., including such topics as committee-floor relations, bicameralism, filibusters, president-Congress relations, presidential vetoes and veto override politics, the appointment process, and congressional (and presidential) control of the bureaucracy. He is also working on models of two-level games in foreign policy decision making and of stability and change in policy choice by presidential and parliamentary systems.

Patricia W. Ingraham is Professor of Public Administration and Political Science at the Maxwell School of Citizenship and Public Affairs at Syracuse University. She is also Director of the Alan K. Campbell Public Affairs Institute and the principal investigator for the institute's Government Performance Project, a four-year initiative funded by the Pew Charitable Trusts to examine government management. A former career civil servant, Dr. Ingraham has spent much of her academic career examining reform of public management systems and structures, and is the author and editor of a number of books and articles related to that issue. Dr. Ingraham also served as a staff member of the National Commission of Public Service and is a Fellow of the National Academy of Public Administration.

Lawrence R. Jones is Wagner Professor of Public Management, Department of Systems Management, Naval Postgraduate School, Monterey, California. Professor Jones is widely published and conducts research on international public management change, public financial management, and public budgeting. He is the recipient of a Fulbright Fellowship and has been a visiting scholar in Australia, Canada, China, the Czech Republic, France, Germany, Poland, New Zealand, Switzerland, and other nations.

Jocelyn M. Johnston is Assistant Professor of Public Administration at the University of Kansas. Her research focuses on intergovernmental programs and policy. She is a field research associate for the Rockefeller Institute's State Capacity Study, contributing to their national studies of welfare and Medicaid reform. She is also examining state-level contracting for social services. In addition, she studies state-local issues, including property tax administration and school finance, and is now involved in a national study of county fiscal capacity. She is co-editor, with H. George Frederickson, of *Public Management Reform and Innovation: Research, Theory and Application* (University of Alabama Press, 1999).

Anne M. Khademian is an independent author and researcher living in Michigan. She was an associate professor of political science and public policy at the University of Wisconsin–Madison (1990–96), and a visiting associate professor of political science and public policy at the University of Michigan (1996–98). She is the author of *The SEC and Capital Market Regulation: The Politics of Expertise* (University of Pittsburgh, 1992) and *Checking on Banks: Autonomy and Accountability in Three Federal Agencies* (Brookings Institution Press, 1996). Her current work is a study of emerging institutions of governance under conditions of limited resources, particularly at the local level.

Gordon Kingsley is an Assistant Professor in the School of Public Policy at the Georgia Institute of Technology. His research focuses upon the interactions of the public and private sectors in implementing public policy. Much of this work is aimed at the performance of state and local governments. Recent studies address policies to create networks among small manufacturers, evaluating the impacts of state science and technology organizations, methods for assessing human capital and social capital impacts, and the implementation of environmental policies by state governments.

Amy E. Kneedler is Instructor of Public Administration at the Maxwell School of Citizenship and Public Affairs at Syracuse University. She is also a senior research associate at the Alan K. Campbell Public Affairs Institute, where she works on the Institute's Government Performance Project. Ms. Kneedler is currently finishing her Ph.D. at the Maxwell School. Her research interests center around the application of the principles of public management to fire and emergency services agencies and the measurement of productive efficiency and performance in local public service provision. Before beginning her graduate studies, Ms. Kneedler served as an operations officer in the United States Army and as an emergency communications center manager.

Jack H. Knott is Director of the Institute of Government and Public Affairs and Professor of Political Science at the University of Illinois. He previously served as chair of the Political Science Department and director of the Institute of Public Policy and Social Research at Michigan State University. He has published articles and books on administrative and budget reform, comparing public and private management, and on models of the policymaking process.

Suzanne Leland is a doctoral candidate at the University of Kansas, Department of Public Administration. Her dissertation stems from the research supported by a National Science Foundation grant in two states with Steven Maynard-Moody and Michael Musheno on the justice norms of street-level workers and is titled "Organizational Misalignment: How and Why It Occurs at the Street Level." She is a faculty member at Kansas State University.

Laurence E. Lynn, Jr., the Sydney Stein, Jr., Professor of Public Management at the University of Chicago, is the author of *Public Management as Art, Science, and Profession* (Chatham House, 1996) and *Teaching and Learning With Cases: A Guidebook* (Chatham House, 1999). He has been leading a research program "Models and Methods for the Empirical Study of Governance and Public Management" supported by the Pew Charitable Trusts. His article "The New Public Management: How to Transform a Theme into a Legacy," was published in the May/June 1998 issue of *Public Administration Review.*

Steven Maynard-Moody is Professor and Chair of the Department of Public Administration at the University of Kansas. His current research has involved three years of National Science Foundation-funded fieldwork in two states. His research uses narratives to examine the justice norms of street-level workers. His chapter (with Suzanne Leland) in this book is based on one research site. With Michael Musheno he is in the early stages of drafting a book manuscript based on this research, tentatively titled, *Citizen Agents: Stories from the Front-Lines of Governing.* His most recent book, *The Dilemma of the Fetus: Fetal Research, Medical Progress, and Moral Politics* (St. Martin's Press 1996), examined a twenty-year social and political controversy over medical research.

Eugene B. McGregor is Professor of Public and Environmental Affairs at Indiana University. His research and teaching interests center on the relationship of the three legs of the public management trichotomy: governance, public policy, and operations. Current achievements include three books (one forthcoming) and over fifty published papers. Research and consulting assignments cover the strategic management of human knowledge, skills, and abilities in the post-industrial era; workforce decision-making strategies and methods of analysis; the relationship between education and economic development; and modern uses of information and information technology in the management of public and nonprofit enterprise.

Kenneth J. Meier is Charles Puryear Professor of Liberal Arts and Professor of Political Science at Texas A&M University. A former editor of the *American Journal of Political Science,* he is currently working on new methods for public policy analysis, reformulating principal-agent models to be useful for students of bureaucracy, and developing theories of policy design. The publication of this chapter puts him third on the all-time list of publishing with people named Jeff (Brudney, Worsham, Gill).

Julia Melkers is an Assistant Professor in the Department of Public Administration and Urban Studies at Georgia State University. Her research focuses on science and technology policy in the states and on performance measurement activities. Her recent work has addressed performance measurement in state science and technology organizations, performance-based budgeting in the states, and legislative information needs regarding research activities.

Laurence J. O'Toole, Jr., is Professor in the Department of Political Science and Senior Research Associate in the Fanning Institute of Leadership and Community Development at the University of Georgia. Much of his research focuses on policy implementation and public management in network settings, particularly in the field of environmental policy. Among his recent books are *Institutions, Policy and Outputs for Acidification* (Aldershot, UK: Ashgate, 1998) and *Participation and the Quality of Environmental Decision Making* (Dordrecht, The Netherlands: Kluwer Academic, 1998). The third edition of his edited volume *American Intergovernmental Relations* (Washington, D.C.: CQ Press) will be published in 2000.

Hal G. Rainey is Professor of Political Science at the University of Georgia specializing in public administration and organizational behavior. He is author of *Understanding and Managing Public Organizations,* which won the 1992 Best Book Award of the Public and Nonprofit Sectors Division of the Academy of Management. His articles have appeared in *Public Administration Review, Academy of Management Review, Administration and Society, Policy Studies Journal, Journal of Public Policy, Social Science Quarterly,* and numerous other journals. In 1995 he received the Levine Award for Excellence in Teaching, Research, and Service, conferred jointly by the American

Society for Public Administration and the National Association of Schools of Public Affairs and Administration.

Nancy C. Roberts is a Professor of Strategic Management at the Naval Postgraduate School in Monterey, California. She has authored and co-authored research on strategic planning and management, organizational and policy change; power and politics; and stakeholder collaborations in multi-organizational domains. Her co-authored book with Paula King, *Transforming Public Policy,* examines the dynamics of policy entrepreneurship and innovation in the public sector. She is currently working on a United Nations project that brings stakeholders together in order to develop relief and development programs for countries in crisis.

Barbara S. Romzek is a Professor of Public Administration at the University of Kansas. She is recognized for her publications on public management and accountability. In addition to her work on privatization, Romzek's most recent work has focused on accountability relationships in government reform and on the commitments and accountability of employees who are directly appointed by elected officials, including congressional staff and city managers.

Fred Thompson is the Grace and Elmer Goudy Professor of Public Management at the Atkinson Graduate School of Management, Willamette University. Previously he taught at the School of International and Public Affairs, Columbia University, UCLA, and the University of British Columbia, and held senior staff positions with the Economic Council of Canada, the State Department of Finance of California, and the California Postsecondary Education Commission. He is the editor of the *International Public Management Journal,* a contributing editor for *Policy Sciences,* and a Mosher Award winner.

James R. Thompson is an Assistant Professor of Public Administration at the University of Illinois at Chicago. Dr. Thompson earned his B.A. from Swarthmore College, his MPA from the State University of New York at Albany, and his Ph.D. in public administration from Syracuse University. Prior to attending Syracuse University, Dr. Thompson worked for fifteen years in local government in upstate New York. His research interests are administrative reform and issues of organizational change in the public sector. He is the co-editor of *Transforming Government: Lessons from the Reinvention Laboratories* (Jossey-Bass, 1998) and the author of several articles addressing issues of strategic change in public organizations.

George A. Waller is a Ph.D. candidate in political science at the University of Wisconson–Milwaukee and the editorial assistant for *American Politics Quarterly.* He has published in the *American Journal of Political Science* and is currently working on his dissertation, which examines the impact of facilities and technology on student performance.

Bibliography

Accountable Cost Advisory Committee. 1986. *Accountable cost study and recommendations of the accountable cost advisory committee to the state board of education.* Austin, Tex.: Texas Education Agency.

Alaska Science and Technology Foundation. 1995. *Annual report.* Anchorage.

Alchian, A., and H. Demsetz. 1972. Production, information costs, and economic organization. *American Economic Review* 62:777–95.

Allison, G. 1969. Conceptual models and the Cuban missile crisis. *American Political Science Review* 63:689–718.

Anthony, R. A., and V. Govindarajan. 1998. *Management control systems.* 9th ed. New York: Irwin/McGraw-Hill.

Appleby, P. 1949. *Big Democracy.* New York: Alfred A. Knopf.

Ashkenas, R., D. Ulrich, T. Jick, and S. Kerr. 1995. *The boundaryless organization: Breaking the chains of organizational structure.* San Francisco: Jossey-Bass.

Ban, C. 1995. *How do public managers manage? Bureaucratic constraints, organizational culture, and the potential for reform.* San Francisco: Jossey-Bass.

Barber, B. 1977. Absolutization of the market: Some notes on how we got from there to here. In *Markets and morals,* eds. G. Dworkin, G. Berman, and P. Brown, 15–31. New York: John Wiley & Sons.

Bardach, E. 1998. *Getting agencies to work together.* Washington, D.C.: Brookings Institution Press.

Barnard, C. 1938. *The functions of the executive.* Cambridge, Mass.: Harvard University Press.

Barzelay, M., and B. J. Armajani. 1992. *Breaking through bureaucracy: A new vision for managing in government.* Berkeley, Calif.: University of California Press.

Barzelay, M., and C. Moukheibir. 1997. Listening to customers. In *Handbook of public administration.* 2nd ed., edited by J. L. Perry. San Francisco: Jossey-Bass.

Beetham, D. 1991. Models of bureaucracy. In *Markets, hierarchies, and networks: The coordination of social life,* eds. G. Thompson, J. Frances, R. Levacic, and J. Mitchell, 128–40. London: Sage Publications.

Behn, R. D. 1988. Management by groping along. *Journal of Policy Analysis and Management* 7:643–63.

———. 1991. *Leadership counts: Lessons for public managers from the Massachusetts Welfare, Training, and Employment Program.* Cambridge, Mass.: Harvard University Press.

———. 1997. The dilemmas of innovation in American government. In *Innovation in American government: Challenges, opportunities, and dilemmas,* eds. A. A. Altshuler and R. D. Behn, 3–27. Washington, D.C.: Brookings Institution Press.

Bellow, G., and M. Minow, eds. 1996. *Law stories.* Ann Arbor, Mich.: University of Michigan Press.

Bendor, J. 1990. Formal models of bureaucracy: A review. In *Public administration: The state of the discipline,* eds. N. Lynn and A. Wildavsky, 373–420. Chatham, N.J.: Chatham House.

Bennett, C., and E. Ferlie. 1996. Contracting in theory and in practice: Some evidence from the NHS. *Public Administration* 74:49–66.

Bennett, W. L. 1997. Why government innovation is not news: The view from the newsroom. In *Innovation in American government: Challenges, opportunities, and dilemmas,* eds. A. A. Altshuler and R. D. Behn, 177–201. Washington, D.C.: Brookings Institution Press.

Boje, D. M., and D. A. Whetten. 1981. Effects of organizational strategies and contextual constraints on centrality and attributions of influence in interorganizational networks. *Administrative Science Quarterly* 26:378–95.

Bolman, L. G., and T. E. Deal. 1991. *Reframing organizations: Artistry, choice, and leadership.* San Francisco: Jossey-Bass.

Boorstin, D. J. 1978. *The republic of technology: Reflections on our future community.* New York: Harper & Row.

Borins, S.F. 1995a. A last word. *Canadian Public Administration* (spring): 137–39.

———. 1995b. The new public management is here to stay. *Canadian Public Administration* (spring):122–32.

———. 1998. *Innovating with integrity: How local heroes are transforming American government.* Washington, D.C.: Georgetown University Press.

Boston, J., J. Martin, J. Pallot, and P. Walsh. 1996. *Public management: The New Zealand model.* Auckland: Oxford University Press.

Boyer, B. D. 1973. *Cities destroyed for cash.* Chicago: Follett Publishing.

Bozeman, B. 1993. Theory, 'wisdom,' and the character of knowledge in public management: A critical view of the theory-practice linkage.

In *Public management: The state of the art,* ed. B. Bozeman, 27–39. San Francisco: Jossey-Bass.

Bozeman, B., S. Bretschneider, M. Meyers, M. Papdakis, G. Kingsley, C. Cimitile, J. Melkers, M. Tyszkiewicz, and K. Coker. 1992. *R & D Impacts at the New York State Energy Research and Development Authority: Final Report.* Syracuse, N.Y.: Syracuse University, Center for Technology and Information Policy.

Bozeman, B., and J. D. Straussman. 1990. *Public management strategies.* San Francisco: Jossey-Bass.

Bradach, J., and R. Eccles. 1991. Price, authority, and trust: From ideal types to plural forms. In *Markets, hierarchies, and networks: The coordination of social life,* eds. G. Thompson, J. Frances, R. Levacic, and J. Mitchell, 277–92. London: Sage Publications.

Bradley, R. T., and K. H. Pribram. 1996. Communication and optimality in biosocial collectives. In *Optimality in biological and artificial networks,* eds. D. S. Levine and W. S. Elsberry. Hillsdale, N.J.: Lawrence Earlbaum Associates.

Bragaw, L. 1980. *Managing a federal agency: The hidden stimulus.* Baltimore, Md.: Johns Hopkins University Press.

Brehm, J., and S. Gates. 1997. *Working, shirking, and sabotage: Bureaucratic response to a democratic republic.* Ann Arbor, Mich.: University of Michigan Press.

Brodkin, E. Z. 1997. Inside the welfare contract: Discretion and accountability in state welfare administration. *Social Service Review* 71:1–3.

Brown, R. 1978. Bureaucracy as praxis: Toward a political phenomenology of formal organizations. *Administrative Science Quarterly* 23:365–82.

Bryson, J. M., F. Ackerman, C. Eden, and C. B. Finn. 1996. Critical incidents and emergent issues in managing large-scale change. In *The state of public management,* eds. D. F. Kettl and H. B. Milward, 267–85. Baltimore, Md.: The Johns Hopkins University Press.

Buck, I., P. Delongchamps, D. Kling, D. Koehn, W. Lincoln, N. McKown, C. Santoni, and J. Winder. 1992. *Bureaucracy: What government agencies do and why they do it,* by James Q. Wilson: A critique by a few bureaucrats. *Public Administration Review* 52:406–7.

Bunker, B., and B. Alban. 1997. *Large group interventions.* San Francisco: Jossey-Bass.

Burns, T., and G. M. Stalker. 1961. *The management of innovation.* London: Tavistock.

Burrell, G., and G. Morgan. 1979. *Sociological paradigms and organisational analysis: Elements of the sociology of corporate life.* London: Heineman.

Burtless, G. 1996. *Does money matter? The effect of school resources on student achievement and adult success.* Washington, D.C.: Brookings Institution Press.

Carnevale, D. G. 1995. *Trustworthy government: Leadership and management strategies for building trust and high performance.* San Francisco: Jossey-Bass.

Caro, R. A. 1974. *The power broker: Robert Moses and the fall of New York.* New York: Alfred A. Knopf.

Carter, N., and P. Greer. 1993. Evaluating agencies: Next steps and performance indicators. *Public Administration* 71:407–16.

Chandler, A. 1962. *Strategy and structure: Chapters in the history of the industrial enterprise.* Cambridge, Mass.: MIT Press.

Charlesworth, J., J. Clarke, and A. Cochrane. 1996. Tangled webs? Managing local mixed economies of care. *Public Administration* 74:67–88.

Chevallier, J. 1996. La Réforme de L'État et La Conception Française du Service Public. *Revue Française d'Administration Publique* (January–March).

Clinton, W., and A. Gore. 1997. *Blair House Papers.* Washington, D.C.: U.S. Government Printing Office, January.

Coburn, C. 1995. *Partnerships: A compendium of state and federal cooperative technology programs.* Columbus, Ohio: Batelle Press.

Cohen, M. D., J. G. March, and J. P. Olsen. 1972. A garbage can model of organizational choice. *Administrative Science Quarterly* 17:1–25.

Cohen, S., and W. Eimicke. 1995. *The new effective public manager: Achieving success in a changing government.* San Francisco: Jossey-Bass.

Davenport, T. H. 1993. *Process innovation: Reengineering work through information technology.* Boston, Mass.: Harvard Business School Press.

Davidow, W. H., and M. S. Malone 1992. *The virtual corporation: Structuring and revitalizing the corporation for the 21st century.* New York: Edward Burlingame Books.

Davis, S. 1998. Interview by J. R. Thompson with Sue Davis, Disability Process Redesign Team, Social Security Administration, June 29, 1998.

Deakin, N., and K. Walsh. 1996. The enabling state: The role of markets and contracts. *Public Administration* 74:33–48.

Deal, T. E., and A. A. Kennedy. 1982. *Corporate cultures.* Reading, Mass.: Addison-Wesley.

DeHann, R. F. 1963. *Accelerated learning programs.* Washington, D.C.: Center for Applied Research in Education, Inc.

DeHoog, R. H. 1984. *Contracting for human services: Economic, political and organizational perspectives.* Albany: State University of New York Press.

Demchak, C. C. 1995. Coping, copying, and concentrating: Organizational learning and modernization in militaries. *Journal of Public Administration Research and Theory* 5:345.

———. 1996. Tailored precision armies in fully networked battlespace. *Journal of Contingencies and Crisis Management* June 4:93–102.

Demchak, C. C., and G. C. Rochin. 1991. *Lessons of the Gulf War: Ascendant technology and declining capability.* Institute of International Studies, University of California, Berkeley, No. 39.

Deming, W. E. 1986. *Out of crisis.* Cambridge, Mass.: MIT Press.

Denhardt, R. B. 1993. *The pursuit of significance: Strategies for managerial success in public organizations.* Belmont, Calif.: Wadsworth Publishing Co.

Department of Defense. 1996. *Reinventing the Department of Defense.* Office of the Secretary of Defense, the Pentagon.

De Pree, M. 1989. *Leadership is an art.* New York: Dell.

Derlien, H.-U. 1995. Germany. In *Learning from experience: Lessons of administrative reform,* eds. J. Olsen and B. G. Peters. Pittsburgh, Penna.: University of Pittsburgh Press.

Derthick, M. 1970. *The influence of federal grants: Public assistance in Massachusetts.* Washington, D.C.: The Brookings Institution Press.

———. 1990. *Agency under stress: The Social Security Administration in American government.* Washington, D.C.: The Brookings Institution Press.

Dienstag, J. F. 1997. *'Dancing in chains': Narrative and memory in political theory.* Stanford, Calif.: Stanford University Press.

DiIulio, Jr., J. J., G. Garvey, and D. F. Kettl. 1993. *Improving government performance: An owner's manual.* Washington, D.C.: The Brookings Institution Press.

———, ed. 1994. *Deregulating the public service: Can government be improved?* Washington, D.C.: The Brookings Institution Press.

DiMaggio, P. 1986. Structural analysis of organizational fields: A blockmodel approach. In *Research in organizational behavior,* eds. B. Staw and L. L. Cummings, 335–70. Greenwich, Conn.: JAI Press.

Doig, J. W., and E. C. Hargrove, eds. 1987. *Leadership and innovation: A biographical perspective on entrepreneurs in government.* Baltimore, Md.: Johns Hopkins University Press.

Donahue, J. D. 1997. *Disunited states.* New York: Basic Books.

Doty, D. H., W. H. Glick, and G. P. Huber. 1993. Fit, equifinality, and organizational effectiveness: A test of two configurational theories. *Academy of Management Journal* 36:1196–250.

Drucker, P. F. 1968. *The age of discontinuity.* New York: Harper & Row.

Eccles, R., and H. White. 1986. Firm and market interfaces of profit center control. In *Approaches to social theory,* eds. S. Lindenberg, J. Coleman, and S. Nowak. New York: Russell Sage.

Edgewood Independent School District v. Kirby. Texas SupCt, No. C–8353, (1989).

Eisenhardt, K. 1989. Agency theory: An assessment and review. *Academy of Management Review* 14:57–74.

Eisner, M. A. 1991. *Antitrust and the triumph of economics: Institutions, expertise, and policy change.* Chapel Hill: University of North Carolina Press.

Ellwood, J. W. 1996. Disciplinary foundations: Political science. In *The state of public management,* eds. D. F. Kettl and H. B. Milward. Baltimore, Md.: Johns Hopkins University Press.

Etzioni, A. 1975. *A Comparative analysis of complex organizations.* New York: The Free Press.

Feldman, M. S. 1989. *Order without design: Information processing and policy making.* Palo Alto, Calif.: Stanford University Press.

Fernandez, R. R., and W. Velez. 1985. Race, color, and language in the changing public schools. In *Urban ethnicity in the United States,* eds. L. Maldonado and J. Moore, 107–40. Beverly Hills, Calif.: Sage Publications.

Fischer, D. H. 1996. *The great wave: Price revolutions and the rhythm of history.* Oxford, UK: Oxford University Press.

Florida, R. 1996. Regional creative destruction: Production organization, globalization, and the economic transformation of the midwest. *Economic Geography* 72: 314–34.

Fountain, J. E. 1994a. A customer service literature review. In *Customer service excellence: Using information technologies to improve service delivery in government,* 13–22. Cambridge, Mass.: John F. Kennedy School of Government, Harvard University.

———. 1994b. Comment: Disciplining public management research. *Journal of Policy Analysis and Management* 13 (2):269–77.

Fountain, J. E., L. Kaboolian, S. Kelman, and J. Mechling. 1994. Report summary, findings, and recommendations. In *Customer service excellence: Using information technologies to improve service delivery in government,* 1–12. Cambridge, Mass.: John F. Kennedy School of Government, Harvard University.

Fox, C. J., and H. T. Miller. 1995. *Postmodern public administration: Toward discourse.* Thousand Oaks, Calif.: Sage Publications.

Frederickson, D. G., and J. L. Perry. 1998. Overcoming employee resistance to change. In *Transforming government: Lessons from the reinvention laboratories,* eds. P. W. Ingraham, J. R. Thompson, and R. P. Saunders, 125–46. San Francisco: Jossey-Bass.

Frederickson, H. G., and J. M. Johnston. 1999. *Public management reform and innovation: Research, theory and application.* Tuscaloosa, Ala.: University of Alabama Press.

Friedman, L. S. 1997. Public sector innovations and their diffusion: Economic tools and managerial tasks. In *Innovation in American government: Challenges, opportunities, and dilemmas,* eds. A. A. Altshuler and R. D. Behn, 332–59. Washington, D.C.: Brookings Institution Press.

Fry, G., A. Flynn, A. Gray, W. Jenkins, and B. Rutherford. 1988. Symposium on improving management in government. *Public Administration* 66:429–45.

Fuller, B., C. Eggers-Pierola, S. D. Holloway, X. Liang, and M. F. Rambaud. 1996. Rich culture, poor markets: Why do Latino parents forego preschooling. *Teachers College Record* 97:400–18.

Gage, R. W., and M. P. Mandell, eds. 1990. *Strategies for managing intergovernmental policies and networks.* New York: Praeger.

Galaskiewicz, J. 1979. *Exchange networks and community politics.* Beverly Hills, Calif.: Sage Publications.

Galaskiewicz, J., and W. Bielefeld. 1998. *Nonprofit organizations in an age of uncertainty: A study of organizational change.* New York: Aldine De Gruyter.

Galbraith, J. R. 1995. *Designing organizations: An executive briefing on strategy, structure, and process.* San Francisco: Jossey-Bass.

Garvey, G. 1993. *Facing the bureaucracy: Living and dying in a public agency.* San Francisco: Jossey-Bass.

Garvin, D. A. 1993. Building a learning organization. *Harvard Business Review* July–August:78–91.

Gill, J. 1997. Generalized substantively reweighted least squares regression. Political methodology Internet site. http://wizard.ucr.edu/polmeth/working_papers97.

———. 1999. The insignificance of null hypothesis significance testing. Cal Poly Working Paper, San Luis Obispo, Calif.

Gill, J., and K. J. Meier. 1998. Ralph's pretty good grocery versus Ralph's supermarket: Separating the excellent agencies from the good ones. http://www.calpoly.edu/~jgill/.

Goggin, M., A. O'M. Bowman, J. P. Lester, and L. J. O'Toole, Jr. 1990. *Implementation theory and practice: Toward a third generation.* Glenview, Ill.: Scott, Foresman/Little, Brown.

Golden, O. 1997. Innovation in the public sector human services programs: The implications of innovation by 'groping along.' In *Innovation in American government: Challenges, opportunities, and dilemmas,* eds. A. A. Altshuler and R. D. Behn, 146–74. Washington, D.C.: Brookings Institution Press.

Golembiewski, R. T. 1995. *Practical public management.* New York: Marcel Dekker.

Goodnow, F. 1900. *Politics and administration: A study in government.* New York: The Macmillan Co.

Goodsell, C. 1994. *The case for bureaucracy: A public administration polemic.* 3rd ed. Chatham, N.J.: Chatham House.

Gore, A. 1993. *From red tape to results: Creating a government that works better and costs less, Report of the National Performance Review.* New York: Times Books/Random House.

———. 1994. The new job of the federal executive. *Public Administration Review* 54:317–21.

———. 1996. *The best kept secrets in government.* Washington, D.C.: U.S. Government Printing Office, September.

Granovetter, M. 1985. Economic action and social structure: The problem of embeddedness. *American Journal of Sociology* 91:481–510.

Gray, A., and B. Jenkins. 1991. The management of change in Whitehall: The experience of the FMI. *Public Administration* 69:41–59.

Gray, B. 1989. *Collaborating.* San Francisco: Jossey-Bass.

Greer, P. 1994. *Transforming central government: The Next Steps initiative.* Buckingham, U.K.: Open University Press.

Gulick, L. 1937. Notes on the theory of organization. In *Papers on the science of administration,* eds. L. Gulick and L. Urwick. New York: Institute of Public Administration.

Halal, W. E. 1994. From hierarchy to enterprise: Internal markets are the new foundation of management. *Academy of Management Executive* 8:69–83.

Hall, P. D. 1994. A historical perspective on nonprofit organization. In *The Jossey Bass handbook of nonprofit leadership and management,* eds. R. D. Herman and Associates, 3–42. San Francisco: Jossey-Bass.

Hamel, G., and C. K. Prahalad. 1994. *Competing for the future.* Boston: Harvard Business School Press.

Hammer, M., and J. Champy. 1993. *Reengineering the corporation: A manifesto for business revolution.* New York: HarperBusiness.

Hammer, M., and S. A. Stanton. 1995. *The reengineering revolution.* New York: HarperBusiness.

Hammond, T. H., and B. D. Humes. 1993. 'What this campaign is all about is . . . ': A rational choice alternative to the Downsian spatial model of elections. In *Information, participation, and choice: An economic theory of democracy in perspective,* ed. B. Grofman. Ann Arbor: University of Michigan Press.

Hammond, T. H., and J. H. Knott. 1996. Who controls the bureaucracy?: Presidential power, congressional dominance, legal constraints, and bureaucratic autonomy in a model of multi-institutional policy-making. *Journal of Law, Economics, & Organization* 12:121–68.

———. 1999. Political institutions, public management, and policy choice. *Journal of Public Administration Research and Theory* 9 (January): 33–85.

Handler, J., and E. J. Hollingsworth. 1971. *The "deserving poor": A study of welfare administration.* New York: Markham.

Handy, C. 1989. *The age of unreason.* Boston: Harvard Business School Press.

———. 1994. *The age of paradox.* Boston: Harvard Business School Press.

Hanushek, E. A. 1986. The economics of schooling: Production and efficiency in public schools. *Journal of Economic Literature* 24:1141–77.

———. 1989. The impact of differential expenditures on school performance. *Educational Researcher* 23:45–65.

———. 1996. School resources and student performance. In *Does money matter? The effect of school resources on student achievement and adult success,* ed. G. Burtless. Washington, D.C.: Brookings Institution Press

Hanushek, E. A., and R. R. Pace. 1995. Who chooses to teach (and why?) *Economics of Education Review* 14:107–17.

Harvard Business Review. 1991. *Revolution in real time: Managing information technology in the 1990s.* Boston: Harvard Business School Publishing Division.

Hedges, L. V., and R. Greenwald. 1996. Have times changed? The relation between school resources and student performance. In *Does money matter? The effect of school resources on student achievement and adult success,* ed. G. Burtless. Washington, D.C.: Brookings Institution Press.

Heimann, C. F. L. 1993. Understanding the Challenger disaster: Organizational structure and the design of reliable systems. *American Political Science Review* 87:421–35.

Hennart, J. 1993. Explaining the swollen middle: Why most transactions are a mix of "market" and "hierarchy." *Organization Science* 4: 529–47.

Hickson, D. J., ed. 1993. *Management in Western Europe: Society, culture and organization in twelve nations.* Berlin: Walter de Gruyter.

Hill, J. S. 1985. Why so much stability? The role of agency determined stability. *Public Choice* 46:275–87.

Hochschild, J. L. 1995. *Facing up to the American dream: Race, class, and the soul of the nation.* Princeton, N.J.: Princeton University Press.

Hoggett, P. 1996. New modes of control in the public service. *Public Administration* 74:9–32.

Hogwood, B. 1993. Restructuring central government: The "Next Steps" initiative in Great Britain. In *Managing public organizations: Lessons from contemporary European experience,* eds. K. Eliassen and J. Kooiman. London: Sage Publications.

Hogwood, B. W., and B. G. Peters. 1985. *The pathology of public policy.* New York: Oxford University Press.

Holzer, M., and K. Callahan. 1997. *Government at work: Best practices and model programs.* Thousand Oaks, Calif.: Sage Publications.

Hood, C. 1983. *The tools of government.* London: Macmillan.

———. 1991. A public management for all seasons. *Public Administration* 69:3–19.

Huber, G. P., and W. H. Glick. 1993. *Organizational change and redesign: Ideas and insights for improving performance.* New York: Oxford University Press.

Hummel, R. P. 1994. *A critique of life in the modern organization.* 4th ed. New York: St. Martin's Press.

Hunt, M. 1995. The Employment Service as an agency: The first three years. In *Next Steps: Improving management in government?,* eds. B. O'Toole and G. Jordan, 74–85. Aldershot, U.K.: Dartmouth.

Huntington, S. E. 1961. *The common defense: Strategic programs in national politics.* New York: Columbia University Press.

Ingersoll, V. H., and G. B. Adams. 1992. *The tacit organization.* Greenwich, Conn.: JAI Press.

Ingraham, P. W. 1995. *The foundation of merit: Public service in American democracy.* Baltimore, Md.: Johns Hopkins University Press.

———. 1996. Reinventing the American federal government: Reform redux or real change? *Public Administration* Autumn 74: 453(23).

———. 1997. Play it again, Sam; It's still not right: Searching for the right notes in administrative reform. *Public Administration Review* 57: 325–31.

Ingraham, P. W., B. S. Romzek, and Associates. 1994. *New paradigms for government: Issues for the changing public service.* San Francisco: Jossey-Bass.

Ingram, H. 1977. Policy implementation through bargaining: The case of federal grants-in-aid. *Public Policy* 25:499–526.

Ingram, H., and A. Schneider. 1993. Constructing citizenship: The subtle messages of policy design. In H. Ingram and S. R. Smith, eds., *Public policy for democracy.* Washington, D.C.: The Brookings Institution Press.

Jeavons, T. H. 1994. Ethics in nonprofit management: Creating a culture of integrity. In *The Jossey Bass handbook of nonprofit leadership and management,* eds. R. D. Herman and Associates, 184–207. San Francisco: Jossey-Bass.

Jencks, C. 1990. Varieties of altruism. In *Beyond self-interest,* ed. J. Mansbridge, 54–67. Chicago: University of Chicago Press.

Johnston, J. M., R. Davis, and M. Fox. 1998. Medicaid reform in Kansas: A cautious approach. In *Medicaid reform and the American states,* eds. M. R. Daniels, 110–34. Westport, Conn.: Auburn House.

Johnston, J. M., and B. S. Romzek. 1997. Privatizing a bureaucracy: Theories, complications and conflicts. Paper presented at the Annual

Meeting of the Midwest Political Science Association, 10–12 April, Chicago, 1997.

Johnston, K. B. 1993. *Beyond bureaucracy: A blueprint and vision for government that works.* Homewood, Ill.: Business One Irwin.

Jordan, F. 1990. *Innovating America.* New York: Ford Foundation.

Kaboolian, L. 1995. Dialogue between advocates and executives agencies: New roles for public managers. Paper presented at the Third Annual Public Management Research Conference. University of Kansas, Lawrence.

Kamensky, J. M. 1996. Role of the 'reinventing government' movement in federal management reform. *Public Administration Review* 56: 247–55.

Kansas Department of Social and Rehabilitation Services. 1997. *Cooperative agreement between the Secretary of Social and Rehabilitation Services and the Secretary of Aging for the transfer of certain long-term care programs from the Kansas Department of Social and Rehabilitation Services to the Kansas Department on Aging.* Topeka, Kans.

Kanter, R. M. 1989. *When giants learn to dance.* New York: Simon and Schuster.

Kantor, B. 1995. *Understanding capitalism: How economies work.* London: Boyars/Bowerdean.

Kaplan, R. S., and D. P. Norton. 1996. *The balanced scorecard: Translating strategy into action.* Boston: Harvard Business School Press.

Katz, D. and R. L. Kahn. 1978. *The social psychology of organizations,* 2d ed. New York: Wiley.

Kaufman, H. 1981. *The administrative behavior of federal bureau chiefs.* Washington, D.C.: The Brookings Institution Press.

Kearney, R. C., and C. Sinha. 1988. Professionalism and bureaucratic responsiveness: Conflict or compatibility. *Public Administration Review* 48:571–79.

Kearns, K. 1996. *Managing for accountability.* San Francisco: Jossey-Bass.

Keiser, L. R. 1997. Controlling the child support enforcement bureaucracy: Organizational characteristics and bureaucratic responses. Paper presented at the Fourth National Public Management Research Conference. October, Athens, Ga.

Keiser, L. R., and K. Meier. 1996. Policy design, bureaucratic incentives, and public management: The case of child support enforcement. *Journal of Public Administration Research and Theory* 6 (July 3): 337–64.

Kemp, P. 1990. Next steps for the British civil service. *Governance* 3 (April), 186–96.

Ketchen, D. J., J. B. Thomas, and C. C. Snow. 1993. Organizational configurations and performance: A comparison of theoretical approaches. *Academy of Management Journal* 36:1278–313.

Kettl, D. F. 1993a. Searching for clues about public management: Slicing the onion different ways. In *Public management: The state of the art,* ed. B. Bozeman, 55–70. San Francisco: Jossey-Bass.

———. 1993b. *Sharing power: Public governance and private markets.* Washington, D.C.: The Brookings Institution Press.

———. 1997. The global revolution in public management: Driving themes, missing links. *Journal of Policy Analysis and Management,* 16 (3 summer):446–62.

Kettl, D. F., and Ingraham, P. W. 1992. *Agenda for excellence: public service in America.* Chatham, N.J.: Chatham House Publishers.

Kettl, D. F., and H. B. Milward. 1996. *The state of public management.* Baltimore, Md.: Johns Hopkins University Press.

Khademian, A. M. 1996. *Checking on banks: Autonomy and accountability in three federal agencies.* Washington, D.C.: The Brookings Institution Press.

Kickbusch, K. 1985. Minority students in mathematics: The reading skill connection. *Sociological Inquiry* 55:402.

Kiel, L. D. 1974. *Managing chaos and complexity in government: A new paradigm for managing change, innovation, and organization renewal.* San Francisco: Jossey-Bass.

Kingsley, G., and B. Bozeman. 1997. Charting the routes to commercialization: The absorption and transfer of energy conservation technologies. *International Journal of Global Energy Issues* 9:8–16.

Kingsley, G., B. Bozeman, and K. Coker. 1996. Technology transfer and absorption: An R&D value mapping approach to evaluation. *Research Policy* 25:967–95.

Kiser, L. L., and E. Ostrom. 1982. The three worlds of action: A metatheoretical synthesis of institutional approaches. In *Strategies of political inquiry,* ed. Ostrom, 179–222. Beverly Hills, Calif.: Sage Publications.

Klijn, E.-H. 1996. Analyzing and managing policy processes in complex networks: A theoretical examination of the concept policy network and its problems. *Administration and Society* 28:90–119.

Kost, J. M. 1996. *New approaches to public management: The case of Michigan.* Washington, D.C.: The Brookings Institution Press.

Kotter, J. P. 1996. *Leading change.* Boston: Harvard Business School Press.

Kreps, D. M. 1990. Corporate culture and economic theory. In *Perspectives on positive political economy,* eds. J. Alt and K. Shepsle, 90–143. Cambridge, Mass.: Cambridge University Press.

Landau, M. 1969. Redundancy, rationality, and the problem of duplication and overlap. *Public Administration Review* 29:346–58.

LaPiere, R. T. 1965. *Social change.* New York: McGraw-Hill.

LaPorte, T. R., and A. Keller. 1996. Assuring institutional constancy: Requisite for managing long-lived hazards. *Public Administration Review* 56:535–44.

LaPorte, T. R., and D. Metlay. 1996. Facing a deficit of trust: Hazards and institutional trustworthiness. *Public Administration Review* 56: 341–47.

Lappé, F. M., and P. M. DuBois. 1994. *The quickening of America: Rebuilding our nation, remaking our lives.* San Francisco: Jossey-Bass.

Lawler, J. R., E. E. Lawler III, & Associates. 1993. *Organizing for the future: The new logic for managing complex organizations.* San Francisco: Jossey-Bass.

Levin, M. A., and M. B. Sanger. 1994. *Making government work: How entrepreneurial executives turn bright ideas into real results.* San Francisco: Jossey-Bass.

Levine, A. S. 1982. *Managing NASA in the Apollo era.* Washington, D.C.: NASA.

Levine, A., and J. Luck. 1994. *The new management paradigm: A review of principles and practices.* Santa Monica, Calif.: Rand.

Lewis, E. 1980. *Public entrepreneurship: Toward a theory of bureaucratic political power: The organizational lives of Hyman Rickover, J. Edgar Hoover, and Robert Moses.* Bloomington: Indiana University Press.

Light, P. C. 1997. *The tides of reform: Making government work, 1945–1995.* New Haven, Conn.: Yale University Press.

———. 1998. *Sustaining innovation: Creating nonprofit and government organizations that innovate naturally.* San Francisco: Jossey-Bass.

Lindblom, C. E. 1959. The science of 'muddling through.' *Public Administration Review* 19:79–88.

———. 1977. *Politics and markets.* New York: Basic Books.

———. 1979. Still muddling, not yet through. *Public Administration Review* 39:517–26.

———. 1990. *Inquiry and change: The troubled attempt to understand and shape society.* New Haven, Conn.: Yale University Press.

Linden, R. M. 1994. *Seamless government: A practical guide to re-engineering in the public sector.* San Francisco: Jossey-Bass.

Liner, E. B., ed. 1989. *A decade of devolution: Perspectives on state-local relations.* Washington, D.C.: The Urban Institute Press.

Lipsky, M. 1980. *Street-level bureaucracy: Dilemmas of the individual in public services.* New York: Russell Sage Foundation.

Lodge, G. C. 1990. *Perestroika for American Restructuring U.S. business-government relations for competitiveness in the world economy.* Boston: Harvard Business School Press.

Long, N. E. 1949. Power and administration. *Public Administration Review* 9:257–64.

Lynn, L. E., Jr. 1994. Public management research: The triumph of art over science. *Journal of Policy Analysis and Management* 13:231–59.

———. 1996. *Public management as art, science and profession.* Chatham, N.J.: Chatham House.

Mandell, M. P. 1990. Network management: Strategic behavior in the public sector. In *Strategies for managing intergovernmental policies and networks,* eds. R. W. Gage and M. P. Mandell, 29–53. New York: Praeger Publishers.

March, J. G. 1995. Should higher education be more efficient? *Stanford Educator* (Fall) 3, 5, 12. Stanford, Calif.: School of Education News.

March, J. G., and J. P. Olsen. 1989. *Rediscovering institutions: The organizational basis of politics.* New York: The Free Press.

Martin, J. 1992. *Cultures in organizations: Three perspectives.* New York: Oxford University Press.

Matland, R. 1995. Synthesizing the implementation literature: The ambiguity-conflict model of policy implementation. *Journal of Public Administration Research and Theory* 5 April:145–74.

Maynard-Moody, S., M. Musheno, and D. Palumbo. 1990. Street-wise social policy: Resolving the dilemma of street-level influence and successful implementation. *Western Political Quarterly* 43:833–48.

Mayntz, R., and F. W. Scharpf. 1995. Der Ansatz des akteruzentrierten Institutionalismus. In *Steuerung und Selbstorganisation in Staatsnahen Sektoren,* eds. Mayntz and Scharpf, 39–72. Frankfurt am Main: Campus.

Mazmanian, D., and P. Sabatier. 1981. *Effective policy implementation.* Lexington, Mass.: D.C. Heath & Co.

———. 1983. *Implementation and public policy.* Glenview, Ill.: Scott, Foresman.

McAuley, M. 1997. Interview by J.R. Thompson with Mike McAuley, General Counsel, Chicago Regional Office, National Treasury Employees Union, May 20, 1997.

McGregor, Jr., E. B. 1991. *Strategic management of human knowledge, skills, and abilities.* San Francisco: Jossey-Bass.

———. 1993. Toward a theory of public management success. In *Public management: The state of the art,* ed. B. Bozeman. San Francisco: Jossey-Bass.

———. 1994. Economic development and public education: Strategies and standards. *Educational Policy* 8:252–71.

McLagan, P., and C. Nel. 1995. *The age of participation: New governance for the workplace and the world.* San Francisco: Berrett-Koehler.

Mechling, J. 1994. Options for policy makers. In *Customer service excellence: Using information technologies to improve service delivery in government,* 23–31. Cambridge, Mass.: John F. Kennedy School of Government, Harvard University.

Meier, K. J., and J. Gill. 2000. *Substantively weighted analytical techniques: A new approach to program and policy analysis.* Boulder, Colo.: Westview.

Meier, K. J., J. Gill, and G. Waller. 2000. Optimal performance vs. risk aversion: An application of substantively weighted least squares. In *Advancing public management: New developments in theory, methods, and practice,* eds. J. L. Brudney, L. J. O'Toole, Jr., and H. G. Rainey. Washington, D.C.: Georgetown University Press.

Meier, K. J., and L. R. Keiser 1996. Public administration as a science of the artificial: A methodology for prescription. *Public Administration Review* 56:459–66.

Meier K. J., and D. R. McFarlane. 1995. Statutory coherence and policy implementations: The case of family planning. *Journal of Public Policy* 15:281–99.

Meier, K. J., and J. Stewart, Jr. 1991. *The politics of Hispanic education.* Albany, NY: State University of New York Press.

Meier, K. J., R. D. Wrinkle, and J. L. Polinard. 1999a. Representative bureaucracy and distributional equity: Addressing the hard question. *Journal of Politics* 61 (forthcoming).

———. 1999b. Equity versus excellence in organizations: substantively weighted least squares analysis. *American Review of Public Administration* 29:5–18.

Melkers, J., and D. Bugler. 1994. Phase I Evaluation: Alaska Science and Technology Foundation, Anchorage AK. *Report to the Alaska Science and Technology Foundation,* May.

———. 1995. Phase II Evaluation: Alaska Science and Technology Foundation, Anchorage, AK. *Report to the Alaska Science and Technology Foundation,* March.

Melkers, J., and S. Cozzens. 1997. Use and usefulness of performance measurement in state science and technology programs. *Journal of Technology Transfer* 22:27–32.

Metcalfe, L., and S. Richards. 1987. *Improving management in government.* London: Sage Publications.

Meyer, A. D., A. S. Tsui, and C. R. Linings. 1993. Introduction: Configurational approaches to organizational analysis. *Academy of Management Journal* 36:1175–95.

Meyer, J. W., and B. Rowan. 1991. Institutionalized organizations: Formal structure as myth and ceremony. In *The new institutionalism in organizational analysis,* eds. W. Powell and P. DiMaggio, 41–62. Chicago: University of Chicago Press.

Meyers, M. K., B. Glaser, and K. MacDonald. 1998. On the front lines of welfare delivery: Are workers implementing policy reforms? *Journal of Policy Analysis and Management* 17:1–22.

Meyers, M. K., and N. Dillon. 1999. Institutional paradoxes: Why welfare workers can't reform welfare. In *Public management reform and innovation: Research, theory, and application,* eds. H. G. Frederickson and J. M. Johnston. Tuscaloosa: University of Alabama Press.

Meyers, R. T. 1996. Is there a key to the normative budgeting lock? *Policy Sciences* 29:171–89.

Miles, R. E., C. C. Snow, and A. D. Meyer. 1978. *Organizational strategy, structure, and process.* New York: McGraw-Hill.

Miller, D., and P. H. Friesen. 1984. *Organizations: A quantum view.* Englewood Cliffs, N.J.: Prentice-Hall.

Miller, G. J. 1992. *Managerial dilemmas: The political economy of hierarchy.* Cambridge, Mass.: Cambridge University Press.

Milward, H. B. 1996. The changing character of the public sector. In *Handbook of public administration.* 2nd ed., ed. J. L. Perry. San Francisco: Jossey-Bass.

Milward, H. B., and L. O. Snyder. 1996. Electronic government: Linking citizens to public organizations through technology. *Journal of Public Administration Research and Theory* 6 (April 2):261–76.

Mintzberg, H. 1996a. The machine organization. In *The strategy process,* eds. H. Mintzberg and J. B. Quinn, 635–49. Upper Saddle River, N.J.: Prentice Hall.

———. 1996b. The innovative organization. In *The strategy process,* eds. H. Mintzberg and J. B. Quinn, 679–703. Upper Saddle River, N.J.: Prentice Hall.

———. 1996c. The professional organization. In *The strategy process,* eds. H. Mintzberg and J. B. Quinn, 704–17. Upper Saddle River, N.J.: Prentice Hall.

———. 1996d. The diversified organization. In *The strategy process,* eds. H. Mintzberg and J. B. Quinn, 666–77. Upper Saddle River, N.J.: Prentice Hall.

———. 1996e. Managing government, governing management. *Harvard Business Review* May–June 74:75(9).

Moe, R. C. 1992. *Reorganizing the executive branch in the twentieth century: Landmark commissions,* report 92–293 GOV. Congressional Research Service, March.

———. 1994. The 'reinventing government' exercise: Misinterpreting the problem, misjudging the consequences. *Public Administration Review* 54:111–22.

Moe, T. M. 1987. An assessment of the positive theory of 'Congressional Dominance.' *Legislative Studies Quarterly* 12:475–520.

———. 1990. Political institutions: The neglected side of the story. *Journal of Law, Economics, & Organization* 6:213–54.

———. 1991a. Politics and the theory of organization. *Journal of Law, Economics, and Organization* 7:106–29.

———. 1991b. The politics of structural choice: Toward a theory of public bureaucracy. In *Organization theory: From Chester Barnard to the present and beyond,* ed. O. Williamson. New York: Oxford University Press.

Moon, M. J., and S. Bretschneider. 1997. Can state government actions affect innovation and its diffusion?: An extended communication model and empirical test. *Technological Forecasting and Social Change* 54:57–77.

Moore, E. G. J., and A. W. Smith. 1986. Sex and race differences in mathematics aptitude: Effects of schooling. *Sociological Perspectives* 29:77.

Moore, M. H. 1995. *Creating public value: Strategic management in government.* Cambridge, Mass.: Harvard University Press.

Moore, M. H., M. Sparrow, and W. Spelman. 1997. Innovations in policing: From production lines to jobs shops. In *Innovation in American government: Challenges, opportunities, and dilemmas,* eds. A. A. Altshuler and R. D. Behn, 274–98. Washington, D.C.: Brookings Institution Press.

Morgan, G. 1997. *Images of organization.* 2nd ed. Thousand Oaks, Calif.: Sage Publications.

Morley, D. 1993. Strategic direction in the British Public Service. *Long Range Planning* 26:77–86.

Mosher, F. C. 1968. *Democracy and the public service.* New York: Oxford University Press.

Murray, S. E. 1995. Two essays on the distribution of education resources and outcomes. Unpublished Ph.D. dissertation, Department of Economics, University of Maryland.

Murray, S. E., W. N. Evans, and R. M. Schwab. 1995. Money matters after all: Evidence from panel data on the effects of school resources (working paper). University of Kentucky and University of Maryland, The Martin School.

Nagel, J. H., ed. 1997. Special issue—The new public management in New Zealand and beyond. *Journal of Policy Analysis and Management* 16:349–56.

Naisbitt, J., and P. Aburdene. 1985. *Re-inventing the corporation: Transforming your job and your company for the new information society.* New York: Warner Books.

National Academy of Public Administration. 1994. *Renewing HUD: A long-term agenda for effective performance.* Washington, D.C.: July.

National Education Goals Panel. 1996. *The national education goals report: Building a nation of learners.* Washington, D.C.: U.S. Government Printing Office.

National Performance Review [NPR]. 1997. *Serving the American public: Best practices in customer-driven strategic planning.* Federal Benchmarking Consortium Study Report.

Nayak, P. R., and J. M. Ketteringham. 1986. *Breakthroughs!* New York: Rawson Associates.

Necochea, J., and Z. Cune. 1996. A case study of within district school finding inequities. *Equity and Excellence in Education* 29:69–77.

Niskanen, W. A. 1971. *Bureaucracy and representative government.* New York: Aldine-Atherton.

Nolan, R. L., and D. C. Croson. 1995. *Creative destruction: A six-stage process for transforming the organization.* Boston: Harvard Business School Press.

Nye, B. A., J. Boyd-Zacharias, B. D. Fulton, and M. P. Wallenhorst. 1992. Smaller classes really are better. *American School Board Journal* May: 31–33.

Nye, Jr., J. S., P. D. Zelikow, and D. C. King. 1997. *Why people don't trust government.* Cambridge, Mass.: Harvard University Press.

Nystrom, P. C., and W. H. Starbuck, eds. 1981. *Handbook of organizational design.* London: Oxford University Press.

Oliver, D., and G. Drewry 1996. *Public service reforms: Issues of accountability and public law.* New York: Pinter.

Osborne, D., and T. Gaebler. 1992. *Re-inventing government: How the entrepreneurial spirit is transforming the public sector.* Reading, Mass.: Addison-Wesley.

Osborne, D., and P. Plastrik. 1997. *Banishing bureaucracy: The five strategies for reinventing government.* Reading, Mass.: Addison-Wesley.

Ostroff, C., and N. Schmitt. 1993. Configurations of organizational effectiveness and efficiency. *Academy of Management Journal* 36:1345–61.

Ostrom, E. 1990. *Governing the commons: The evolution of institutions for collective action.* Cambridge: Cambridge University Press.

———. 1996. Institutional rational choice: An assessment. Paper presented at the annual meetings of the American Political Science Association, 31 August, San Francisco.

O'Toole, L. J., Jr. 1983. Interorganizational cooperation and the implementation of labour market training policies: Sweden and the Federal Republic of Germany. *Organization Studies* 4:129–50.

———. 1986. Policy recommendations for multi-actor implementation: An assessment of the field. *Journal of Public Policy* 6:181–210.

———. 1996. Rational choice and the public management of interorganizational networks. In *The state of public management,* eds. D. F. Kettl and H. B. Milward, 241–63. Baltimore, Md.: The Johns Hopkins University Press.

———. 1997a. Implementing public innovations in network settings. *Administration and Society* 29:115–38.

———. 1997b. Treating networks seriously: Practical and research-based agendas in public administration. *Public Administration Review* 57: 45–52.

———. 2000. Different public managements? Implications of structural context in hierarchies and networks. In *Advancing public management: New developments in theory, methods, and practice,* eds. J. L. Brudney, L. J. O'Toole, Jr., and H. G. Rainey. Washington, D.C.: Georgetown University Press.

O'Toole, L. J., Jr., and R. S. Montjoy. 1984. Interorganizational policy implementation: A theoretical perspective. *Public Administration Review* 44:491–503.

Ott, J. S. 1989. *The organizational culture perspective.* Pacific Grove, Calif.: Brooks/Cole.

Painter, C. 1995. The Next Steps reforms and current orthodoxies. In *Next Steps: Improving management in government?,* eds. B. O'Toole and G. Jordan, 17–36. Aldershot, U.K.: Dartmouth.

Pate-Bain, H., C. M. Achilles, J. Boyd-Zacharias, and B. McKenna. 1992. Class size does make a difference. *Phi Delta Kappan,* November: 253–56.

Pennings, J. M., and A. Buitendam. 1987. *New technology as organizational innovation: The development and diffusion of microelectronics.* Cambridge, Mass.: Ballinger Publishing Co.

Pennings, P. S., and J. M. Goodman. 1977. Toward a workable framework. In *New perspectives on organizational effectiveness,* eds. P. S. Pennings and J. M. Goodman, 146–84. San Francisco: Jossey-Bass.

Peters, B. G. 1993. Models of governance for the 1990s. Paper presented at the Third National Public Management Research Conference, University of Madison–Wisconsin, September 30–October 2, 1993.

———. 1996. *The future of governing.* Lawrence: University of Kansas Press.

Peters, B. G., and M. O. Heisler. 1983. Thinking about public sector growth. In *Why governments grow: Measuring public sector size,* ed. C. L. Taylor, 177–98. Beverly Hills, Calif.: Sage Publications.

Peters, B. G., and D. Savoie. 1994. Civil service reform: Misdiagnosing the patient. *Public Administration Review* 54:418–25.

———. 1996. Managing incoherence: The coordination and empowerment conundrum. *Public Administration Review* 56:281–90.

Peters, T., and R. Waterman, Jr. 1982. *In search of excellence.* New York: Harper and Row.

Peterson, P., B. Rabe, and K. Wong. 1986. *When federalism works.* Washington, D.C.: The Brookings Institution Press.

Pfeffer, J. 1992. *Managing with power: Politics and influence in organizations.* Boston, Mass.: Harvard Business School Press.

Pierce, N. R., and R. Guskind. 1993. *Breakthroughs: Re-creating the American city.* New Brunswick, N.J.: Center for Urban Policy Research, Rutgers University.

Pindyck, R. S., and D. L. Rubinfeld. 1991. *Econometric models and economic forecasts.* 3rd ed. New York: McGraw-Hill.

Pollitt, C. 1993. *Managerialism and the public services: Cuts or cultural change in the 1990s.* Oxford, U.K.: Blackwell.

Porter, M. E. 1980. *Competitive strategy: Techniques for analyzing industries and competitors.* New York: The Free Press.

———. 1985. *Competitive advantage: Creating and sustaining superior performance.* New York: The Free Press.

———. 1990. *The competitive advantage of nations.* New York: The Free Press.

Powell, W. W. 1990. Neither market nor hierarchy: Network forms of organization. In *Research in organizational behavior,* Vol. 12, eds. B. M. Staw and L. L. Cummings, 295–336. Greenwich, Conn.: JAI Press.

Powell, W., and P. DiMaggio, eds. 1991. *The new institutionalism in organizational analysis.* Chicago: The University of Chicago Press.

Pressman, J. L., and A. Wildavsky. 1984. *Implementation: How great expectations in Washington are dashed in Oakland.* Berkeley: University of California Press.

Provan, K. G., and H. B. Milward. 1995. A preliminary theory of interorganizational network effectiveness: A comparative study of four community mental health systems. *Administration Science Quarterly* 40:1–33.

Quinn, J. B. 1980. *Strategies for change: Logical incrementalism.* Homewood, Ill.: Richard D. Irwin, Inc.

———. 1992. The intelligent enterprise: A new paradigm. *Academy of Management Executive* 6:48–63.

Quinn, J. B., P. Anderson, and S. Finkelstein. 1996. Leveraging intellect. *Academy of Management Executive* 10:7–27.

Quinn, R. E., and K. S. Cameron, eds. 1988. *Paradox and transformation.* Cambridge, Mass.: Ballinger.

Quinn, R. E., and J. Rohrbaugh. 1981. A competing values approach to organizational effectiveness. *Public Productivity Review* 5: 122–40.

———. 1983. A spatial model of effectiveness criteria: Towards a competing values approach to organizational analysis. *Management Science* 29:363–77.

Quirk, P. J. 1980. Food and Drug Administration. In *The Politics of Regulation*, ed. J. Q. Wilson, New York: Basic Books.

Radin, B., and B. S. Romzek. 1996. Accountability expectations in an intergovernmental arena: The National Rural Development Partnership. *Publius: The Journal of Federalism* 26 (spring, 2):59–81.

Rago, W. 1996. Struggles in transformation: A study in TQM, leadership, and organizational culture in a government agency. *Public Administration Review* 56:227–34.

Rainey, H. G. 1993. Important research questions. In *Public management: The state of the art*, ed. B. Bozeman, 9–12. San Francisco, Calif.: Jossey-Bass.

———. 1996. Building an effective organizational culture. In *The Handbook of Public Administration*. 2nd ed., ed. James Perry. San Francisco, Calif.: Jossey-Bass.

———. 1997. *Understanding and managing public organizations*. 2nd ed. San Francisco, Calif.: Jossey-Bass.

Reich, R. B. 1990. *Public management in a democratic society*. Englewood Cliffs, N.J.: Prentice Hall.

Report of the National Performance Review. 1993. Washington, D.C.: U.S. Government Printing Office.

Rheingold, H. 1993. *The virtual community: Homesteading on the electronic frontier*. Reading, Mass.: Addison-Wesley.

Riker, W. H. 1986. *The art of political manipulation*. New Haven, Conn.: Yale University Press.

Rivlin, A. 1992. *Reviving the American dream: The economy, the states & the federal government*. Washington, D.C.: The Brookings Institution Press.

Roberts, A. 1995. 'Civic discovery' as rhetorical strategy. *Journal of Policy Analysis and Management* 14:291–307.

———. Command performance. *Government Executive* 28:20–26.

Roberts, N. C. 1985. Transforming leadership: A process of collective action. *Human Relations* 38:1023–46.

———. 1997. Public deliberation: An alternative approach to crafting policy and setting direction. *Public Administration Review* 124–32.

Roberts, N. C., and R. T. Bradley. 1991. Stakeholder collaboration and innovation: A study of policy initiation at the state level. *Journal of Applied Behavioral Science* 27:209–27

Roberts, N. C., and P. J. King. 1996. *Transforming public policy: Dynamics of policy entrepreneurship and innovation*. San Francisco, Calif.: Jossey-Bass.

Roberts, N. C., and J. Menker. 1998. Strategic management in the federal government: Necessary and sufficient conditions. In *Handbook of strategic management*, eds. J. Rabin, G. J. Miller, and W. Bartley Hildreth. New York: Marcel Dekker.

Roberts, N. C., and L. Wargo. 1994. The dilemma of planning in large-scale public organizations: The case of the United States Navy. *Journal of Public Administration Research and Theory* 4:469–91.

Roessner, D. 1977. Incentives to innovate in public and private organizations. *Administration and Society* 9 (November):341–65

Rogers, E. M. 1995. *Diffusion of innovations.* New York: The Free Press.

Romzek, B., and M. J. Dubnick. 1987. Accountability in the public sector: Lessons for the Challenger tragedy. *Public Administration Review* 47:227–38.

Rong, X. L., and L. Grant. 1992. Ethnicity, generation, and school attainment of Asians, Hispanics, and non-Hispanic whites. *Sociological Quarterly* 33:625.

Rose, R. 1991. *The postmodern president: George Bush meets the world.* 2nd ed. Chatham, N.J.: Chatham House Publishers.

Rosenbloom, D. H. 1989. *Public administration: Understanding management, politics and law in the public sector.* New York: Random House.

Rourke, F. 1984. *Bureaucracy, politics and public policy.* 3rd ed. Boston: Little-Brown.

Rourke, F. E. 1992. Responsiveness and neutral competence in American bureaucracy. *Public Administration Review* 52:539–46.

Rouse, M. J., and U. Fleising. 1995. Miners and managers: Workplace cultures in a British Columbia coal mine. *Human Organization* 54:238–48.

Rowe, L. A., and W. B. Boise, eds. 1973. *Organizational and managerial innovation: A reader.* Pacific Palisades, Calif.: Goodyear Publishing Co.

Sabatier, P. A. 1988. An advocacy coalition framework of policy change and the role of policy-oriented learning therein. *Policy Sciences* 21:129–68.

Sabatier, P. A., and H. C. Jenkins-Smith. 1996. The advocacy coalition framework: An assessment. Paper presented at the annual meetings of the American Political Science Association, San Francisco, Calif.: 31 August.

Salamon, L. 1995. *Partners in public service: Government-nonprofit relations in the modern welfare state.* Baltimore, Md.: Johns Hopkins University Press.

San Antonio Independent School District v. Rodriguez. 411 U.S.1 (1973).

Sanders, R. P., and J. R. Thompson. 1996. Laboratories of reinvention. *Government Executive* (Special Supplement, March), 1–12.

Sanger, M. B., and M. A. Levin. 1992. Using old stuff in new ways: Innovation as a case of evolutionary tinkering. *Journal of Policy Analysis and Management* 11:88–115.

Savas, E. S. 1987. *Privatization: The key to better government.* Chatham, N.J.: Chatham House Publishers.

Savoie, D. J. 1995a. Just another voice from the pulpit. *Canadian Public Administration* (spring):133–36.

———. 1995b. What is wrong with the new public management? *Canadian Public Administration* (spring):112–21.

———. 1998. Making government reform stick: Lessons learned. In *Transforming government: Lessons from the reinvention laboratories,* eds. P. W. Ingraham, J. R. Thompson, and R. P. Saunders, 220–40. San Francisco, Calif.: Jossey-Bass.

Schall, E. 1995. APPAM: Learning to love the swamp: Reshaping education for public service. *Journal of Policy Analysis and Management* 14: 202–20.

Schall, E., and K. Feely. 1992. Guidelines to grope by: Reflections from the field. *Innovating* 2 (spring):3–11.

Scharpf, F. W. 1997. *Games real actors play: Actor-centered institutionalism in policy research.* Boulder, Colo.: Westview Press.

Schein, E. H. 1990. Organizational culture. *American Psychologist* 45: 109–19.

———. 1992. *Organizational culture and leadership.* 2nd ed. San Francisco, Calif.: Jossey-Bass.

———. 1993. Legitimating clinical research in the study of organizational culture. *Journal of Counseling and Development* 71: 703–8.

Schneider, A. L., and H. Ingram. 1997. *Policy design for democracy.* Lawrence: University Press of Kansas.

Schumpeter, J. 1942. *Capitalism, socialism, and democracy.* New York: Harper and Row.

Schwartz, H. N. 1997. Reinvention and retrenchment: Lessons from the application of the New Zealand model to Alberta, Canada. *Journal of Policy Analysis and Management* 16:405–22.

Scott, G., I. Ball, and T. Dale. 1997. New Zealand's public management reform: Implications for the United States. *Journal of Policy Analysis and Management* 16 (summer):357–81.

Scott, P. G. 1997. Assessing determinants of bureaucratic discretion: An experiment in street-level decision making. *Journal of Public Administration Research and Theory* 7:35–57.

Scott, W. R. 1990. Symbols and organizations: From Barnard to the institutionalists. In *Organization theory: From Chester Barnard to the present and beyond,* ed. O. Williamson, 38–55. New York: Oxford University Press.

Scott, W. R., and J. W. Meyer. 1983. The organization of societal sectors. In *Organizational environments: Ritual and rationality,* eds. J. Meyer and R. Scott. Beverly Hills, Calif.: Sage Publications.

Secretary's Commission on Achieving Necessary Skills. 1992. *Learning a living: A blueprint for high performance.* Washington, D.C.: U.S. Department of Labor.

Selznick, P. 1957. *Leadership in administration.* Evanston, Ill.: Row, Peterson.

Senge, P. M. 1990. *The fifth discipline: The art and practice of the learning organization.* New York: Doubleday/Currency.

Senge, P. M., C. Roberts, R. B. Ross, B. J. Smith, and A. Kleiner. 1994. *The fifth discipline fieldbook: Strategies and tools for building a learning organization.* New York: Doubleday.

Sentell, G. D. 1994. *Fast, focused & flexible: Bold new imperatives for the high performance organization.* Knoxville, Tenn.: Pressmark International.

Shapiro, J. P. 1993. *No pity: People with disabilities forging a new civil rights movement.* New York: Times Books.

Simon, H. 1947. *Administrative behavior.* New York: Free Press.

———. 1976. *Administrative behavior.* 3rd ed. New York: The Free Press.

———. 1981 (1957). *The sciences of the artificial.* Cambridge, Mass.: MIT Press.

———. 1995. Organizations and markets. *Journal of Public Administration Research and Theory* 5:275–94.

Sjoberg, G., R. A. Brymer, and B. Farris. 1966. Bureaucracy and the lower class. *Sociology and Social Research* April:325–27.

Smircich, L. 1983. Concepts of culture and organizational analysis. *Administrative Science Quarterly* 28:339–58.

Smith, H. 1995. *Rethinking America: Innovative strategies and partnerships in business and education.* New York: Avon Books.

Smith, K. B., and K. J. Meier. 1994. Bureaucrats, markets, and schools. *Public Administration Review* 54:511–58.

Smith, K. B., K. J. Meier, and J. Gill. 1998. SWAT in pooled analysis. http://www.calpoly.edu/~jgill/.

Smith, S. R., and M. Lipsky. 1993. *Nonprofits for hire: The welfare state in the age of contracting.* Cambridge, Mass.: Harvard University Press.

Snow, C. C., and L. G. Hrebiniak. 1980. Strategy, distinctive competence, and organizational performance. *Administrative Science Quarterly* 25:317–36.

Snow, C. C., R. E. Miles, and H. J. Coleman. 1992. Managing 21st century network organizations. *Organizational Dynamics* (winter):5–20.

Sparrow, M. K. 1994. *Imposing duties: Government's changing approach to compliance.* Westport, Conn.: Praeger.

Stevens, J. M. 1997. Public governance ideals and models: An existential search—or manager for all seasons. Unpublished paper, Pennsylvania State University, University Park, Penna.

Stillman II, R. J. 1996. *The American bureaucracy: The core of modern government.* 2nd ed. Chicago: Nelson-Hall Publishers.

Stivers, C. 1994. The listening bureaucrat: Responsiveness in public administration. *Public Administration Review* 54:364–69.

Stone, D. 1997. *Policy paradox: The art of political decision making.* New York: W. W. Norton.

Talbot, C. 1997a. UK civil service personnel reform: Devolution, decentralisation, and delusion. Unpublished manuscript, University of Glamorgan, Wales.

———. 1997b. The politics of performance—contexts, complexity and contradictions. Paper presented at the Symposium on Performance-Based Management and Its Training Implications, Caserta, Italy, September 1997.

Tapscott, D., and A. Caston. 1993. *Paradigm shift: The new promise of information technology.* New York: McGraw-Hill.

Taylor, F. W. 1911. *Principles of scientific management.* New York: Norton.

Tellier, 1990. Public service 2000: The renewal of the public service. *Canadian Public Administration* 33:123–32.

Texas Research League. 1986. Bench marks for 1986–87 schools district budgets in Texas. Austin, Tex.: Texas Research League.

Theodore, J. 1997. Telephone interview by J. R. Thompson with Julie Theodore, Quality Analyst with the Office for Strategic Process Improvement and Reengineering, Internal Revenue Service, 18 June.

Thomas, J. C. 1995. *Public participation in public decisions: New skills and strategies for public managers.* San Francisco, Calif.: Jossey-Bass.

Thompson, F. 1997. Book Review of Donald F. Kettl and H. Brinton Milward eds. *The State of Public Management. Journal of Policy Analysis and Management,* 16: 484–89.

———. 1999. Cost analysis. In *Handbook of public budgeting,* eds. A. Schick and R. Meyers. San Francisco, Calif.: Jossey-Bass.

Thompson, F., and L. R. Jones. 1994. *Reinventing the Pentagon: How the new public management can promote institutional renewal.* San Francisco, Calif.: Jossey-Bass

Thompson, G., J. Frances, R. Levacic, and J. Mitchell, eds. 1991. *Markets, hierarchies, and networks: The coordination of social life.* London: Sage Publications.

Thompson, J. D. 1967. *Organizations in action.* New York: McGraw-Hill.

Tichy, N. 1983. *Managing strategic change: Technical, political, and cultural dynamics.* New York: Wiley.

Trice, H. M., and J. M. Beyer. 1993. *The cultures of work organizations.* Englewood Cliffs, N.J.: Prentice Hall.

Tsebelis, G. 1990. *Nested games.* Berkeley, Calif.: University of California Press.

Tushman, M. L., and W. L. Moore, eds. 1988. *Readings in the management of innovation.* Cambridge, Mass.: Ballinger.

Tyler, T. R. 1990. Justice, self-interest, and the legitimacy of legal and political authority. In *Beyond self interest,* ed. J. Mansbridge, 171–79. Chicago: University of Chicago Press.

U.S. General Accounting Office. 1996. *SSA disability redesign: More testing needed to assess feasibility of new claim manager position* (HEHS-96-170). Washington, D.C.: Government Printing Office.

———. 1997. *SSA disability redesign: Focus needed on initiatives most crucial to reducing costs and time* (HEHS-97-20). Washington, D.C.: Government Printing Office.

Utterback, J. M. 1994. *Mastering the dynamics of innovation: How companies can seize opportunities in the face of technological change.* Boston: Harvard Business School Press.

Valente, T. W. 1995. *Network models of the diffusion of innovations.* Cresskill, N.J.: Hampton Press.

Vancil, R. 1978. *Decentralization: Managerial ambiguity by design.* Homewood, Ill.: Dow Jones Irwin.

Van de Ven, A., H. Angle, and M. S. Poole. 1989. *Research on the management of innovation.* New York: HarperCollins.

Van de Ven, A. H., and R. Drazin. 1985. The concept of fit in contingency theory. In *Research in organizational behavior,* eds. L. L. Cummings and B. M. Staw, 333–65. Greenwich, Conn.: JAI Press 7.

Van Horn, C. 1979. *Policy implementation in the federal system: National goals and local implementors.* Lexington, Mass.: D.C. Heath & Co.

Van Meter, D., and C. Van Horn. 1975. The policy implementation process: A conceptual framework. *Administration and Society* 6:445–88.

Venkatraman, N. 1991. IT-induced business reconfiguration," in *The corporation of the 1990s: Information technology and organizational transformation,* ed. M. S. Scott Morton, 122–58. New York: Oxford University Press.

Vinzant, J. C., and L. Crothers. 1999. *Street-level leadership: Discretion and legitimacy in front-line public service.* Washington, D.C.: Georgetown University Press.

Waller, G. A. 1998. For want of a modem and a comfortable chair: A research note. *American Journal of Political Science* 42 (April):704–08.

Walsh, D. F. 1998. American politics in transition: The 1980s and 1990s. In *America in the 21st century: Challenges and opportunities in domestic politics,* eds. K. B. Rai, D. F. Walsh, and P. J. Best, 1–20. Upper Saddle River, N.J.: Prentice-Hall.

Walton, R. E. 1987. *Innovating to compete: Lessons for diffusing and managing change in the workplace.* San Francisco, Calif: Jossey-Bass.

Wamsley, G. L., and J. F. Wolf, eds. 1996. *Refounding democratic public administration: Modern paradoxes, postmodern challenges.* Thousand Oaks, Calif.: Sage Publications.

Warren, C. R. 1992. Policy making and innovation in the American states: The case of economic development. Bloomington, Ind.: Indiana University, Unpublished Ph.D. dissertation.

Warwick, D. P. 1975. *A theory of public bureaucracy: Politics, personality, and organization in the State Department.* Cambridge, Mass.: Harvard University Press.

Webb, J. E. 1969. *Space age management: The large-scale approach.* New York: McGraw-Hill.

Weber, M. 1946. *From Max Weber: Essays in sociology,* eds. H. H. Gerth and C. W. Mills. New York: Oxford University Press.

———. 1947. *The theory of social and economic organization.* Translated by A. M. Henderson and T. Parsons. New York: The Free Press.

Webster's third new international dictionary. 1971. Springfield, Mass.: G&C Marum Co.

Weick, K. E. 1984. Small wins: Redefining the scale of social problems. *American Psychologist* 39 (January):40–49.

Weiher, G. R. 1998. Why redistribution doesn't work: State educational reform policy and governmental decentralization in Texas. *American Politics Quarterly* 16:193–210.

Weiss, J. A. 1994. Comment: Public management research—the interdependence of problems and theory. *Journal of Policy Analysis and Management* 13:278–85.

White, L. D. 1948. *The Federalists: A study in administrative history 1789–1801.* New York: The Free Press.

———. 1951. *The Jeffersonians: A study in administrative history 1801–1829.* New York: The Free Press.

———. 1954. *The Jacksonians: A study in administrative history 1829–1861.* New York: The Free Press.

———. 1958. *The Republican Era: A study in administrative history 1869–1901.* New York: The Free Press.

White, L. G. 1988. Public management in a pluralistic arena. *Public Administration Review* May/June:735–42.

Wiesbrod, B. A. 1997. The future of the nonprofit sector: Its entwining with private enterprise and government. *Journal of Policy Analysis and Management* 16 (fall):541–55.

Wilkins, A. L., and W. G. Ouchi. 1983. Efficient cultures: Exploring the relationship between culture and organizational performance. *Administrative Science Quarterly* 28:468–81.

Williams, W. 1980. *The implementation perspective: A guide for managing social service delivery programs.* Berkeley: University of California Press.

Williamson, O. E. 1985. *The economic institutions of capitalism.* New York: Free Press.

———, ed. 1990. *Industrial Organization.* Aldershot, Hants, England: F. Elger Publishers.

Wilson, J. 1989. *Bureaucracy: What government agencies do and why they do it.* New York: Basic Books.

Wolman, H. 1971. *The politics of federal housing.* New York: Dodd, Mead.

Worsham, J., E. Ringquist, and M. A. Eisner. 1997. "Assessing the assumptions: A critical analysis of agency theory." *Administration and Society* 28: 419–40.

Wright, D. 1988. *Understanding intergovernmental relations.* 3rd ed. Pacific Grove, Calif.: Brooks/Cole.

———. 1990. Federalism, intergovernmental relations and intergovernmental management: Historical reflections and conceptual comparisons. *Public Administration Review* March/April: 168–78.

Yanow, D. 1996. *How does a policy mean? Interpreting policy and organizational actions.* Washington, D.C.: Georgetown University Press.

Yates, D. 1991. Management in public and private organizations: Similarities and differences. In *Public management: The essential readings,* eds. J. S. Ott, A. C. Hyde, and J. M. Shafritz. Chicago: Lyceum Books.

Yin, R. K. 1984. *Case study research: Design and methods.* Beverly Hills, Calif.: Sage Publications.

Zifcak, S. 1994. *New managerialism: Administrative reform in Whitehall and Canberra.* Buckingham: Open University Press.

Index

www.ingramcontent.com/pod-product-compliance
Lightning Source LLC
LaVergne TN
LVHW090805070826
844660LV00022B/1084

9780878408597